BUILDING CLASSROOM DISCIPLINE

FOURTH EDITION

C. M. Charles
San Diego State University

Collaboration by
Karen Blaine Barr

Longman

Building Classroom Discipline, 4th Edition

Longman, 10 Bank Street, White Plains, N.Y. 10606

Associated companies:
Longman Group Ltd., London
Longman Cheshire Pty., Melbourne
Longman Paul Pty., Auckland
Copp Clark Pitman, Toronto

Senior editor: Ray O'Connell
Production editor: Marcy Gray
Cover design: Irmgard Lochner
Photo research: Helena Frost
Production supervisor: Anne Armeny
Photo Credits
p.   3: The University Archives,
           Wayne State University
p.   21: The University Archives,
           Wayne State University
p.   33: Courtesy of Harvard University
p.   47: AP/Wide World Photos
p.   61: Courtesy of the Alfred Adler
           Institute of Chicago
p.   79: AP/Wide World Photos
p.   93: Courtesy of Lee Canter & Associates
p. 111: Courtesy of William Glasser Inc.

Library of Congress Cataloging in Publication Data

Charles, C. M.
    Building classroom discipline : from models to practice / C.M.
Charles. — 4th ed.
        p.   cm.
    Includes index.
    ISBN 0-8013-0788-0
    1. School discipline.   2. Classroom management.   I. Title.
LB3012.C46   1991
371.5—dc20   91-29400
                                                                CIP

4 5 6 7 8 9 10-AL-95 94 93

Contents

PART TWO From Models to Classroom Practice 127

Introduction

The scene is an inner-city school. Classroom 314 is quiet as students listen attentively to the teacher's questions about a recent lesson. Suddenly, eager hands begin
to wave and bodies twist out of their seats amidst shouts of "ooh me," "I know,"
"ooh-oh." Quiet returns when one student is chosen to answer. As soon as she has
responded, others begin to yell out refutations or additions and compete again for
teacher recognition. As they participate wholeheartedly in class, several students are
simultaneously but secretly passing notes and candy and signaling to each other in
sign and face language. When the questions end and seat work begins, some students offer to help others who are unsure of how to proceed.

But across the hall in room 315, chaos reigns. The room is noisy with the
shouting, laughter, and movement of many children. Though most students are
seated, many are walking or running aimlessly around the classroom. Some stop at
others' desks, provoke them briefly, and move on. Several students who are lining
up textbooks as "race courses" for toy cars laugh when the teacher demands their
attention.

As the teacher struggles to ask a question over the noise, few if any students
volunteer to answer. When one student does respond correctly, others yell out, "You
think you're so smart." (Schwartz, 1981)

By most teachers' standards, the discipline in Classroom 314 is good, while that
in Classroom 315 is poor. But what is the difference? In both rooms, students are
making noise and doing things usually considered unacceptable. Yet the teacher in 314
is probably quite satisfied with the lesson while the teacher in 315 is probably
frustrated and laboring with stress. Why?

One purpose of this book is to help you answer that question, an answer that
begins with the distinction between behavior and misbehavior.

BEHAVIOR AND MISBEHAVIOR

Behavior is defined as all the physical and mental acts that humans perform. Thus, behavior is whatever one does, whether good or bad, right or wrong, helpful or useless, productive or wasteful. In contrast, *misbehavior* is a label applied to any behavior that is considered to be inappropriate to the setting or situation in which it occurs. Most classroom misbehavior is considered to be done intentionally by students, when they know they should not do it. An inadvertent hiccup during quiet work time is not misbehavior, but when feigned for the purpose of disrupting a lesson the same behavior is justifiably disapproved.

Five Types of Misbehavior

Teachers contend with five broad types of misbehavior. In descending order of seriousness, as judged by social scientists, they are

1. *Aggression*—physical and verbal attacks by students on the teacher or other students.
2. *Immorality*—acts such as cheating, lying, and stealing.
3. *Defiance of authority*—where students refuse, sometimes hostilely, to do what the teacher tells them to do.
4. *Class disruptions*—talking loudly, calling out, walking about the room, clowning, tossing objects, and so forth. (Most class behavior rules focus on this category of misbehavior.)
5. *Goofing off*—fooling around, not doing assigned tasks, daydreaming, and so forth.

Teachers agree with the levels of social seriousness shown here for the five categories of misbehavior. Indeed, they are very concerned about aggression, immorality, and defiance, and dread having to deal with them. But in practice, the effort they expend on misbehavior falls mostly on the less serious problems, such as goofing off and talking.

Thus, in a sense, the less nocuous behaviors are the more serious for teachers because such behaviors waste instructional time and interfere with learning. Lee Canter, whose Assertive Discipline is one of the most widely-used discipline systems, was asked how he could justify sending a student to the office for a misbehavior as mild as (repeatedly) talking without permission. He replied that it was precisely such behaviors, which no one considers that bad, that drive teachers crazy because they so strongly interfere with teaching and learning.

DISCIPLINE AND MISBEHAVIOR

The word "discipline" has several different meanings, but throughout this book it is used to refer to steps taken to cause students to behave acceptably in school. You can see that discipline is tied directly to misbehavior—where there is no misbehavior, no discipline is required. Teachers dream of such classes but rarely encounter them.

Discipline is intended to suppress, control, and redirect misbehavior—behavior that is aggressive, immoral, or disruptive to learning. All teachers know that students sometimes behave with sweetness, kindness, gentility, consideration, helpfulness, and honesty. Their doing so makes teaching one of the most satisfying and rewarding of all professions. But teachers also know, though they fervently wish it weren't so, that students sometimes behave with hostility, abusiveness, disrespect, disinterest, and cruelty, all of which reduce effectiveness of and pleasure in teaching and learning.

Ultimately, the purpose of discipline in the classroom is to reduce the need for teacher intervention over time by encouraging students to develop self-control over their own behavior. When teachers understand and apply appropriate models of discipline, the hope is that students will internalize the need for self-discipline not only in the classroom but beyond its walls. The lessons learned will have long-range consequences for students, and ultimately for the world in which we all must live.

IS DISCIPLINE ALL THAT SERIOUS?

Each year since 1969, Phi Delta Kappa has sponsored a Gallup Poll of the public's attitudes toward education. One question on the survey asks: "What do you think are the biggest problems with which the public schools in this community must contend?" In the vast majority of the years since 1969, the public has listed discipline as the number one problem. Though in recent years the public has named drugs as the most difficult problem with which schools must contend, overall no other concern has come close to that of discipline.

Let it be recognized that public opinion can be suspect because it is so influenced by the sensational—events such as physical attacks on teachers and severe vandalism of schools. In the case of discipline, however, little disagreement exists between teachers and the public. Further, most teachers maintain that student misbehavior interferes significantly with their teaching (Elam, 1989). The resultant frustration produces stress that in some teachers becomes so severe that it has been likened to battle fatigue experienced by soldiers in combat, symptoms of which include lethargy, exhaustion, tension, high blood pressure, depression, and alcoholism.

The concern about discipline is not waning; rather, it is growing stronger. Numerous recent studies have listed discipline as one of the major problems with which teachers must contend and a major factor in the high numbers of teachers leaving the profession—now almost 40% departure during teachers' first three years ("Study backs," 1987). Adding to the problem is that experienced teachers gravitate away from schools that have high levels of misbehavior, leaving those schools to beginning teachers who are not yet skilled in discipline.

THE INTENT AND ORGANIZATION OF THIS BOOK

The primary purpose of this book is to help you develop practical skills needed for maintaining effective discipline in your classroom. Ultimately you must give strong attention to three aspects of discipline, which are labeled:

Preventive Discipline—referring to what you can do to prevent misbehavior from occurring in the first place.

Supportive Discipline—referring to what you can do to assist students when they show first signs of incipient misbehavior.

Corrective Discipline—referring to what you do to suppress and positively redirect misbehavior once it does occur.

In order to have effective discipline, you must weave these three facets into a coordinated system, one that your students will support and that you can implement humanely and consistently.

The information, activities, and suggestions presented in the following chapters will enable you to organize and implement such an effective system. Throughout, you will be urged to construct your system so that it not only attends to the realities of students and locale where you teach, but is also consistent with your own personality and philosophy. Only in that way will your discipline system serve you as intended.

The book is organized to provide the following experiences: First is an examination of eight important and established systems of discipline. Referred to as "models of discipline," they have historical, theoretical, and practical value. Some are widely used today, and all can contribute to your thinking about discipline. Following each model is a set of application exercises to help you better understand the elements of the models and how they are applied. Within those exercises are a repetitive set called "Concept Cases," which allow you, for purposes of comparison, to apply different model concepts to the same instances of misbehavior.

Second, you will find two chapters that supplement the models with additional information. Chapter 9 describes classroom conditions that encourage good, rather than bad, behavior. Implementation of the suggestions provided will dramatically reduce the incidence of misbehavior. Chapter 10 gives attention to working with students-at-risk, who often require special understandings and techniques. Emphasis is given to discipline from multicultural and special education perspectives.

Third, following the models and supplements, you will find suggestions for building your own personal system of discipline. Chapter 11 provides specific guidelines for organizing your personal system, culminating with 17 steps to personalized discipline. Chapter 12 provides details of six discipline systems organized and used by experienced classroom teachers. Those systems are presented as exemplars, to be used for analysis and further guidance for your own personal system. Chapter 13 consists of 10 classroom scenarios that depict instances of behavior considered troublesome by most teachers. Those scenarios can provide further practice with the models of discipline and, ultimately, situations against which to test your system.

REFERENCES

Elam, S. (June, 1989). The second Gallup/Phi Delta Kappa poll of teachers' attitudes toward the public schools. *Phi Delta Kappan 70*, 10:785–798.

Schwartz, F. (1981). Supporting or subverting learning: peer group patterns in four tracked schools. *Anthropology and Education Quarterly, 12*, 2:99–120.

Study backs induction schools to help new teachers stay teachers. (1987). *ASCD Update, 29*, 4:1.

PART I
Eight Models of Discipline

CHAPTER 1

The Redl and Wattenberg Model:
Dealing with the Group

REDL AND WATTENBERG
BIOGRAPHICAL SKETCHES

Fritz Redl immigrated to the United States from Austria in 1936. He worked as a therapist, researcher, and professor of behavioral science at Wayne State University. In 1973 he became a consultant to the department of criminal justice at the State University of New York at Albany, dealing with deviant juveniles. His writings in the field of education consist of *Mental Hygiene in Teaching,* co-authored with William Wattenberg (1951), *Discipline for Today's Children,* co-authored with George Sheviakov (1956), and *When We Deal with Children* (1972).

William W. Wattenberg, born in 1911, received his PhD degree from Columbia University in 1936. He specialized in educational psychology, which he has taught at Northwestern University, Chicago Teacher's College, and Wayne State University. Dr. Wattenberg's writings include *Mental Hygiene in Teaching,* co-authored with Fritz Redl (1951), *The Adolescent Years* (1955), and *All Men Are Created Equal* (1967).

In their book *Mental Hygiene in Teaching,* Redl and Wattenberg provided insights into the forces—psychological and social—that affect student behavior in classroom groups. They were among the first to offer teachers specific disciplinary techniques that can be used in everyday situations—techniques designed to maintain classroom control and strengthen emotional development in students.

REDL AND WATTENBERG'S CENTRAL FOCUS

Group behavior differs from individual behavior. Teachers can learn how to use influence techniques to deal with undesirable aspects of group behavior.

Redl and Wattenberg's Key Ideas

1. People in groups behave differently than they do individually. Group expectations influence individual behavior, and individual behavior affects the group. Teachers need to be aware of the characteristic traits of group behavior.
2. Groups create their own psychological forces that influence individual behavior. Teacher awareness of *group dynamics* is important to effective classroom control.
3. Group behavior in the classroom is influenced by how students perceive the teacher. Students see teachers as filling many psychological roles.
4. Dealing with classroom conflict requires diagnostic thinking by the teacher. This thinking involves: (1) forming a first hunch, (2) gathering facts, (3) applying hidden factors, (4) taking action, and (5) being flexible.
5. Teachers maintain group control through various *influence techniques*. These techniques include: (1) supporting self-control, (2) offering situational assistance, (3) appraising reality, and (4) invoking pleasure and pain.
6. *Supporting self-control techniques* are low-keyed. They address the problem before it becomes serious. They include eye contact, moving closer, encouragement, humor, and ignoring.

7. *Situational assistance* techniques are necessary when students cannot regain control without assistance from the teacher. Techniques to provide assistance include: (1) helping students over a hurdle, (2) restructuring the schedule, (3) establishing routines, (4) removing the student from a situation, (5) removing seductive objects, and (6) physical restraint.

8. *Appraising reality* techniques involve helping students understand underlying causes for misbehavior and foresee probable consequences. Teachers "tell it like it is," offer encouragement, set limits, and clarify situations with post-situational follow-up.

9. *Pleasure-pain* techniques involve rewarding good behavior and punishing bad behavior. Punishment should be used only as a last resort because it is too often counterproductive.

GROUP LIFE IN THE CLASSROOM

Understanding motivations, the basic causes behind behavior and conflict, is half the battle of classroom control. Our knowledge of individual behavior is growing daily. Teachers know better than ever before why individuals behave as they do, and that outward behavior has roots in identifiable needs. They know that students are contin- . ually torn between personal desires and expectations of society.

However, teachers seldom deal with students on a purely individual basis. Instead, they must concern themselves with groups—the entire class, large groups, and smaller groups. This does not mean that teachers cannot use their valuable insights into individual behavior, but that they must instead transfer those insights into group behavior. This presents a major problem: group psychology is different from individual psychology. People simply behave differently when in groups.

Redl and Wattenberg view the group as an organism. "A group creates conditions such that its members will behave in certain ways because they belong to it; at the same time, the manner in which the parts function affects the whole" (Redl and Wattenberg, 1959, p. 267). In other words, group expectations strongly influence individual behavior, and individual behavior in turn affects the group. Redl and Wattenberg describe several roles that are available to individuals in groups. The following are some of the roles that can cause trouble in the classroom.

Leaders

A leadership role is available in almost every group. The role varies according to the group's purpose, makeup, and activities. Within the same group, different people may act as leaders in different activities. For example, a student who is a leader in physical education may fill a different role in music.

Group leaders tend to share certain qualities. They are above average in most respects (intellect, responsibility, social skills, and socioeconomic status). They generally have a highly developed understanding of others, and they embody group ideals.

Teachers must be aware that the leaders they appoint are not necessarily the group's natural leaders. Such mismatches often lead to conflict within the group.

Clowns

Clowns are individuals who take the position of entertainer in the group. Students sometimes take this role in order to mask feelings of inferiority, thinking it best to make fun of themselves before others have a chance. Clowns sometimes help the group and sometimes hinder it. Clowning can be beneficial to both teacher and the group, especially when students are anxious, frustrated, or in need of relief from tension. At times, however, group members may support the disruptive antics of the clown as a way of expressing hostility to the teacher.

Fall Guys

A fall guy is an individual who takes blame and punishment in order to gain favor with the group. Members of the group feel free to misbehave knowing that they can set up the fall guy to suffer the penalties. Teachers need to be aware of this kind of manipulation and be sure to focus their corrective actions on the instigators of misbehavior.

Instigators

Instigators are individuals who cause trouble, but appear not to be involved. They often solve their inner conflicts by getting others to act them out. They may even feel that they are benefiting the victim in some way. Teachers need to look into recurring conflicts carefully to see if there is an unnoticed instigator. It may be necessary to point out this role to the group, as it is often undetected by them. The group may need help in recognizing and discouraging this role.

Comment on Group Roles

All of the roles described here are played by individuals in groups either because the role fills a strong personal need or because the group expects or enjoys it. By playing a role, an individual finds a place within the group—one of the main desires of almost all students—and becomes a functioning part of the organism.

GROUP DYNAMICS

Previous paragraphs explained how roles and role expectations influence behavior. Membership in groups can affect individuals in other ways, too. Groups create their own psychological forces that strongly influence individuals. These forces are called "group dynamics." Redl and Wattenberg describe some of the dynamics that cause difficulties in the classroom.

Contagious Behavior

Undesired behavior sometimes, but not always, spreads quickly in the classroom. One student's misbehavior may be a good sign of what other students are itching to do also. Once the ice is broken, other students may follow, especially if the perpetrator has high status.

Before reacting to misbehavior, teachers should evaluate its potential for spread. If the potential is high, teachers should squelch the misbehavior at once. If the potential is low, it may be safe to ignore the behavior or use a low-pressure technique, such as suggesting the correct behavior.

Teachers can reduce contagion by giving attention to negative factors that foster it, including poor seating arrangements, boredom, restlessness, lack of purpose in lessons, and poor student manners. On the positive side, desirable behavior can also be contagious. Teachers can encourage positive behavior by approving it, reinforcing it, and giving status to those who display it.

Scapegoating

Scapegoating takes place when a group seeks to displace its hostility onto an unpopular individual or subgroup. The group will select a target person who is weak or outcast, often unable to cope with normal occurrences in the classroom. Scapegoating has undesirable consequences for everyone concerned. Teachers must guard against it and stifle it when it occurs. In so doing, they should be sure that their approach does not cause even more dislike for the target.

Teacher's Pets

When a group believes that a teacher is playing favorites, it reacts with jealousy and resentment. These emotions manifest themselves in hostile behavior toward the favored individual or group. Hostility may also be directed toward the teacher. When teachers need to give individual students extra help, they should be sure that the actions are seen as impartial, necessary, and professional.

Reactions to Strangers

It is common in most schools for strangers to enter the classroom occasionally. Teachers notice a marked change in student behavior when this occurs. Unknown visitors increase tension for teachers and students alike.

If the stranger is a new student, the group code may become exaggerated in order to show the newcomer how to act. For example, if the group prizes cooperation, they might go to great lengths to be helpful to the newcomer and each other. On the other hand, the group may set off a series of behaviors intended to test the new child. Individuals or subgroups may vie for friendship, offer status positions, or taunt each other.

If the stranger is an adult, the students may rally to support their teacher, if that person is liked and respected. If they do not respect their teacher, the students may misbehave rudely and boisterously. All teachers are well advised to set up a standard procedure to be followed whenever a stranger enters the classroom.

Teachers should note the class reactions when a stranger enters the room. Extreme behaviors provide clues to underlying motivations and feelings that are operating within the group.

Group Disintegration

Groups serve many purposes, and good group behavior is highly desirable. Teachers hope to establish groups that will prosper, grow in maturity, and serve everyone well. Even the strongest group, however, will show strain in time.

Consider Mrs. Brown's discouraging situation. Early in the year her class worked strongly together, pulling toward goals as one. Later there was a decline in cohesion. One day when directing a lesson, Mrs. Brown noticed with dismay that some students were looking out the window, a small group was discussing the football game, and one student was writing a letter to a friend. The students had to be coerced into participating, one individual at a time.

Teachers frequently encounter such situations. Not knowing the cause, they are at a loss as to what to do or how to correct the situation. Redl and Wattenberg suggest that when a formerly effective group begins to disintegrate, teachers should ask themselves the following questions:

1. Are there long, unnecessary periods of waiting time in which students could be getting more direction?
2. Are the assigned tasks relevant and within the students' ability?
3. Is there too much emphasis on competition between groups?
4. Are there too many unexpected changes in leadership, environment, schedules, and so forth?
5. Are the classroom activities stimulating and thought-provoking?
6. Are students given ample opportunity to experience success, or are there too many failures?
7. Is there more criticism than praise from the teacher?

Each of these factors can cause problems within the group. As they appear, control problems appear with them. Group disintegration causes insecurity among members, especially weaker ones, in terms of knowing their places and their expected roles. This in turn causes deviant behavior and loss of mutual support within the group.

Comment on Group Dynamics

Group dynamics are psychological forces that influence individuals' behavior as members of a group. They are the forces behind the group's unwritten codes of conduct. When these codes run counter to teachers' codes, conflict occurs. Teachers are powerful, and they may seem to win out. However, the group code usually prevails under the surface, forming lasting attitudes that are the opposite of what the teacher desired.

PSYCHOLOGICAL ROLES OF TEACHERS

The ways in which groups and individuals behave in the classroom are greatly influenced by how they perceive the teacher. Like it or not, teachers fill many different roles and present many different images. Some of these roles and images are:

1. *Representatives of society*. Teachers reflect and develop values, moral attitudes, and thinking patterns typical of the community.
2. *Judges*. Teachers judge students' behavior, character, work, and progress.
3. *Source of knowledge*. Teachers are the primary source of knowledge, a resource from which to obtain information.
4. *Helpers in learning*. Teachers help students learn by giving directions, furnishing information, requiring that work be done, removing obstacles to learning, and facilitating problem solving.
5. *Referees*. Teachers arbitrate and make decisions when disputes arise.
6. *Detectives*. Teachers maintain security in the classroom, discover wrongdoing, and hand out consequences.
7. *Models*. Teachers model customs, manners, values, and beliefs that students are to imitate.
8. *Caretakers*. Teachers reduce anxiety by maintaining standards of behavior, consistent environments, regular schedules, and freedom from danger or threat.
9. *Ego supporters*. Teachers support student egos by building student self-confidence and bettering self-images.
10. *Group leaders*. Teachers facilitate harmonious and efficient group functioning.
11. *Surrogate parents*. Teachers are a source of protection, approval, affection, and advice.
12. *Targets for hostility*. When student hostility cannot be appropriately expressed to other adults, it may be displaced onto teachers.
13. *Friends and confidants*. Teachers can be talked with and confided in.
14. *Objects of affection*. Teachers are often objects of affection and esteem, as well as crushes and hero worship.

Comment on Psychological Roles of Teachers. As you can see, teachers are assigned many roles by students. Sometimes teachers have little choice about those roles, but normally they have some measure of choice concerning the roles they will adopt and how they will assume them. They may enter into some roles wholeheartedly while avoiding others completely, depending on how they wish to relate to students, and they may adopt or avoid roles in accordance with strong needs of the group. In any event, the class functions better when teachers remain consistent in the roles they do assume.

DIAGNOSTIC THINKING IN THE CLASSROOM

So far we have examined several of Redl and Wattenberg's contentions: group makeup and functioning; group dynamics and how they affect class behavior; how group expectations can cause role-playing in individuals; and some of the many roles that students assign to teachers. Given this knowledge and an understanding of group motivation, how do teachers act on them?

Redl and Wattenberg suggest *diagnostic thinking* as a general approach to facing challenging situations. You will see that their approach is not a magical formula. It requires diligence and persistence. With practice, diagnostic thinking becomes second nature and allows teachers to add insights about psychological forces that influence group behavior and, in turn, permit efficient classroom management. Their diagnostic thinking approach involves *first hunch, fact gathering, hidden factors, acting,* and *flexibility.* They describe the approach as follows.

When conflict first becomes apparent, it is natural to form a *preliminary hunch* about its underlying cause. This hunch is not based on specific data, but is simply a general feeling about the incident.

Next, the teacher gathers *obvious facts.* Is there a student on the floor? Is he or she screaming and pointing at someone else? Is there something broken?

To these obvious facts the teacher adds *hidden factors* of which he or she may be aware. Hidden factors might be such things as background information on the students involved, knowledge of psychological, mental, or moral development, or knowledge of a previous volatile situation.

When teachers believe they have identified the facts, motivations, and other hidden factors behind a conflict, they are ready to *act* on the situation. This step is akin to testing a hypothesis; they apply a solution and see whether it works. The attempt may or may not solve the problem. After observing the effect of their actions, teachers may want to revise their appraisal or solution.

This uncertainty points out the need for teachers to be *flexible* in the diagnostic procedure. They may have assessed the situation incorrectly, or by their actions have altered its dynamics, thus creating a new situation that requires further action. Redl and Wattenberg suggest that a single action is not enough. Teachers must act in a series of steps, all leading ultimately to a resolution of the problem.

Redl and Wattenberg offer a final word of advice concerning diagnostic problem solving: Feelings are very important. Teachers should not rely solely on their own feelings, but should try to put themselves in the students' place, see how the students feel, and modify their actions accordingly.

See if you understand Mr. Bryant's use of diagnostic thinking in the following episode:

> Three girls come into the classroom. Bonnie and Susan are in tears. Trish is shouting angrily. Class cannot proceed. There have been similar incidents during the last few weeks.
>
> Mr. Bryant has a hunch that Trish is consistently instigating trouble between the other two. He examines the facts: Bonnie and Susan are usually upset; Trish is usually very vocal; these problems occur at the end of the week. From their exchanges Mr. Bryant deduces a hidden factor—Trish wants Bonnie to go to the football game with her, not with Susan.
>
> Mr. Bryant now must decide on a course of action, knowing that it may or may not work. He asks himself, "Should I give some sort of situational assistance? Would reality appraisal work? Is punishment called for in this case?" He is trying to decide on "influence techniques." Look for descriptions of what he has in mind in the next section.

INFLUENCE TECHNIQUES

Redl and Wattenberg have given much attention to the kinds of acts that teachers use to resolve problem behavior. Acts are only a part of diagnostic thinking, but are the obvious manifestations of the process. Redl and Wattenberg called these acts "influence techniques."

Every teacher uses several different techniques to maintain classroom control. Some of those techniques are based on school disciplinary policies; some are selected because they reflect teachers' personalities and philosophies; and others are used because teachers have found them to work well in the past. Some are very effective and some are not effective at all. Many are applicable in certain situations but not in others.

Situations arise regularly that call for corrective action. Teachers use a variety of means for making those corrections. Some shout, some remove students from the class, some suggest alternative behaviors, some ignore the misbehavior. Redl and Wattenberg urge teachers to learn to ask themselves a series of rapid-fire questions before they take action:

1. What is the motivation behind the misbehavior?
2. How is the class reacting?
3. Is the misbehavior related to interaction with the teacher?
4. How will the student react when corrected?
5. How will the correction affect future behavior?

Answers to these questions help ensure first that teachers understand the situation, and then that they will be able to choose a corrective technique that has positive influence on the misbehaving student. Redl and Wattenberg describe four categories of influence techniques from which teachers can choose in accord with the answers to the questions above. The categories are: (1) supporting self-control, (2) offering situational assistance, (3) appraising reality, and (4) invoking the pain-pleasure principle. It must be remembered that if any of these techniques is to be most effective, students must know exactly what the issues are and how they are expected to behave. Expectations and consequences should be made clear at the beginning of the class.

Supporting Self-Control

Most students, most of the time, want to behave correctly and gain the teacher's approval. They do not misbehave simply because they want to be unpleasant. When misbehavior occurs, it is due to some other reason (that is why teachers should appraise the situation). Often it is nothing more than a lapse in self-control, and in that case the best corrective technique is to help students regain control of their own behavior.

Techniques for supporting self-control are low-keyed. They are not forceful, aggressive, or punitive, but aim at helping students help themselves. Teachers should use them when they feel that students are on the verge of losing control. In this way behavior is checked before it becomes unacceptable.

Redl and Wattenberg describe five techniques for supporting self-control. The first technique is *sending signals*. With this technique, teachers use signs that show they know what is going on and that they don't approve. Examples are making eye contact, frowning, shaking the head. These signals are most effective during the earliest stages of misbehavior.

If students fail to respond to a signal, teachers may want to try *proximity control*. By moving closer to the offender, teachers communicate that they are aware and want to help. This allows the student to draw strength from the nearness of the teacher and use that strength to regain self-control. It is usually enough simply to move closer to the student, but sometimes a friendly touch on the shoulder or head might be needed.

Sometimes students who have good self-control will begin to misbehave when they lose interest in an assignment. Teachers can correct this by going to students and *showing interest* in their work. A teacher might say to one, "I see you've finished the first five problems. I'll bet you'll finish them all before the end of the period." This technique is not effective, of course, if the student is lost or feels unable to do the assignment.

A pleasant way to make students aware of a lapse in control is with *humor*. It is important that this humor be gentle and always accompanied by a smile from the teacher. An example of humor would be, "My, there is so much chattering, I almost forgot for a minute that I was in a classroom." Teachers must be careful that they do not use sarcasm or ridicule in such statements. Those are punishing techniques, not supporting techniques.

Occasionally, *ignoring* is one of the most appropriate support techniques, especially if a student is testing a situation. When the teacher ignores inappropriate behavior it often cues other students in the class to follow suit, thus discouraging behavior used to gain attention. However, teachers should make it plain that they are ignoring misbehavior intentionally; otherwise, students will interpret it as insecurity or indecisiveness.

Comment on Supportive Techniques. Techniques that support self-control are useful, but they also have disadvantages. When used in the early stages of misbehavior, they can eliminate the need to dole out penalties, and they give students much needed opportunities to work on controlling their own behavior. It should be remembered, however, that these techniques are effective only in situations where misbehavior is mild or just beginning. If supportive techniques don't get the message across, firmer, more direct techniques are required.

Providing Situational Assistance

When misbehavior reaches the point that students cannot regain self-control, teachers must step in with assistance to guide students back onto the proper course. Redl and Wattenberg describe several techniques for providing situational assistance.

Hurdle help is one such technique. Suppose a math assignment has been made. Susan begins working only to discover she has no understanding of the procedure required. She begins to talk to another student. In this case, the teacher needs only to help Susan over the hurdle, not attack her because she is talking and not working.

Another technique in providing situational assistance is *restructuring* or *rescheduling the situation*. Mr. James's students have come in to class after participating in a particularly exciting volleyball match. He knows that it will be difficult for the students to get to work in his math class. Instead of the routine math assignment, he decides to use the game's scores to solve some computation problems. Why did he change his plans?

When behavior problems are caused by restlessness or over-excitement teachers should recognize the cause—perhaps students have been made to sit too long, or have had too many exciting activities in too short a time. Teachers can restructure situations by giving a brief period of rest, changing the nature of the activities, or rescheduling the work for a more appropriate time.

On the other hand, a lack of established routines can also cause problems because students do not know exactly what they should be doing, or when. Teachers assist in this situation by *establishing routines* and thus adding consistency and predictability to the curriculum. Routines are especially helpful in activities that are apt to become complex or confusing, or where there are many students involved.

If one student has temporarily lost self-control and is disturbing the rest of the class, the teacher might decide to *remove the student from the situation*. Travis refuses to take his seat for a lesson. The teacher takes his hand and leads him to the far corner of the room telling him, "When you decide to sit down, you may return to join us. . . ."

This should always be done in a nonpunitive way. The teacher should emphasize that the student is only exiled until self-control is regained. When a student must be removed from the group, it is important to follow up later with a private talk. Feelings of both teacher and student should be discussed.

Attractive objects that students have in their possession—photographs, toys, and the like—can sometimes overpower self-control. In such cases teachers need only *remove the seductive object*. This is a temporary measure and should be explained to the student as such, together with provisions for returning the object to the student.

Sometimes a lapse in self-control may cause a student to become a danger to her or himself and others. When this happens, the teacher may have to use *physical restraint*. When restraint is used as a situational assistance technique, great care must be taken not to hurt the student. Restraint should be neither rough nor punitive, but should be merely containing or restraining until control is regained. [Author's note: Any physical restraint brings as an inherent danger the possibility of lawsuit against the teacher. Use it only when absolutely necessary to prevent students' harming themselves or others.]

Comment on Providing Situational Assistance. Many different situations can cause students to lose self-control temporarily. In such cases, punitive measures are not needed; in fact, punishment is counterproductive. Instead, the teacher provides only the assistance needed to help students regain control. This approach has many advantages, such as reducing confusion, allowing students to keep energy and attention focused on learning, and establishing the teacher's posture as one of helpfulness and kindliness.

Reality Appraisal

Student misbehavior often escalates for reasons that are not evident even to the students who are misbehaving. Behavior can be improved markedly when teachers help students to examine a behavior situation, see the underlying causes, and foresee the probable consequences. This is what Redl and Wattenberg refer to as reality appraisal, and they have suggested a variety of things teachers should keep in mind when using this approach.

Too often teachers overlook the simplest method for dealing with students, which is to *tell it like it is.* Teachers do this by explaining exactly why behavior is inappropriate and outlining clear connections between conduct and consequences. Teachers should not underestimate students' ability to comprehend statements such as: "If everyone talks at once, no one gets heard"; or "Pushing and horsing around can cause injuries"; or "If you don't keep up with assignments, you simply won't learn very much." Students usually respond well to rules whose reasons they understand, and they judge teachers who take time to explain the rules to be just and fair.

Obviously, one key to reality appraisal is *clarity.* Teachers must make it very clear to students which behaviors are inappropriate, why they are inappropriate, what the probable consequences will be, and what students should do instead.

When using reality appraisal, teachers often must give criticism. Since few people respond positively to criticism, teachers must strive to express it in ways that *show encouragement.* Criticism should be offered in ways that stimulate efforts to try harder; it should not frustrate students with impossible expectations. Neither should it attack students' personal values, humiliate them, or otherwise hurt their self-image or prestige. The teacher's role is to support, not to attack or blame.

Students often misbehave for no other reason than to test limits. They need the security of knowing exactly how far they will be able to go. *Setting limits* provides this security by telling students clearly what is expected, what is unacceptable, and why. Teachers should remember that setting limits and enforcing rules are separate issues. Making threats while setting limits indicates that the teacher expects violations.

Comments on Reality Appraisal. Appraising the reality of a situation helps students to see underlying aspects of situations, themselves, and others, thereby assisting them in developing their own values. This enables them to act more appropriately in future situations.

At times, especially during disturbing incidents, emotions run strong, and both teacher and students are apt to make inappropriate comments. It is difficult for both parties to listen to what is being said. For that reason, Redl and Wattenberg believe discussions about the incident should be held sometime afterward, when both parties are calmer and better able to talk over what happened. This talk is not a time for lecturing or scolding, but rather a time to sort out causes and feelings. It is important for teachers to understand why students acted as they did, and equally important for students to understand the teacher's actions. Such discussions may make it easier to handle similar situations in the future.

Invoking the Pain-Pleasure Principle

When behavior problems persist despite the teacher's attempts to support student self-control, provide situational assistance, and appraise reality, it becomes necessary to move to the strongest measure in Redl and Wattenberg's suggestions—invoking the pain-pleasure principle. The meaning of this approach is evident, but becomes clearer through the understanding that they are really referring to a "pain principle," with little to say about the effects of pleasure.

Pain, for Redl and Wattenberg, is not harsh punishment, but rather consequences that are unpleasant to the student. They do use the word punishment; therefore it is important to recognize the benign nature of the unpleasant consequences they suggest. In contrast, pleasure refers to consequences that are pleasant to the student. Let us examine these meanings a bit further:

Punishment. When students lose the battle for self-control, it sometimes becomes necessary to resort to punishment. Punishment should consist of planned, unpleasant consequences, the purpose of which is to modify behavior in positive directions. Punishment should not be physical, nor should it involve angry outbursts that indicate lack of self-control on the part of the teacher. Neither should it be actions taken to get back at misbehaving students, or to "teach them a lesson." Instead, it should require them to make amends for breaking rules, do correctly what was done incorrectly, forego activities they enjoy, and so forth.

Even when punishing, teachers should try to communicate the idea that they like the students and are trying to help them. Students should be made to see punishment as a *natural and understandable consequence* of unacceptable behavior. If students sense good intentions from the teacher, they will be at least partly angry at themselves for losing self-control, not at the teacher who is trying to help them regain it.

Punishment should be used only as a last resort, when other approaches have failed. That is because there are many things that can go wrong when punishment is used, such as:

1. Punishment is used as revenge or release from tension.
2. It has detrimental effects on student self-concept and relations with the teacher.
3. Over time, it reduces student ability to maintain self-control.
4. Students may use it to raise status with peers.
5. It presents an undesirable model for solving problems.

Threats and Promises

The pain principle should be seen by students and teachers as a *promise,* an assurance that unpleasant consequences will follow repeated inappropriate behavior. Promises can be made without negative emotion, and they do not promote undue fear or other negative reactions in students.

Threats, on the other hand, make students anxious and fearful, which may interfere with learning and certainly work to the detriment of a positive classroom climate. Threats tend to be harsh and negative, taking the form of "If you don't . . . I will. . . ." Teachers who make dire threats seldom carry them out, and that is often their undoing; their ability to control misbehavior erodes, as does their ability to relate positively with the class.

Instead of making threats, teachers should simply state which behaviors are unacceptable and explain exactly what the consequences will be for those behaviors. Unlike threats, these calm assertions lend security to the classroom and help students maintain their own self-control.

FRITZ REDL'S SUGGESTIONS

Essentially, Redl and Wattenberg's suggestions are based on commonsense applications of humane personal relations. Their overall view is summarized nicely by Fritz Redl in his book *When We Deal with Children* (1966):

1. Give students a say in setting standards and deciding consequences. Let them tell how they think you should handle situations that call for punishment.
2. Keep students' emotional health in mind at all times. Punished students must feel that the teacher likes them. *Always* talk to students about their feelings after the situation has calmed down.
3. Be helpful, not hurtful. Show students you want to support their best behaviors.
4. Punishment does not work well. Use it as a last resort. Try other approaches first.
5. Don't be afraid to change your course of action if you get new insights into a situation.
6. Remember: mistakes in discipline need not be considered disastrous, unless they are repeated.
7. Be objective, maintain humor, and remember that we are all human.

COMMENTS ON THE REDL AND WATTENBERG MODEL

Fritz Redl and William Wattenberg made two landmark contributions in helping teachers work more effectively with students. First, they pointed out that humans behave differently in groups than they do individually. They clarified many of those differences and made valuable suggestions for dealing with them. Second, they provided the first well-organized, systematic approach to improving behavior in the classroom. Prior to that time, teachers acquired their control techniques, which were in the main aversive, through tradition and trial and error.

Redl and Wattenberg also provided in their system a procedure for diagnosing the causes of student misbehavior, in the belief that by dealing with causes teachers could correct misbehavior, a procedure consistent with psychoanalytic techniques then in use. While there is validity in that procedure, it is unrealistic to expect that teachers have either the time or expertise to carry out in-depth diagnoses and remediations with the large numbers of students under their direction.

Aside from that shortcoming, the Redl and Wattenberg model not only sets the stage for other models to come, but provides many of the elements you will see in later models, especially regarding the support of student self-control, the provision of situational assistance, and the systematic invocation of principles of reward and punishment.

Application Exercises

Concept Cases

For each of the eight models, the same four concept cases—nonworking Kris, talkative Sara, show-off Joshua, and hostile Tom—will be provided so that you may practice and compare each authority's advice on dealing with misbehavior.

CASE #1. KRIS WILL NOT WORK:

There is a common behavior that frustrates teachers at all levels. It is one in which students do not participate in classroom activities. The students are neither disruptive nor hostile; the problem is simply that it is very difficult to get them to complete their assignments or even join in the classroom happenings. They just sit there like bumps on a log.

Kris, in Mr. Jake's class, behaves in that manner. She is quite docile. She never disrupts class and does little socializing with other students. She rarely completes an assignment. She is simply there, putting forth almost no effort.

How would Redl and Wattenberg deal with Kris? Redl and Wattenberg would suggest that teachers take the following steps in attempting to improve Kris's classroom behavior.

1. Follow the steps in diagnostic thinking: develop a hunch; gather facts; try to discover hidden factors; apply a solution; try out another solution if the first does not work. That might lead to questions such as: Does Kris have emotional problems? Are things difficult for her at home? Is she withdrawing into a fantasy life? Will a warm, caring approach help?
2. Depending on the conclusions reached in diagnostic thinking, the teacher would try out one or more of the following solutions:
   a) Sending signals to Kris (I know you are not working).
   b) Moving closer to prompt Kris into action.
   c) Showing a special interest in Kris's work.
   d) Employing humor (I know you'll want to finish this in my lifetime!).
   e) Offering assistance to Kris.
   f) Telling it like it is (Each incomplete assignment causes you to fall further behind and affects your grade!).
   g) Removing Kris from the situation (You can return when you have completed your work.).

CASE #2. SARA CANNOT STOP TALKING:

Sara is a pleasant girl who participates in class activities and does most, though not all, of her assigned work. She cannot seem to refrain from talking to classmates, however. Her teacher, Mr. Gonzales, has to speak to her repeatedly during lessons, to the point that he often becomes exasperated and loses his temper.

Application Exercises (continued)

What suggestions would Redl and Wattenberg give Mr. Gonzales for dealing with Sara?

CASE #3. JOSHUA CLOWNS AND INTIMIDATES:

Joshua, larger and louder than his classmates, always wants to be the center of attention, which he accomplishes through a combination of clowning and intimidation. He makes wise remarks, talks back (smilingly) to the teacher, utters a variety of sound effect noises such as automobile crashes and gunshots, and makes limitless sarcastic comments and put-downs of his classmates.

Other students will not stand up to him, apparently fearing his size and verbal aggression. His teacher, Miss Pearl, has come to her wits' end.

Using Redl and Wattenberg's suggestions, how would you deal with Joshua?

CASE #4. TOM IS HOSTILE AND DEFIANT:

Tom has appeared to be in his usual foul mood ever since arriving in class. He gets up and on his way to sharpen his pencil he bumps into Frank. Frank complains. Tom tells him loudly to shut up. Miss Baines, the teacher, says, "Tom, go back to your seat." Tom wheels around, swears loudly, and says heatedly, "I'll go when I'm damned good and ready!"

How would Redl and Wattenberg have Miss Baines deal with Tom?

QUESTIONS:

1. Were Kris, Sara, Joshua, and Tom playing any of the roles identified by Redl and Wattenberg?
2. What psychological roles might the four students expect their teachers to fill?
3. What roles are the following students playing?
   a) Cheryl strolls into Spanish class five minutes late. "¿Qué pasa?" she says nonchalantly to the teacher. The class laughs.
   b) The auto shop teacher notices a group of boys squirting oil at one another. The boys point to Shaun who is watching from the sidelines. "He started it," they all agree. Although untrue, Shaun grins and does not deny it.
4. How would Redl and Wattenberg suggest that the respective teachers deal with the Cheryl and Shaun situations?

FURTHER ANALYSIS AND APPLICATION:

Examine scenario #1 in Chapter 13. What advice from Redl and Wattenberg would best help Mrs. Miller provide a better learning environment for her students?

REFERENCES

Redl, F. (1972). *When we deal with children: selected writings.* New York: Free Press.

Redl, F., & Wattenberg, W. (1951; 1959). *Mental hygiene in teaching.* New York: Harcourt, Brace and World.

Sheviakov, G., & Redl, F. (1956). *Discipline for today's children*. Washington, DC: Association for Supervision and Curriculum Development.

Wattenberg, W. (1955). *The adolescent years*. New York: Harcourt Brace.

Wattenberg, W. (1967). *All men are created equal*. Detroit: Wayne State University Press.

CHAPTER 2

The Kounin Model:
Withitness, Alerting, and Group Management

KOUNIN: BIOGRAPHICAL SKETCH

Jacob Kounin (1912–   ) was born in Cleveland, Ohio. He earned his doctorate from Iowa State University in 1939, and in 1946 was appointed to a professorship at Wayne State University, where he served a long tenure as professor of educational psychology. Dr. Kounin made numerous presentations to the American Psychological Association, the American Educational Research Association, and many other organizations. He served often as a consultant and visiting professor at other universities.

Dr. Kounin is best known for his work *Discipline and Group Management in Classrooms* (1971/1977), a book that grew out of two decades of research. In the earlier years, his studies focused on group management, with emphasis on how handling the misbehavior of one student affected other students. Kounin observed that a general effect occurred in the group, which he called the *ripple effect*.

From ripple effect studies came subsequent research on disciplinary and group management techniques. This research involved videotapes made in 80 different classrooms. Kounin analyzed the thousands of hours of tape and discovered several dimensions of group management that promoted student involvement and reduced the amount of misbehavior.

KOUNIN'S CENTRAL FOCUS

Good classroom behavior depends on effective lesson management, especially on pacing, transitions, alerting, and individual accountability.

Kounin's Key Ideas

1. When teachers correct misbehavior in one student, it often influences the behavior of nearby students. This is known as the ripple effect.
2. Teachers should know what is going on in all parts of the classroom at all times. Kounin called this awareness, "withitness."
3. The ability to provide smooth transitions between activities and to maintain consistent momentum within activities is crucial to effective group management.
4. Teachers should strive to maintain group alertness and to hold every group member accountable for the content of a lesson, which allows optimal learning to occur.
5. Student satiation (boredom) can be avoided by providing a feeling of progress and by adding variety to curriculum and classroom environment.

THE RIPPLE EFFECT

Kounin's research on the ripple effect started accidentally one day when he reprimanded a college student for reading a newspaper during the lecture. Immediately afterward, he noticed a difference in the behavior of other students in the class. They sat up straighter and paid closer attention. Kounin's observation led him to believe that the way in which teachers issue desists (remarks intended to stop misbehavior) also influences the behavior of students who merely witness the desist. The effect of the desist ripples from the target student outward to others.

Kounin then tested the ripple effect in four different settings—college, kindergarten, high school, and summer camp. In the college study, he set up an experiment to compare the effects of a "supporting desist" (offering to help) versus a "threatening desist" (chastising the student). Both produced a ripple effect.

In the kindergarten study, Kounin tried to determine whether the *quality* of a desist influenced the degree of conforming behavior. The three qualities tested were (1) *clarity,* with information that named the deviant, specified the unacceptable behavior, and gave reasons for the desist; (2) *firmness,* that is, projecting an "I mean it" attitude until the misbehavior stopped; and (3) *roughness,* in which the desist included anger, physical handling, and punishment. Kounin found that:

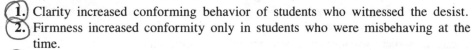

1. Clarity increased conforming behavior of students who witnessed the desist.
2. Firmness increased conformity only in students who were misbehaving at the time.
3. Roughness did not improve behavior at all; it simply upset the audience children, making them restless and anxious.

Kounin also found that the ripple effect was very pronounced on the first day of school but tended to diminish as the year wore on.

In the summer camp study, Kounin attempted to measure the ripple effect with children from 7 to 13 years of age. He could find no measurable effect and decided that this was due to the fact that misconduct at camp was considered more acceptable than at home or school and resulted in fewer consequences. Children in summer camp did not take desists seriously.

In the high school study, Kounin found that the type of desist had no effect on the amount of misbehavior exhibited by the audience students. He found that an extremely angry outburst by the teacher caused some emotional discomfort in students witnessing the desist. What did influence behavior in high school students was the degree to which the teacher was liked. High regard for the teacher coupled with high motivation to learn created maximum work involvement and minimum misbehavior among students.

From these studies one can conclude the following: The ripple effect may occur as the teacher gives encouragement ("Good, I see that many of you are almost finished") and as the teacher gives reprimands ("I see a few people who may have to stay in after class to finish"). The ripple effect is most powerful at the elementary level. It is weaker at the secondary and college levels where it depends on the popularity or prestige of the teacher.

WITHITNESS

Kounin coined the term "withitness" to describe teachers' knowing what was going on in all areas of the classroom at all times. It is akin to the familiar "eyes in the back of the head." Kounin determined that this trait is communicated more effectively by teachers' behaviors than by their words, and further, that it is effective only if students are convinced that the teacher really knows what is going on. If Bob and Bill are not working, the teacher's behavior or words must clearly communicate, "I see you have not started. This must be done today!"

Kounin found two elements of withitness that contributed to effectiveness. The first is the ability to select the correct student for a desist. Suppose Bob and Bill are teasing Mary while the teacher is at work elsewhere with a small group. Mary finally says in a loud voice, "Stop that, you two!" The teacher tells Mary to go sit alone, giving no attention to the instigators of the incident. This tells the students that the teacher does not know what is really going on.

The second element is attending to the more serious deviancy when two are occurring simultaneously. To illustrate: Jill is playing with a toy at her desk. Meanwhile, James and Eric are pushing each other violently at the drinking fountain. The teacher looks up and says, "Jill, bring that toy up to me and get back to work." The teacher failed to take any action against the fight at the drinking fountain. If mistakes like this occur often, students begin to realize that the teacher is not truly aware. This encourages them to misbehave without fear of being caught.

Timing also influences withitness. A major mistake in timing is to wait until the misbehavior spreads before taking action. Mark crumples paper into a ball and throws it at the wastebasket. Ian sees this and decides to try it. Three or four others join into the shooting contest. This situation never would have occurred if their teacher had corrected the misbehavior when it first occurred. Proper timing shows students that the teacher knows exactly what is going on.

Another timing mistake is to allow the misbehavior to increase in seriousness before stopping it. Let's return to the example of the two boys at the drinking fountain. James went there to get a drink. Eric pushed his way in front of James. James pushed him out of the way claiming he himself was there first. Eric hit James, James hit back, and they began to scuffle. The teacher had waited too long to intervene. If she had been aware of what was happening, she could have spoken to the boys early and stopped the misbehavior.

Kounin found that if students perceive that teachers are with it (in that they immediately choose the right culprit and correct the misbehavior), they are less likely to misbehave, especially in teacher-directed lessons. Handling the correct deviant on time is more important to classroom control than is firmness or clarity of a desist.

OVERLAPPING

In his videotaped studies, Kounin became aware of a group-management technique that he labeled *overlapping*. Overlapping is the ability to attend to two issues at the same time. Here is an example. A teacher is meeting with a small group and notices that two students at their seats are playing cards instead of doing their assignment. The teacher could correct this either by:

 1. Stopping the small group activity, walking over to the cardplayers and getting them back on task, and then attempting to reestablish the small-group work; or

2. Having the small group continue while addressing the cardplayers from a distance, then monitoring the students at their desks while conducting the small-group activity.

As you can tell, the second approach involves overlapping. Teachers are often interrupted while working with groups or individuals. A student may approach with a paper that must be reviewed before the student can continue. Teachers adroit in overlapping can check the paper while glancing at the small group and adding encouraging remarks such as "Go on," or "That's correct." Thus, the teacher attends to two issues simultaneously.

Not surprisingly, Kounin found that teachers who were adept at overlapping were also aware of the broader scope of happenings in the classroom. They were more with-it. Overlapping loses its effectiveness if the teacher does not also demonstrate withit-ness. If students working independently know that the teacher is aware of them and able to deal with them, they are more likely to remain on task.

MOVEMENT MANAGEMENT

Kounin's research revealed an important relationship between student behavior and *movement* within and between lessons. He did not mean physical movement of students or teachers. He meant lesson movement—*pacing, momentum, and transitions.* Teachers' ability to move smoothly from one activity to the next and to maintain momentum within an activity has a great deal to do with their effectiveness in controlling behavior in the classroom. In smooth transitions, student attention is turned easily from one activity to another, thus keeping student attention on the task at hand.

Kounin discovered two transition mistakes—jerkiness and slowdowns—that seem to encourage student misbehavior. *Jerkiness* describes the failure to move smoothly from one activity to another. Suppose high school students are working on an art project. Unexpectedly, the teacher says, "Put your supplies away and get ready for a visitor." Half the class does not hear and the other half starts to move around in confusion. Or suppose an elementary class has just begun a math lesson. The teacher calls on three students to go to the board. On their way up, she suddenly asks, "How many of you brought your money for the field trip?" She then counts the raised hands, goes to her desk, and writes down the number.

Kounin gives many other examples of jerkiness in moving from one activity to another. They cause confusion, unnecessary activity, noise, delay, and misbehavior. These problems are minimized with smooth transitions, resulting from routines, clear directions, and completing one task before beginning another.

A second transition mistake Kounin discovered was one he called *slowdowns.* These are delays that waste time between activities. A typical slowdown comes from what Kounin called "overdwelling," that is, spending too much time giving directions and explanations or lecturing students about inappropriate behavior. Another type of slowdown occurs when teachers spend too much time on the details, rather than the main idea of a lesson. Suppose Mr. Anderson is doing a math lesson with the class. He writes some problems on the board for students to complete. He stops them frequently to insert comments such as "Make sure you leave space at the margins," "Remember to skip lines between problems," "Don't forget to number each problem," "Don't put more than three problems on a line," "Be sure to put boxes around your answers." These comments break student concentration and slow their progress.

Transitions may seem at first to be minor concerns, but Kounin concluded from his investigations that *teachers' ability to manage smooth transitions and maintain momentum was more important to work involvement and classroom control than any other behavior-management technique.*

GROUP FOCUS

Teachers have few opportunities to work exclusively with one student. Mostly they work with groups, sometimes the entire class, and sometimes several smaller groups concurrently. Kounin found that the ability to maintain a concerted group focus—that is, keeping students paying attention to the same thing at the same time—is essential to a productive, efficient classroom. Teachers are better able to maintain group focus when they take into account the (1) *group format*, (2) *degree of accountability* of each student for the content of the lesson, and (3) effective focus of group *attention*.

Group Format

Group format refers to grouping students in such a manner that maximum active participation is encouraged. Generally speaking this is obtained through larger, rather than smaller groups. Larger groups allow teachers to call on many different students instead of a few. When responses are desired, the teacher may ask the group to respond in unison, or one student may be asked to do an activity at the chalkboard or on the overhead projector while the remaining members of the group follow by doing the activity at their seats. Having everyone involved in an activity eliminates the group waiting for one member to perform.

Accountability

Accountability refers to each student in the group being responsible for learning each of the facts, concepts, or procedures being taught in a lesson. It is enhanced when teachers know exactly how each student is progressing. Kounin recommends several techniques for holding all members of a group accountable:

1. All students hold up response props for the teacher to see.
2. The teacher asks all members to observe and check on accuracy while one group member performs.
3. The teacher asks all members to write the answer and then, at random, calls on various students to respond.
4. The teacher circulates and observes the responses of nonreciters.

5. The teacher calls for a unison response and then checks individuals at random.

Group accountability has much in common with overlapping. The teacher is able to deal with the entire group and yet have individuals show accountability for their progress. When students perceive that the teacher will definitely and immediately hold them accountable for the content of the lesson, they are more likely to pay attention and remain involved in the activity.

Attention

Attention is a third element in group focus. All group members are expected to focus on the activity at all times. Kounin suggests the following for maintaining attentive group focus:

1. The teacher attracts attention by looking around the group in a suspenseful manner, or saying "Let's see who can . . . "
2. The teacher keeps in suspense who will be called on next and avoids a predictable pattern of response.
3. The teacher varies unison responses with individual responses.
4. Nonreciters are alerted that they may be called on in connection with a reciter's response: "Listen to Jim as he reads and see if you can guess who took the crystal ball."

All of these practices draw the attention of the group to the lesson, alerting every member.

Kounin also examined some common mistakes that contribute to inattention within the group:

1. The teacher focuses on one student at a time and excludes the other members from the lesson.
2. The teacher chooses a reciter before asking a question, allowing others to stop listening because they know they won't have to respond.
3. The teacher calls on students to respond in a predictable sequence, such as going clockwise around a circle. Students then only need to be ready to respond after their neighbor. This permits them to allow their attention to wander. (It is interesting to note that recent research casts some doubt on points 2 and 3. Some studies have shown slightly higher achievement in classes where students are called on in a predictable sequence.)

Of the three elements of group focus, Kounin found maintaining attention to be the most important. Teachers who held the attention of every member throughout the lesson were more successful at inducing work involvement and preventing misbehavior. As one might suspect, group accountability and attention accompany each other, and both come into play to a greater extent in teacher-directed lessons than in lessons where students work independently.

AVOIDING SATIATION

Satiation means getting filled up with something, getting enough of it. Kounin used the term to describe a change in the dynamics of an activity where students show progressively less interest, leading to boredom. Other behaviors may begin to surface, as well. For instance, students may introduce spontaneous variations into the activity. If made to write multiplication facts 10 times each, they may after a time start writing the top line of the problem across the paper, then adding the multiplication sign, then adding the bottom digits, and so on, rather than completing each problem separately.

Satiation causes careless work that results in increased errors. Students begin to do the work mechanically, devoting little thought to the process. The result is a breakdown in meaning. When students break up an activity in a different way to add variety, they may also lose their grasp of the process or concept being learned.

Satiated students not only tend to become less involved in an activity, they may try to escape from it. This is often shown in behaviors such as looking out the window, tying shoes, poking a neighbor, or needlessly sharpening a pencil. They look for anything to initiate some new type of stimulation.

Since satiation may interfere seriously with learning and good behavior, teachers are admonished to prevent its occurrence. As remedies, Kounin suggests providing progress, challenge, and variety.

Progress

Kounin studied many different classrooms to determine why some teachers induced more satiation than did others. One element that more effective teachers used to reduce satiation was providing the students a feeling of progress. Students who saw they were making definite progress took longer to become satiated. Those who did the same task over and over, without feeling they were progressing, satiated quickly.

Challenge

Kounin also noticed that teachers who offered challenges throughout a lesson forestalled satiation. One of the many ways they provided challenges was to show enthusiasm for the lesson with remarks like "I have a special magical math formula to teach you today." Another way was to elicit positive feelings about the lesson by saying something like "I know you'll all get the answer to the next one!" Teachers might make comments such as "Don't be fooled by this one. It's tricky!" These techniques work if the teacher is genuinely enthusiastic and positive.

Variety

Variety is not only the spice of life; it is the spice of most lessons. Kounin felt that variety plays a crucial role in reducing satiation and suggested that teachers vary their classroom activities. Elementary teachers, for example, might have a quiet reading time, followed by physical education, followed by math, and then a spelling game. Secondary teachers might alternate reading, discussion activities, creative production, and independent inquiry.

Within lessons, teachers may change the level of intellectual challenge. Sometimes, students may simply listen. At other times, they may practice a skill or demonstrate comprehension of concepts. The teacher may challenge them by having them engage in abstract thinking or exhibit some sort of creativity.

Teachers can also vary the way they present lessons. They can demonstrate, direct an activity, ask questions for discussion, or have students solve problems on their own. While monitoring the students, teachers may circulate among them or participate in the activities. Students enjoy variety in styles or presentation as well as variety among lessons, even when covering the same material.

Variety can also be provided in the materials used to enhance or extend learning. Some activities call for the usual pencil and paper, but others can make excellent use of slides, tape recorders, or such unusual things as live snakes or real musicians.

Finally, restructuring groups can add variety. One may start a lesson with the entire class, break into small groups for close interaction, and then reconvene into the whole class. The focus changes from teacher to students and back to teacher. Variety is provided through movement and different kinds of interacting and thinking.

COMMENTS ON KOUNIN'S MODEL

The techniques advocated by Kounin for class control are all intended to create and maintain a classroom atmosphere conducive to learning. By keeping students busily (and happily) engaged, behavior problems are reduced to a minimum.

In order to function as Kounin suggests, teachers must be able to deal with the entire class, various subgroups, and individual students, often at the same time. Kounin does not believe that teachers' personality traits are particularly important in classroom control. What is important, he insists, is teachers' ability to manage groups and lessons. To reiterate, teachers must:

1. Know what is happening in every area of the classroom at all times and communicate that fact to students.
2. Be able to deal with more than one issue at a time.
3. Correct the appropriate target before misbehavior escalates.
4. Ensure smooth transitions from one activity to another.
5. Maintain group focus through alerting and accountability.
6. Provide nonsatiating learning programs by emphasizing progress, challenge, and variety.

Kounin's ideas have been widely acknowledged and received. Most of today's discipline systems incorporate his findings, as will become evident as the remaining models are presented. There is no doubt of the value of his suggestions in maintaining a good learning environment, one that also prevents misbehavior. For that reason his suggestions fit best into the *preventive* facet of discipline. As an entire system of discipline, however, teachers find that Kounin's suggestions are of less help in supportive discipline and almost no help at all in the techniques of *corrective* discipline, where misbehavior must be stopped and redirected positively.

Application Exercises

The Concept Cases: Kris, Sara, Joshua, and Tom.

CASE #1. KRIS WILL NOT WORK:

Kris, in Mr. Jake's class, is quite docile. She never disrupts class and does little socializing with other students. But despite Mr. Jake's best efforts, Kris rarely completes an assignment. She doesn't seem to care. She is simply there, putting forth virtually no effort.

How would Kounin deal with Kris? Kounin would suggest to teachers that they use the following sequence of interventions until they find one that is effective with Kris.

1. Use the ripple effect. "I see many people have already completed half their work." Look at Kris. Later comment, "I'm afraid a few people will have to stay late to complete their work."
2. Let Kris know you are aware she is not working. Say to her, "I see you have barely started. This work must be done today!"
3. Call on Kris in discussions preceding independent work, as a means of involving her in the lesson.
4. Point out Kris's progress when it occurs: "Good! Now you are on the track! Keep up the good work."
5. Provide variety. Continually challenge Kris to accomplish more.
6. Hold Kris accountable with group focus techniques. Do not disregard her just because she has been unproductive.

CASE #2. SARA CANNOT STOP TALKING:

Sara is a pleasant girl who participates in class activities and does most, though not all, of her assigned work. She cannot seem to refrain from talking to classmates, however. Her teacher, Mr. Gonzales, has to speak to her repeatedly during lessons, to the point that he often becomes exasperated and loses his temper.

What suggestions would Kounin give Mr. Gonzales to help stop Sara's misbehavior?

CASE #3. JOSHUA CLOWNS AND INTIMIDATES:

Joshua, larger and louder than his classmates, always wants to be the center of attention, which he accomplishes through a combination of clowning and intimidation. He makes wise remarks, talks back (smilingly) to the teacher, utters a variety of sound effect noises such as automobile crashes and gunshots, and makes limitless sarcastic comments and put-downs of his classmates.

Other students will not stand up to him, apparently fearing his size and verbal aggression. His teacher, Miss Pearl, has come to her wits' end.

Do you find anything in Kounin's work that might help Miss Pearl deal with Joshua?

CASE #4. TOM IS HOSTILE AND DEFIANT:

Tom has appeared to be in his usual foul mood ever since arriving in class. He gets up and on his way to sharpen his pencil he bumps into Frank. Frank complains. Tom tells him loudly to shut up. Miss Baines, the teacher, says, "Tom, go back to your seat."

Tom wheels around, swears loudly, and says heatedly, "I'll go when I'm damned good and ready!"

What advice has Kounin provided to help Miss Baines deal with Tom?

QUESTIONS:

1. How do you think withitness and the ripple effect would work with Kris, Sara, Joshua, and Tom?
2. How might Sara's behavior affect others in the class? How could the bad effects, if any, be reduced?
3. According to Kounin's findings, (a) which students in the class would be most affected by the following teacher actions and comments, and (b) how would they be affected?

    Mr. Kent says, "Kevin, I see you bothering Brian while you are supposed to be working. In this class we keep our hands to ourselves."

    Mr. Kent says, "Kevin, stop that immediately! I will not allow that in my classroom!"

    Mr. Kent grabs Kevin by the arm and sits him in a chair, shouting, "You stop that!"
4. Evaluate the following to determine where, and to what extent, satiation might become a problem. Explain your conclusions.

    Mr. Kent does not allow students to move ahead into a new unit of work until all students have completed the old unit with passing scores. Those who pass early are given review and practice pages until the others catch up.

    Mr. Grant allows students to move on to the next unit as soon as they can get a passing score. He helps slower students who need more work to learn the concepts.

    During his 50-minute period, Mr. Smith usually provides some direct instruction, some small-group activity, and some independent work.
5. One of the things Ms. Alletto's students like best about her is that she never pressures them to move quickly from one activity to the next. She seems to understand their need to talk with each other about nonschool matters. She always waits until all the class gets ready before she begins a new lesson or activity. What would Kounin say about Ms. Alletto's tolerant approach?

FURTHER ANALYSIS AND APPLICATION:

Examine scenario #4 (elementary) or #5 (secondary) in Chapter 13. Which of Kounin's suggestions would be helpful to Mrs. Desmond or Mrs. Reed in establishing a more productive and pleasant learning environment?

REFERENCES

Kounin, J. (1971; 1977). *Discipline and group management in classrooms.* New York: Holt, Rinehart and Winston.

CHAPTER 3

The Neo-Skinnerian Model:
Shaping Desired Behavior

SKINNER BIOGRAPHICAL SKETCH

B. F. Skinner (1904–1990) is considered by many authorities to have been the greatest behavioral psychologist of all time. Born in Susquehanna, Pennsylvania, he earned his PhD in psychology at Harvard in 1931 and spent most of his academic career at that university. There, he conducted his famous experimental studies in learning.

Earlier behaviorism had been concerned with stimulus-response connections. Skinner looked at the learning process in the opposite way, investigating how learning was affected by stimuli presented *after* an act was performed. He found that certain stimuli caused the organism to repeat an act more frequently. He called stimuli with that effect *reinforcers*. He found that by providing reinforcers in a systematic way (called reinforcement) one could shape behavior in desired directions.

Skinner's work was not confined to laboratory animals. He drew worldwide attention for his ideas about raising infants inside glass enclosures called air cribs where the child was kept dry, warm, and comfortable, with all needs satisfied. He raised his own daughter in an air crib.

Skinner drew much attention, too, with the publication of his novel *Walden Two* (1948), which described the workings of a utopian community that made extensive use of the principles of reinforcement. It is still widely read and has served as a model for communes in various places.

In 1971, Skinner's book *Beyond Freedom and Dignity* was published, and again world attention turned to him. He challenged traditional concepts of freedom and dignity as inadequate, insisting they are outmoded, useless, and incorrect. We are not free to choose, he asserted. Our choices are made, instead, on the basis of what has happened to us in the past; that is, on which of our various behaviors have been reinforced. Instead of concentrating on free choice, we should turn our efforts to providing conditions that improve human behavior in general.

Teachers have benefited most from Skinner's fundamental work in reinforcement as a means of controlling and motivating student behavior. Skinner's work has been enlarged, extended, and modified by numerous psychologists and educators. Its various applications to classroom practice are commonly called *behavior modification,* a technique that many teachers consider to be one of their most valuable tools for improving both learning and behavior of their students.

SKINNER'S MAIN FOCUS

Human behavior can be shaped along desired lines by means of the systematic application of reinforcement.

Skinner's Key Ideas

The model presented in this chapter is called neo-Skinnerian to indicate that it is made up of new applications of Skinner's basic ideas. Skinner himself never proposed a model of school discipline. Other writers, such as Sharpley (1985), McIntyre (1989), and Macht (1989), have taken his ideas on learning and adapted them to controlling the behavior of students in school. The following ideas reveal the essence of the neo-Skinnerian model:

1. Behavior is shaped by its consequences, by what happens to the individual immediately afterward.
2. Systematic use of reinforcement (rewards) can shape students' behavior in desired directions.
3. Behavior becomes weaker if not followed by reinforcement.
4. Behavior is also weakened by punishment.
5. In the early stages of learning, constant reinforcement produces the best results.
6. Once learning has reached the desired level, it is best maintained through intermittent reinforcement, provided only occasionally.
7. Behavior modification is applied in these two main ways:
   a) The teacher observes the student perform a desired act; the teacher rewards the student; the student tends to repeat the act.
   b) The teacher observes the student perform an undesired act; the teacher either ignores the act or punishes the student, then praises a student who is behaving correctly; the misbehaving student becomes less likely than before to repeat the act.
8. Behavior modification successfully uses various kinds of reinforcers. They include social reinforcers such as verbal comments, facial expressions, and gestures; graphic reinforcers such as marks and stars; activity reinforcers such as free time and collaborating with a friend; and tangible reinforcers such as prizes and printed awards.

Remember that the model of discipline described in this chapter was not proposed by B. F. Skinner, but rather is a composite of his ideas and their extensions made by many people following in his footsteps. It is a powerful model for classroom teachers, one that can be easily modified and implemented with students of all ages and backgrounds. The model will be examined by: (1) considering essential terminology; (2) noting beneficial aspects of the model; (3) reemphasizing the dangers of punishment; (4) explaining various types of reinforcers; (5) exploring systems of behavior modification; (6) showing how a plan of behavior modification is formulated; and (7) showing how a plan of behavior modification is implemented.

ESSENTIAL TERMINOLOGY

Skinner established precise definitions of terms he used, such as *operant behavior, reinforcing stimuli, schedules of reinforcement, successive approximations, positive reinforcement,* and *negative reinforcement.* You must understand the meanings of these terms if you are to understand the model well. We need not be overly concerned about the exact wording of Skinner's definitions, but the fundamental concepts inherent in each are of basic importance.

Operant behavior is simply behavior that the student produces. It comes not as a response, reaction, or reflex but as purposeful voluntary action. Operant behaviors may be any of the immense variety of actions that individuals are able to perform voluntarily, such as entering the room quietly, taking a seat, completing an assignment, listening during a lesson, and so on.

Reinforcing stimuli are stimuli that the individual receives immediately after performing an operant behavior. In school, they include such things as smiles, nods, praise, points, and free time. We can think of reinforcers as rewards. When we see a student exhibit any behavior (operant) that we think especially worthy of attention we can immediately give that individual a reward. Receiving the reward pleases the student, who will likely repeat the behavior. The process of supplying rewards is called *reinforcement*.

Schedules of reinforcement were important in Skinner's experimental work. Different schedules were shown to produce different effects. Constant reinforcement, provided every time a desired act is seen, is most effective in establishing new learnings. Every time all students in the class enter quietly, sit down, and look at the teacher, they are awarded a team point that goes toward earning a specific benefit at a later time. Individuals work hard and fast to earn prized rewards. Once new learning is acquired it can be maintained indefinitely by using intermittent reinforcement, in which reward is supplied only occasionally. The individual knows that reward will come sooner or later and so keeps on trying.

Successive approximations refers to a progression in which actions (operants) come closer and closer to a preset goal. Teachers have to work toward many learnings and behaviors in gradual ways, taking one small step at a time. Successive approximations are small-step improvements leading to the overall learning. For example, the class enters the room and sits down. There is still too much chatter but the teacher gives the class a point for improvement, in that everyone is seated. Later, the students will have to be seated and quiet to earn a point. Teachers reinforce the small improvements to help the students progress more rapidly.

Positive reinforcement is the process of supplying a reward that the student wants, something that will spur greater effort. In classrooms, teachers provide effective reinforcement by means of comments (good job; nice work), stickers, and points. For classroom purposes we need not confuse ourselves about positive and negative reinforcement. We can simply call all rewards reinforcers.

Negative reinforcement is a term that is misunderstood (and used incorrectly) by most classroom teachers. They think of negative reinforcement as meaning harsh punishment that will suppress behavior. Just the opposite is true. Negative reinforcement *increases* the likelihood of behavior, just as does positive reinforcement. Negative means taking away something that the student doesn't like, rather that adding something that the student does like. Negative reinforcement has only limited application in classrooms. Tauber (1982) illustrates the process with the following examples: "If you score 80 percent or higher on the exam, you will not have to turn in a final paper." (The final paper is "taken away" as a reward for scoring well on the exam.) "If you get all of your assignments in on time . . . you will be allowed to drop your lowest grade" (p. 66). These examples show how negative reinforcement is provided through the removal of an "aversive"—the removal of something students dislike.

BENEFICIAL ASPECTS OF BEHAVIOR MODIFICATION

Since the beginning of human history, parents and teachers have used punishment to motivate learning in the young. Learners did what they were supposed to do or suffered harsh lectures or even physical punishment from their teachers. This punitive system of motivation persists to the present day and is still evident in some class-rooms. But is it effective?

Skinner found in his experiments that animals worked harder and learned more quickly if given rewards for doing something right than if given punishment for doing wrong. This made sense when working with rats and pigeons because there was no way to tell them what we wanted them to do and what would happen to them if they didn't comply.

When the notion of providing rewards for desired behavior was applied to school students, an interesting fact came to light. Students, like rats and pigeons, responded better to positive rewards than they did to punishment. Of course, there were, and are, exceptions. But generally speaking, rewards spur interest and effort. Moreover, they help clarify what is expected.

Behavior modification is based almost entirely on rewards. It gives teachers power to work with students in positive ways. It lets them get away from harshness and punishment, which neither students nor teachers like. It allows them to maintain control within classroom environments that are warm, supportive, and positive, in-stead of cold, harsh, and punitive. This coincides with a growing trend toward humaneness in all walks of life.

Behavior modification is good for speeding the learning of academic material as well as enhancing good personal behavior. It has the advantage of allowing the teacher to work in a supportive manner, emphasizing the positive and reducing the negative. It also helps students build desired behavior. A little reward given as each step is accomplished helps spur interest and desire to behave acceptably.

THE DANGERS OF PUNISHMENT

Punishment is effective in stopping undesired behavior. It works quickly, much more quickly than positive reinforcement. When students are fighting, it is ludicrous to think of allowing the fight to continue while looking for a student who is sitting quietly so you can say, "Thank you, Susan, for sitting quietly and not fighting." Instead, we do whatever is necessary to stop the fight and suppress students' inclina-tion to continue, even if that means punishing the offenders.

Skinner did not, at first, believe that punishment weakened misbehavior. He stated that punishment could suppress misbehavior but not eradicate it. He later had to change his mind, based on experiments he conducted.

But punishment has its dark side. While it suppresses unwanted behavior, it produces side effects that sometimes override the best educational intents. If students see punishment as unwarranted, malicious, or excessive, bad feelings result that are very difficult to overcome. Those feelings may provoke retaliation toward the teacher and other students, or withdrawal. Meanwhile, punishment reteaches that might makes right.

For these reasons, teachers are advised to use punishment as little as possible, to try the positive approach first. Of course, students must know what they are doing wrong, if it is not evident to them. And they must also know how they are supposed to behave.

An effective middle ground is to use punishment depicted as the logical consequence that follows misbehavior. Students may be punished (not harshly), but only after they have previously been informed of exactly what is expected of them, what will happen when they comply, and what will happen (the logical consequences) when they do not. In this fashion, students come to understand that they themselves choose the punishment that invariably accompanies misbehavior.

TYPES OF REINFORCERS

Bear in mind that reinforcers can be anything that an individual wants badly enough to do something to earn them. They can range from such mundane things as a breath of fresh air to such rarities as Pulitzer prizes. Many of the things that students want cannot be dispensed in school, and while that puts limitations on what teachers can use as reinforcers, they still have a powerful arsenal at their disposal. Reinforcers commonly used in schools fall into four categories: social, graphic, activity, and tangible.

Social reinforcers consist of words, gestures, and facial expressions. Many students work diligently just to get a smile, pat, or kind word from the teacher. Some examples are:

Verbal

- Okay. Wow! Excellent. Nice going. Exactly. Right. Thank you. I like that. Would you share that?

Nonverbal

- Smiles, winks, eye contact, nods, thumbs up, touches, pats, handshakes, walk beside, stand near.

Graphic reinforcers include marks of various kinds, such as numerals, checks, happy faces, and special symbols. Teachers make these marks with felt pens and rubber stamps. They may enter them on charts or use a paper punch to make holes in cards kept by the students. They may attach stars or stickers that are commercially available in large quantities and varieties.

Activity reinforcers include those activities that students prefer in school. Any school activity can be used as a reinforcer if students prefer it to another. Examples of activities that usually reinforce academic learning are:

For younger students

- Being a monitor, sitting near the teacher, choosing the song, caring for the pet, sharing a pet or toy.

For middle students

- Playing a game, free reading, decorating the classroom, having extra recess time, going to an assembly.

For older students

- Working with a friend, being excused from a test, working on a special project, being excused from homework.

Tangible reinforcers are real objects that students can earn as rewards for desired behavior and are more powerful for some students than other types of reinforcers. They are widely used with students who have special behavior problems. Many elementary teachers use tangible reinforcers regularly. Examples of inexpensive reinforcers are: popcorn, raisins, chalk, crayons, felt pens, pencils, badges, decals, pennants, used books, old magazines, stationery, posters, rubber stamps, certificates, notes, letters, and plastic tokens.

SYSTEMS OF BEHAVIOR MODIFICATION

Behavior modification works even when done sporadically, but it is best approached in a systematic way. A random approach has been used for decades, based on teachers' praising students for doing good work. That fact causes many teachers to say, when behavior modification is introduced, "But I've always done that." In truth, however, few teachers in the past used reinforcement systematically as a means of shaping desired behavior. They used praise on a hit-or-miss basis. Behavior modification is maximally effective when used in an organized, systematic, and consistent manner.

Systems of behavior modification are legion. Every teacher adds a personal twist. Such flexibility is a strength because it allows teachers to apply reinforcement in ways consistent with their personalities and those of their students. The multitude of systems fits roughly into five categories: (1) informal "catch 'em being good"; (2) rules-ignore-praise (RIP); (3) rules-reward-punishment (RRP); (4) contingency management; and (5) contracting.

Catch 'Em Being Good

This approach rests solely on rewarding students who are doing what is expected. The teacher says, "Class, take out your math books." Several students get their books at once. Others waste time talking. The teacher picks out students who acted as directed and says: "Thank you, Helen, for being ready. Thank you, Ted. I like the way Ramon got his book immediately." Many other students then open their books at once and pay attention. This strategy offers two benefits. First, it reinforces the proper behavior of Helen, Ted, and Ramon, and second, it shapes behavior of other students as well. The catch 'em being good approach is highly effective in primary grades. Teachers through third grade use it extensively. By fourth grade it begins to lose effectiveness, and by junior high students find it laughable. Older students do, however, tend to respond well when reinforced as a group rather than being singled out individually. There are, however, still better approaches to be used with older students.

Rules–Ignore–Praise (RIP)

The RIP approach is used as follows. The teacher, perhaps with student involvement, formulates a set of rules for class behavior. The rules might be:

1. Be courteous to others.
2. Keep hands, feet, and objects to yourself.
3. Complete all assignments.
4. Work without disturbing others.
5. Follow all directions.

These rules are made very clear and understandable to the students. They may be written on a chart and posted at the front of the room. This list is kept short—five or six rules, few enough that students, with reminders, can keep them in mind.

Once the rules are established, the teacher watches for people who are complying with them. She might say, "Row 1 is doing an excellent job of following directions!" Students who comply with the rules receive praise, and every student is praised as often as possible. Student behavior that breaks the rules is ignored. That is, no direct attention at all is given to the student. No reinforcement comes from the teacher. Instead, the teacher immediately finds a student who is following the rules and praises that student. When Mrs. Jenet sees Tim poke his neighbor, she goes to an adjacent student, Sally, who is following the rules, gives Sally a sticker, and says, "Thank you Sally for working without bothering others."

This system works fairly well at the elementary level, provided that the class is relatively well-behaved to begin with. But it is not effective at the secondary level. Students speak derisively of peers who receive public praise from the teacher, calling them pets and "kiss-ups." Moreover, secondary students when misbehaving are not shaped well through praise given to others. They are already getting enough positive reinforcement in the form of peer attention, teacher attention, and laughter.

Rules–Reward–Punishment (RRP)

The RRP approach builds limits and consequences into behavior modification. As with RIP, RRP begins with rules and emphasizes rewards, but it does not ignore inappropriate behavior. The added factor of limits and consequences makes this approach especially effective with older students and with students who have behavior problems.

The rules phase is the same as described earlier. Rules, as few in number as possible, are established, understood, and put on written display. The teacher becomes very direct about compliance. Students who follow the rules will be rewarded in various ways. They will receive praise, if appropriate. They will receive laudatory notes to take home to their parents. They will earn points that count toward a larger reward, either for the individual or for the class as a whole.

Students are clearly informed about what will happen if the rules are broken. They realize that it is their prerogative to break the rules. But if they do so, they simultaneously choose the consequences that follow and punishment is invoked immediately in accord with procedures described fully and carefully to the class. When Jane refuses to begin her work, Mr. Trammel tells her that, in accord with the rules and consequences, she must sit at the table in the rear of the room until she completes her assignment. In a sense the teacher does not punish misbehavior; students punish themselves. They have chosen to behave in ways that automatically bring undesired consequences.

This system is quite effective with older students. It clearly sets expectations, rewards, and punishments. Students consider it fair, know that they have the power to choose consequences through their behavior, and that the responsibility for good behavior rests directly on their shoulders.

Contingency Management

Mrs. Vickers explained that she uses a "token economy" in her classroom. If the students stay in their seats, raise their hands, finish their work, and so on, she rewards them with plastic chips. The chips can be exchanged later for desired rewards.

Mrs. Vickers' plan is an example of contingency management, which involves an elaborate system of tangible reinforcers. It has been used widely with all types of students at kindergarten through high school. It has been shown to be especially effective for working with behavior-problem students and with the mentally retarded.

Sometimes referred to as token economies, contingency management systems use tokens that students earn for desired behaviors such as staying in their seats, raising their hands, finishing their work, improving over past performance, and so forth. The tokens may be exchanged for tokens of higher value or cashed in for prizes such as food, toys, comic books, magazines, badges, privileges, and other activities. In actual practice, teachers find that the tokens often become sufficiently rewarding in themselves. Students have no desire to cash them in, preferring simply to amass and possess the tokens. Plastic discs and poker chips are often used for tokens. Some teachers print up play money in different denominations, as well as special certificates of various types.

Teachers who use token economies must be sure to award the tokens fairly and consistently. They must have an adequate supply of tokens, provide a manageable way for students to keep their tokens, and be sure that counterfeiting and extortion do not occur. They must set aside a time every few weeks for students to cash in their tokens. Students can buy "white elephants" that other students have brought from home, the teacher can obtain free materials from various shops and stores, and vouchers can be made for special activities and privileges. Each object and voucher has its price in tokens. Some teachers like to have auctions in which students bid for the items available.

Teachers who use this plan should explain it very carefully to the principal, the students, and the parents before putting it into practice. This ensures that everyone approves and understands what is taking place, thus preventing objections that are otherwise likely to occur.

Contracting

Behavior contracts are widely used with older students, and are especially favored in working with individual students of all ages who are hard to manage. Contracts specify work to be done or behavior to be established, with deadlines for completion. They indicate what the payoff will be for successful accomplishment, and they indicate what input the teacher will give. They lend an air of legality, promise, and responsibility. Student and teacher both sign the agreement. Sometimes parents cosign with the student.

Mr. Lex has a contract with Jesse, who has been continually remiss in bringing needed materials to class. Jesse has agreed to bring paper, pencil, and textbook to class every day. If he does this five days in a row, he gets five points. When he has accumulated 15 points he can exchange them for a special pen from Mr. Lex's collection.

Contract forms can be prepared and duplicated in quantity. For older students quasi-legal terminology adds a pleasing touch, as do filigree and official stamps of gold foil or contact paper. While contracts are fun to use, they must be seen as serious commitments, the terms of which must be lived up to by all who have signed.

PLANNING AND IMPLEMENTING
BEHAVIOR MODIFICATION

Teachers who intend to use behavior modification need to spend some time planning in advance. According to various experts, the planning should focus on two things: (1) analysis of the behaviors one wants to change, and (2) development of a specific plan to change those behaviors.

Analysis consists of identifying the behaviors to be changed or improved, deciding what is wrong with them at present, and determining what they should be in the future. It should include consideration of *antecedents,* conditions in the classroom that encourage misbehavior, and *consequences,* the system of rewards and punishments that will be used to motivate and guide student behavior. Antecedents include such factors as distractions, boredom, poor models, awkward transitions between lessons, and so forth. Consequences include, as reinforcers, any of the many factors already described in this chapter as well as the logical-consequence punishers that suppress misbehavior. This analysis may at first appear to be a complicated process, but in fact it can be done adequately within a few minutes.

Implementation refers to formulating the behavior modification plan and putting it into practice. The plan follows from the analysis of behavior and the identification of desired reinforcers and punishers. It may be written in outline form, providing reminders of specific things to be done, and it can be used jointly by teachers and students.

Target behaviors are the new behaviors that one wishes to see exhibited by students. Systematic reinforcement shapes classroom behavior in the direction of those targets. If a target behavior is to prevent students from talking out in class without permission, the teacher might reward people who raise their hands and wait to be called on before they speak. Verbal praise can be used for reinforcement, such as, "Thank you, Maria, for raising your hand." If the target behavior is to stay on task for the entire work period, reinforcements are given for that behavior. Reinforcement is given very frequently at first, and as the behavior improves rewards are given less frequently.

The implementation plan calls for correcting antecedent conditions that might be contributing to poor behavior, things such as uncertainty about rules, forgetfulness, poor peer models, inadequate teacher models, awkward times between lessons, poor lesson pacing, boredom, frustration, and lack of interesting activities for students. Removal of such conditions gives the behavior modification plan a much greater chance of success.

Students who chronically misbehave do so in part because their misbehavior is bringing them some type of reinforcement. These reinforcers might include teacher and peer attention, laughter, sense of power, and getting one's own way. This pattern must be changed so that misbehavior brings negative consequences rather than positive ones. Negative consequences range from ignoring (by both teacher and students) to isolation from the group. Positive consequences meanwhile must be supplied for desired behavior. Teachers can always find someone doing what they are supposed to do. Teachers identify that person by name (at primary grade levels) and tell what the person was doing right. At secondary levels, teachers reinforce the behavior anonymously, for example: "Class, I really appreciate the way many of you helped us get started by having your work ready."

Students can also learn to reinforce themselves, a tactic that can be quite powerful. Suggestions for self-reward have been put forth by several authorities. One of the earliest was Ogden Lindsley ("Precision Teaching," 1971) who described a technique he called precision teaching that involves graphing student performance, whether academic or personal behavior. The graph documents performance, but it has a great additional advantage: Students can graph their own performance, which greatly increases their interest in improving. Seeing improvement serves additionally to reinforce students' efforts to do well.

Another example of student self-reinforcement comes from Mahoney and Thoresen (1972), who described a system in which students set up their own systems of reward and punishment, which they apply as consequences to their own behavior. Kindergarten students who finish their artwork may go on their own to the play area. Fifth graders who have not disrupted for the entire math period may go to the reinforcement area and pick up a permit for 10 minutes of free reading. Secondary students who complete assignments accurately before they are due allow themselves to work together with a friend.

Self-rewarding is, of course, subject to misuse. Students will not always earn the reinforcement they select. In this event, teachers must first inspect the student's work or behavior, then signal an okay for the reinforcement. The student then selects the reinforcer.

COMMENTS ON BEHAVIOR MODIFICATION

Teachers who once begin using behavior modification in a systematic way tend to stick with it, appreciating its powerful effects. They come to see it not as manipulating students but as freeing them to behave in ways that bring success and positive recognition. Systematic attention and reinforcing become natural parts of the teaching act, occurring automatically. After a while, teachers do not even have to think of them. That natural spontaneity makes reinforcement even more effective. Students feel that the teacher is simply kind, considerate, and friendly, not designing or manipulative.

But do teachers see behavior modification for what it really is? And if they do, are its inherent dangers evident to them?

Considerable controversy over these questions began decades ago and continues to the present time. One of the most perplexing questions has to do with whether, and to what extent, behavior modification amounts to blatant teacher control of students' thoughts and actions. Related to that question is the concern over free will, which most people believe to be the essential quality that sets mankind apart from other organisms. Skinner rejected the concept of free will, which he considered to be a formidable roadblock to understanding human behavior.

In recent years, research has cast doubt on whether rewards, the keystone of behavior modification, actually serve to strengthen desired learning and behavior. Some contend that rewards serve to reduce intrinsic motivation, supplanting it with a control-system of compliance and external motivation (Hill, 1990).

In truth, not all teachers like behavior modification, but those who do, say it makes teaching easier and more enjoyable. With regard to discipline, they find behavior modification especially effective in preventive and supportive control, though they admit it is slow and cumbersome (and often ineffective) when it comes to correcting misbehavior.

Application Exercises

Concept Cases: Kris, Sara, Joshua, and Tom.

CASE #1. KRIS WILL NOT WORK:

Kris, in Mr. Jake's class, is quite docile. She never disrupts class and does little socializing with other students. But despite all his efforts, Mr. Jake can hardly get Kris to participate in class activities. She rarely completes an assignment. She is simply there, like a bump on a log, putting forth no effort.

How would Skinner deal with Kris? Skinner would suggest that Mr. Jake try the following approaches with Kris.

1. Catch Kris being good (doing anything that is appropriate). Reward her whenever she participates or works.
2. Reiterate the class rules regarding work. Praise Kris whenever she follows the rules.
3. Consider stronger reinforcers. If praise is ineffective, use points, tokens, or other tangible objects to reinforce and shape Kris's improvement.
4. Set up a contract with Kris. Identify a reward that is exceptionally attractive to her. Outline what she must do in order to earn the reward. Share the contract with Kris's parents to enlist their support. Reinforce every improvement Kris makes.

CASE #2. SARA CANNOT STOP TALKING:

Sara is a pleasant girl who participates in class activities and does most, though not all, of her assigned work. She cannot seem to refrain from talking to classmates, however. Her teacher, Mr. Gonzales, has to speak to her repeatedly during lessons, to the point that he often becomes exasperated and loses his temper.

What techniques of behavior modification might help Mr. Gonzales in dealing with Sara?

CASE #3. JOSHUA CLOWNS AND INTIMIDATES:

Joshua, larger and louder than his classmates, always wants to be the center of attention, which he accomplishes through a combination of clowning and intimidation. He makes wise remarks, talks back (smilingly) to the teacher, utters a variety of sound effect noises such as automobile crashes and gunshots, and makes limitless sarcastic comments and put-downs of his classmates. Other students will not stand up to him, apparently fearing his size and verbal aggression. His teacher, Miss Pearl, has come to her wits' end.

What approach to behavior modification do you believe would be most appropriate for working with Joshua?

CASE #4. TOM IS HOSTILE AND DEFIANT:

Tom has appeared to be in his usual foul mood ever since arriving in class. He gets up and on his way to sharpen his pencil he bumps into Frank. Frank complains. Tom tells him loudly to shut up. Miss Baines, the teacher, says, "Tom, go back to your seat." Tom wheels around, swears loudly and says heatedly, "I'll go when I'm damned good and ready!"

How would Skinner have Miss Baines deal with Tom?

QUESTIONS AND ACTIVITIES:

1. In general terms, how would effective systems of behavior modification differ between primary grades and high school?
2. Ms. Wong is having problems in her classroom. The students enter boisterously and take a long time to settle down. They call out answers and make smart remarks during the lessons. Many do not pay attention when Ms. Wong is talking. Describe how you would set up a behavior modification system with Ms. Wong's class. (You may prepare it as if Ms. Wong's class were a first-, sixth-, or tenth-grade class.)

Application Exercises (continued)

3. Describe how you would create an effective contract with a student (you choose the grade level) who is chronically tardy to class.

FURTHER ANALYSIS AND APPLICATION:

Examine scenario #7 (elementary) or #8 (secondary) in Chapter 13. Explain how principles of behavior modification might improve the behaviors of specific students in Mrs. Bates's or Mr. Jaramillo's class.

REFERENCES

Firth, G. (1985). *Behavior management in the schools: A primer for parents.* New York: Thomas.

Hill, D. (1990). Order in the classroom. *Teacher, 1*(7), 70–77.

Ladoucer, R., & Armstrong, J. (1983). Evaluation of a behavioral program for the improvement of grades among high school students. *Journal of Counseling Psychology, 30,* 100–103.

Macht, J. (1989). *Managing classroom behavior: An ecological approach to academic and social learning.* White Plains, NY: Longman.

Mahoney, M., & Thoresen, C. (1972), Behavioral self-control—Power to the person, *Educational Researcher, 1,* 5–7.

McIntyre, T. (1989). *The behavior management handbook: Setting up effective behavior management systems.* Boston: Allyn & Bacon.

Precision teaching in perspective: an interview with Ogden R. Lindsley. (1971). *Teaching Exceptional Children, 3,* 114–119.

Sharpley, C. (1985). Implicit rewards in the classroom. *Contemporary Educational Psychology, 10,* 349–368.

Skinner, B. F. (1948). *Walden Two.* New York: Macmillan.

Skinner, B. F. (1971). *Beyond freedom and dignity.* New York: Knopf.

Tauber, R. (1982). Negative reinforcement: A positive strategy in classroom management. *Clearing House, 56,* 64–67.

CHAPTER 4

The Ginott Model:

Addressing the Situation with Sane Messages

GINOTT BIOGRAPHICAL SKETCH

Haim Ginott (1922–1973) was born in Tel Aviv, Israel. He earned his PhD at Columbia University in 1952 and went on to become a professor of psychology at New York University Graduate School and a professor of psychology at Adelphi University. He also served in Israel as a UNESCO consultant, was a resident psychologist on television's "Today Show," and wrote a weekly syndicated column entitled "Between Us," that dealt with interpersonal communication.

Among educators, Ginott is best known for three books that dealt with relationships between adults and the young. In the first two, *Between Parent and Child* (1965) and *Between Parent and Teenager* (1969), he offered solutions to communication breakdowns that occur between parents and their offspring. He believed that adults vitally impact children's self-esteem through the messages they send. In an attempt to make that impact positive, he developed specific skills for dealing with parent-child conflicts. As a fundamental principle, Ginott emphasized addressing the situation while avoiding attacks on the child's character. He urged parents to show their offspring that they still like them even when they disapprove of their children's behavior.

In a later book, *Teacher and Child* (1971), Ginott showed how those ideas are extended to the classroom. Teachers, like parents, he said, hold the power to make or break a child's self-concept. *Teacher and Child* deals with methods of communication that maintain a secure, humanitarian, and productive classroom environment.

GINOTT'S MAIN FOCUS

Discipline is a series of little victories, brought about when teachers use *sane messages*—messages that address the situation rather than the students' character—to guide students away from inappropriate behavior toward behavior that is appropriate and lasting.

Ginott's Key Ideas

The following is a list of key ideas advocated in Ginott's model of discipline. The remainder of the chapter elaborates on these ideas.

1. Discipline is a series of little victories, not something that occurs overnight.
2. The most important ingredient in classroom discipline is the teacher's own self-discipline.
3. The second most important ingredient is using sane messages when correcting misbehaving students. Sane message are messages that address the situation and do not attack students' characters.
4. Teachers at their best use *congruent communication,* communication that is harmonious with students' feelings about situations and themselves.
5. Teachers at their worst attack and label students' characters.
6. Teachers should model the behavior they hope to see in their students.

7. Inviting cooperation from students is vastly preferable to demanding it.
8. Teachers should express anger but in appropriate (sane) ways.
9. Labeling students disables them—they tend to live up to the label.
10. Sarcasm is almost always dangerous, and praise is often dangerous. Use both with great care.
11. Apologies from students should be accepted with the understanding that students intend to improve.
12. The best teachers help students to build their own self-esteem and to trust their own experience.

THE GINOTT MODEL OF DISCIPLINE

Teachers are a decisive, powerful element in the classroom. They create and maintain the environment. They have the power to humanize or dehumanize their students. Their effectiveness depends on their ability to establish an educational climate that promotes optimal learning. Children who are in constant emotional turmoil cannot learn. To reduce this turmoil, Ginott advocates using *congruent communication,* a harmonious and authentic way of talking in which teacher messages to students match the students' feelings about situations and themselves.

Ginott claims that the principle of congruent communication is the crucial factor in classroom climate. Teachers must constantly endeavor to use it. When they do so, they convey an attitude of helpfulness and acceptance and are continually aware of the impact of their messages on students' self-esteem. Congruent communication incorporates many different elements that we see expressed in Ginott's descriptions of teachers at their best and at their worst.

Teachers at Their Best

Ginott wrote at length about teachers at their best and at their worst. At their best, teachers use congruent communication, evidenced when they:

1. Send sane messages, addressing the situation rather than the student's character.
2. Express anger appropriately.
3. Invite cooperation.
4. Accept and acknowledge student feelings.
5. Avoid labeling students.
6. Correct students by directing them appropriately.
7. Avoid the perils of praise.
8. Are brief when correcting students.
9. Are models of humane behavior.

Teachers at Their Worst

Teachers at their worst fail to use congruent communication, as shown when they:

1. Are caustic and sarcastic.
2. Attack students' characters.
3. Demand, rather than invite, cooperation.
4. Deny students' feelings.
5. Label students as lazy, stupid, and so forth.
6. Give long and unnecessary lectures.
7. Lose their tempers and self-control.
8. Use praise to manipulate students.
9. Are poor models of humane behavior.

Let us look further at some of Ginott's suggestions for helping teachers function at their best.

Sane Messages

Sane messages address situations rather than students' characters. They *accept and acknowledge* how students feel. Sanity, according to Ginott, depends on people's ability to trust their own perception of reality. Too often, adults send insane messages, telling the young to distrust or deny their feelings or inner reality. They blame, preach, command, accuse, belittle, and threaten. In so doing, they tell children to deny their feelings about themselves and to build their feelings of self-worth from the judgments of others.

Ginott (1973) repeatedly reiterates his cardinal principle of the sane message. When a student gets in trouble, the teacher should always address the situation and never judge the student's character or personality. *By simply describing the scene of concern*, teachers allow students to appraise the situation, consider what is right and wrong, and decide how they feel about the situation and themselves.

Here is an example of a sane message: Two students are talking during a quiet time, violating class rules. The teacher says, "This is a quiet time. It needs to be absolutely silent." An insane message, by contrast, might be: "You two are being very rude. You have no consideration for others who are trying to work."

Ginott maintained that teachers' manners of talking with students reveal how they truly feel about them. Their ways of responding to students can build or destroy self-concept. Poor teacher responses can contradict a student's perception of self. Good teacher responses simply state the facts, letting students decide for themselves if their behavior is in keeping with what they expect of themselves.

Expressing Anger

Teaching is a tough job. Fatigue, frustration, and conflict make teacher anger inevitable. Most people, adults and students alike, expect teachers to be saints. Ginott maintained that such expectations are wrong and even damaging to teachers. Teachers should never deny human feelings, either their students' or their own. Their behavior should always be genuine. That includes how they talk, behave, and respond to students. However, they need to learn to express anger, even displeasure, without damaging the students' character.

When situations arise that cause teachers to feel angry, they should simply (and sanely) describe what they see. They should address the situation and tell how they feel about it. When they need to tell how they feel, Ginott (1972) says they should use *I-messages*. "I am angry." "I am disappointed." These I-messages are much more appropriate expressions of anger than are you-messages: "You are not being good." "You are messy." "You only think of yourself." I-messages tell how the teacher feels about the situation. You-messages attack the student.

When angry, good teachers state their demands clearly and firmly, avoiding language that insults or humiliates. Their messages are as brief as possible. It is important that teachers be good models of civilized behavior. When tempted to explode with wrath, they should ask themselves, "Am I dealing with anger in the same way I expect my students to? Am I modeling behavior I want to see replicated in my classroom?"

One last item about expressing anger: Ginott points out that an anger situation is one of those times when teachers have the full attention of students. The situation affords an opportunity to enrich vocabulary by expressing anger in eloquent terms, such as "I am appalled, indignant, chagrined. I see inexcusable and intolerable behavior. I wish to terminate the situation at once." The teacher conveys two messages, one about the students' behavior and another about the power of descriptive language. Ginott notes that using words that students understand only vaguely increases the shock value of teacher expressions of anger.

Inviting Cooperation

Ginott urges teachers to invite cooperation rather than demand it. One of the ways to issue the invitation is to decide with the class before an activity is started what kinds of personal behavior are required during the activity. Another is to stop an activity that has gotten out of control and say, "We can watch the movie in silence, or we can do another math assignment. You decide." If the students continue to disrupt, the teacher must follow through with the alternative, making it clear that such was the students' decision.

Teachers who do not invite cooperation must use ordering, bossing, and commanding. Ginott stresses the need to avoid direct commands, which frequently induce hostility. Again, Ginott says to describe the situation and let students decide what their course of action should be. Too often, teachers use long, drawn-out directions or explanations such as: "Close your library books. Put them in your desks. Get out your math book. Get a pencil. Turn to page sixty. Start on the assignment." Ginott suggests a simple declaration such as, "It is now math time. The assignment is on page sixty." With that kind of message, teachers show that they respect students' ability to behave autonomously. They invite cooperation, promote self-choice, and foster responsibility. Self-image improves through independent choice of productive behavior.

By inviting cooperation, teachers begin to break down students' dependency on the teacher. Of course, we all depend on others in many ways, but if that dependency is too strong it creates problems. This is certainly true when students are made too dependent on teachers, as strong dependency often makes students lethargic and indecisive, even resentful and hostile. Ginott recommends reducing dependency problems by providing many opportunities for students to behave independently. One of the ways suggested by Ginott is to present students with several possible solutions to a problem and let them decide on the one they want to adopt. This helps them feel they have some control over happenings in the classroom. They can also decide how they want to proceed in applying the solution they have chosen. Given these opportunities to make decisions, they come to depend less on the teacher for motivation and direction. Also, they are more likely to live up to standards of behavior they have set for themselves.

Accepting and Acknowledging Feelings

Students are in an awkward position in that they recognize they have their own feelings about themselves and situations, but at the same time are also told how they *should* feel by adults. Ginott believes teachers can be especially useful in helping students sort out feelings. He would like for teachers to minimize student confusion by withholding their opinions and merely acting as sounding boards for students with problems.

Consider young children as an example. Their perceptions of reality are much different from those of adults. Youngsters routinely exaggerate the truth, and their opinions often have little basis in reality. Teachers should not argue with children's perceptions, even when they are obviously wrong. This only causes feelings of belittlement and rejection. Instead, teachers should strive to acknowledge and understand children's feelings.

Here is an example: Suppose Juan comes running in from the playground crying, "José threw a ball at me and hit me in the head on purpose. Everyone started laughing at me. No one likes me." The teacher could argue with the child's experience and deny his feelings, saying, "That's silly. I'm sure it was an accident. The others were laughing at something else." Or she could respond with sympathy and understanding, offering no judgment on the situation, saying, "You seem very upset. You feel that no one likes you. Your feelings are hurt when others laugh at you." In this way, the child's feelings are acknowledged and respected. He is not put on the defensive or told how he should feel.

Ginott suggests that teachers add another comment to such situations: "How can I help you?" This provides an opportunity for the student to come up with a solution to the problem and reveals the teacher's confidence in the student's ability to cope. By acknowledging feelings and offering to be helpful, the teacher does not deny feelings, reject opinions, attack a student's character, or argue with the student's experience. Students must have an opportunity to decide how they feel and what they are going to do about it.

Children's fears are another matter that should be treated carefully. Adults have the tendency to make light of them. When they do this, they tell children that their feelings are not real. Adults also may cause them to believe that people are not supposed to feel that way. Ginott says to avoid the standard adult phrase, "There is nothing to be afraid of," which only makes children feel worse. They are now stuck with both the original fear and a new fear of showing fear. Telling children not to be afraid, angry, or sad does not dispel those emotions, but it does cause them to doubt their own inner feelings. It causes them to doubt the teacher's ability to understand and teaches them that adults are not to be trusted during times of trouble.

Labeling Is Disabling

Teachers are sometimes heard to make statements to students such as, "You're lazy, irresponsible, and sloppy. You'll never amount to anything if you don't change." By now you realize that Ginott is adamant about there being no place in the classroom for such labels, diagnoses, or prognoses of students' character.

Labeling is disabling, Ginott avows, because it tells students how to think about themselves. When subjected to these messages often enough they begin to believe them. They start to live up to a negative self-image. This is especially true when adults attempt to predict a student's future. When teachers tell students to forget about going to college, the students may do just that. The very art of teaching demands that teachers open vistas, encourage growth and achievement, provide enlightenment, and stimulate imagination. Labeling and diagnosing a student's character only limit visions of the self and the future.

In difficult situations, teachers can avoid labeling while striving to be helpful and encouraging. They can offer statements like, "Your grades are low, but I know if we work together we can improve them." "You want to be veterinarian? Did you know there is a career information section in the media center?" Statements such as these do not tell students what you think they can or cannot do. They encourage students to set goals for themselves and they assure them that the teacher will support and assist in the attainment of those goals. When teachers believe in students, the students begin to believe in themselves.

Correction Is Direction

Throughout every day, situations arise in the classroom that require correcting comments from the teacher. Tim and Mary may throw erasers. A group of boys may discuss baseball instead of doing seatwork. Brian may stare out the window instead of completing his math assignment. In these situations Ginott recommends directing as the method of correcting.

When correcting by directing, teachers describe the situation and offer acceptable alternative behaviors. Often students simply need to be told what they could be doing differently. In the case of Tim and Mary, the teacher might say, "Erasers are not for throwing. This is reading time."

When correcting misbehavior, teachers should avoid attacking a student's character. They should not rant and rave about what they dislike in it. When teachers tell what they see and suggest acceptable alternatives, students know how the teacher feels about the current behavior and exactly how they are supposed to behave differently. They become more likely to follow the teacher's suggestions and correct their own behavior.

Sarcasm

Ginott has a word of advice for teachers who are tempted to use sarcasm in the classroom—don't. Many adults use sarcasm as a form of wit. Teachers often do so with students, intending only to be clever and witty. All too often, however, their sarcasm sounds clever only to themselves and not to the students receiving the comments, who end up with hurt feelings and damaged self-esteem. Students often do not understand the sarcasm and feel that they are being made fun of or belittled. It is better to avoid sarcasm altogether than to risk hurting feelings.

The Perils of Praise

Who would ever think that praise could damage a student's self-concept? Don't we all need to be told we are great, terrific, valuable? Ginott makes some provocative observations about praise. He does not deny its value, but he sees a danger there, too. The danger is that teachers can use it to manipulate students' feelings about themselves. As with negative comments, praise can have detrimental effects on forming a positive self-image, especially if the praise is *judgmental*. Such praise—"You are a good boy!"—creates a dependence on others for approval and validation of self-worth.

Again, Ginott is emphatic about the importance of describing the circumstances and letting a student decide what behavior is appropriate. When praising, teachers need to concentrate on applauding *specific acts* without including adjectives about the personality.

An example of Ginott's point is seen in these comments that Mrs. Richards wrote on her student's paper: "This is an exceptional description of human emotions. This paper truly has poetic qualities." She did not make the mistake of attributing qualities of the paper to the student's personality. Instead, she allowed the student to come to his own conclusions about himself from the comments on the paper.

Another way teachers use praise inappropriately is by telling students that they are good because they know the correct answer. A logical conclusion could then be drawn by other students—that they are bad because they do not know the answer. Ginott says: "Knowledge does not make one good. The lack of it does not make one bad." Appropriate responses for correct answers are "fine," "exactly," or "that's correct." These comments carry no evaluation of the student's personality.

Praising good behavior can have its drawbacks, too. When teachers praise students for behavior they are supposed to show, it may appear that the teacher is surprised by good behavior, implying that poor behavior is expected. Sometimes, students decide to live up to negative expectations.

Teachers should express their feelings of appreciation without words that evaluate the students' behavior. Ginott would have the teacher say, "Thank you for entering quietly," or "I enjoyed working with you today." He would not want them to say, "You were so good at the assembly," or "You can really behave when you want to." Ginott insists that evaluative praise inevitably puts teachers in a judgmental position. It causes them to appear condescending. Persons on a higher status level are at liberty to praise those on a lower level, but not vice versa. Students would seem disrespectful if they said, "You can do a fine job, Mr. Green, when you really want to."

Another danger that should be recognized in evaluative praise is that it so easily manipulates student behavior. When teachers give profuse praise, they are trying to ensure repetition of a desired behavior. Students, especially older ones, sometimes resist such obvious manipulation. They feel that the praise is not sincere, but is only delivered to coerce them into certain behavior.

On the other hand, praise correctly used can be productive. Such is the case when teachers describe their own feelings or describe the efforts of students, for example, "It makes me feel good to see such quality work," or "The amount of work that has gone into this drawing is obvious." These are honest recognitions without value judgments about the students' personalities. In summary, praise well used supports, motivates, and encourages; it does not judge people. Teachers should use it to recognize effort and show appreciation, while letting students make their own evaluations about themselves.

GINOTT'S SPECIAL VIEWS ON DISCIPLINE

Ginott describes discipline as "a series of little victories" that accrue over time, a small-step process, ongoing, and never-ending. When done properly, it ultimately brings about student self-direction, responsibility, and concern for others.

Of course, teachers can influence student behavior through threats and punishment, but that produces ill will, rebellion, and subversion. The better way is to influence behavior through compassion and understanding, which can turn volatile situations into victories for students and teacher alike. Students often misbehave in order to get reactions from adults, who almost always react negatively. These negative reactions support students' negative opinions of themselves and also their opinions of adults. Good teachers talk and act in ways that do not confirm negative expectations.

Ginott states that the most important ingredient of effective discipline is the teacher's own self-discipline. Teachers with self-discipline do not lose their tempers, insult others, or resort to name calling. They are not rude, sadistic, or unreasonable. Rather, they strive to model the behavior they expect of their students. They are polite, helpful, and respectful. They handle conflict calmly and reasonably. In the face of crisis, they show civilized behavior. Students continually watch to see how teachers handle difficult situations, and—not surprisingly—tend to imitate them.

Ginott presents many vignettes on discipline that describe disciplinary methods that are inappropriate as well as those that are appropriate. To begin with the negative, he asserts that teachers using inappropriate discipline:

1. Lose their tempers (shout, slam books, use verbal abuse).
2. Call students names ("You are like pigs! Clean that up!").
3. Insult students' character ("John, you are nothing but lazy!").
4. Behave rudely ("Sit down and shut up!").
5. Overreact (When Mary accidentally drops a sheaf of papers being handed out: "Oh for heaven's sake! Can't you do anything right?!!").
6. Show cruelty ("Watch carefully on your way home from school, Jack. You're a little short on brains.").

7. Punish all for the sins of one ("Since certain people couldn't listen during the assembly, we will all have to miss the next one.").
8. Threaten ("If I hear one more voice, we will all stay 10 minutes after school.").
9. Deliver long lectures ("It has come to my attention that several students think the trash can is a basketball hoop. We can throw things out on the grounds, but in the classroom . . ." etc., etc.).
10. Back students into a corner ("What are you doing? Why are you doing that? Don't you know any better? Apologize at once!").
11. Make arbitrary rules (Rules are made without any student input or discussion).

In contrast, teachers who use appropriate discipline:

1. Recognize feelings ("I can see that you are angry because you have to stay after school").
2. Describe the situation ("I can see coats all over the closet floor. They need to be hung up.").
3. Invite cooperation ("Let's all help to be quiet, so we can go to the performance").
4. Are brief ("We do not throw paper").
5. Do not argue (They stick to a decision, but remain flexible enough to change it if they are wrong. Arguing is always a losing proposition for teachers).
6. Model appropriate behavior (They show through example how they want students to behave).
7. Discourage physical violence ("In our class we talk about our problems. We do not hit, kick, or pull hair").
8. Do not criticize, call names, or insult (A student interrupts the teacher. Teacher: "Excuse me. I will be with you as soon as I can").
9. Focus on solutions ("I am seeing unsportsmanlike conduct here. What can we do about that?").
10. Allow face-saving exits ("You may remain at your desk and read quietly, or you may sit by yourself in the back of the room").
11. Allow students to help set standards ("What do we need to remember when we are using this paint?").
12. Are helpful (Mathew yells, "Roger and Joe are teasing me!" Teacher responds, "You sound upset. What would you like me to do?").
13. De-escalate conflicts (Susan, crumpling her paper: "I'm not going to do this assignment! It's too hard!" Teacher: "You feel this assignment is too difficult. Would you like me to go over a few problems with you?").

COMMENT ON GINOTT'S VIEWS

Ginott believes it is the teacher's job to provide an environment conducive to learning. An important part of this environment is the social-emotional atmosphere in the classroom. He believes that discipline problems will diminish markedly if teachers show concern for students' feelings and recognize that their messages have strong impact on students' feelings and self-esteem.

His suggestions for congruent communication are similar in some ways to Kounin's "withitness." When teachers address the situation rather than the student's character, they communicate that: (1) they know what is going on, (2) they know what they want changed, and (3) they are aware of the student's feelings.

But far more than the models considered previously, Ginott's model emphasizes how teachers should deal positively with students' emotions and exemplify good behavior in their own personal conduct.

To a far greater extent than most authorities, Ginott reminds teachers that students are people, too. Being bossed or labeled gives students justification for distrusting adults and being rebellious. Teachers should treat students as they themselves would like to be treated—by giving them choices, being helpful, and inviting rather than demanding cooperation. They should ask themselves, "How do I want my students to relate to me and each other, and how should I treat them in order that they will do so?"

Most teachers will obtain better behavior from students, and will enjoy teaching more, if they incorporate Ginott's suggestions into their teaching styles. However, even after becoming adept in the techniques Ginott advocates, many teachers find that still more is required when they must face hostile, defiant students who refuse to work or behave properly. In short, they find Ginott's ideas good for preventive and supportive control, but weak for corrective control, especially in hard-to-manage classes.

Application Exercises

The Concept Cases: Kris, Sara, Joshua, and Tom.

CASE #1. KRIS WILL NOT WORK:

Kris, a student in Mr. Jake's class, is quite docile. She does little socializing with other students and never disrupts class. Mr. Jake simply cannot get her to do her work. She never completes an assignment, but just sits there like a bump on a log, putting forth no effort at all.

How would Ginott deal with Kris?   Ginott would advise teachers to use a number of gentle tactics to encourage Kris to do her work. These would include:

- Sane messages (Students in my class are expected to complete all assignments).
- Inviting cooperation (All students who finish their work can then choose to play a game with a friend).
- Accepting and acknowledging Kris's feelings (Kris, I can tell you find it difficult to begin work on your assignment. How can I help you?).
- Correct by directing (You need to finish 10 problems within the next 30 minutes).
- Focus on solutions (This cannot continue. What do you think we might be able to do about it?).

Application Exercises (continued)

CASE #2. SARA CANNOT STOP TALKING:

Sara is a pleasant girl who participates in class activities and does most, though not all, of her assigned work. She cannot seem to refrain from talking to classmates, however. Her teacher, Mr. Gonzales, has to speak to her repeatedly during lessons, to the point that he often becomes exasperated and loses his temper.

What suggestions would Ginott give Mr. Gonzales for dealing with Sara?

CASE #3. JOSHUA CLOWNS AND INTIMIDATES:

Joshua, larger and louder than his classmates, always wants to be the center of attention, which he accomplishes through a combination of clowning and intimidation. He makes wise remarks, talks back (smilingly) to the teacher, utters a variety of sound effect noises such as automobile crashes and gunshots, and makes limitless sarcastic comments and put-downs of his classmates. Other students will not stand up to him, apparently fearing his size and verbal aggression. His teacher, Miss Pearl, has come to her wits' end.

What do you think Ginott would advise in this case?

CASE #4. TOM IS HOSTILE AND DEFIANT:

Tom has appeared to be in his usual foul mood ever since arriving in class. He gets up and on his way to sharpen his pencil he bumps into Frank. Frank complains. Tom tells him loudly to shut up. Miss Baines, the teacher, says, "Tom, go back to your seat." Tom wheels around, swears loudly and says heatedly, "I'll go when I'm damned good and ready!"

How would Ginott advise Miss Baines to deal with Tom?

QUESTIONS AND ACTIVITIES:

1. The following statements illustrate some of Ginott's main points about talking with students. Identify the main point with which each statement is associated.
   a) You boys head the list of my all-time laziest students.
   b) Yes, I'm just *sure* you didn't do your assignment because your mother was sick last night.
   c) I am so disappointed and angry I could pop!
   d) Alicia, you are the most intelligent kid I have ever known!
2. Peggy and June are each accusing the other of taking personal items without permission. What would Ginott have the teacher say to the girls?
3. Miss Tykes is dealing with a group of boys who were shouting obscenities in the hall. "That's the worst thing I have ever witnessed!" she yells. "Where do you think you are? Are you allowed to behave like hoodlums at home? You will all report to my room after school for the next two weeks!" How would Ginott advise that Miss Tykes change her approach?

FURTHER ANALYSIS AND APPLICATION:

Examine scenario #6 in Chapter 13. What, specifically, would Ginott have Mr. Carnett say to his misbehaving students?

REFERENCES

Ginott, H. (1965). *Between parent and child.* New York: Avon.

Ginott, H. (1969). *Between parent and teenager.* New York: Macmillan.

Ginott, H. (1971). *Teacher and child.* New York: Macmillan.

Ginott, H. (1972). I am angry! I am appalled! I am furious! *Today's Education, 61,* 23–24.

Ginott, H. (1973). Driving children sane. *Today's Education, 62,* 20–25.

Kounin, J. (1971; 1977). *Discipline and group management in classrooms.* New York: Holt, Rinehart and Winston.

CHAPTER 5

The Dreikurs Model:
Confronting Mistaken Goals

DREIKURS BIOGRAPHICAL SKETCH

Rudolf Dreikurs (1897–1972) was born in Vienna, Austria. He received his medical degree from the University of Vienna and entered into a long association with the renowned psychiatrist, Alfred Adler, with whom he conducted studies dealing with family and child counseling. Dreikurs immigrated to the United States in 1937 and eventually became director of the Alfred Adler Institute in Chicago. He also served as professor of psychiatry at the Chicago Medical School. Throughout his career, he continued to focus on family-child counseling. He became known as an expert in the area of classroom behavior through his books *Psychology in the Classroom* (1968), *Discipline Without Tears* with P. Cassel (1972), and *Maintaining Sanity in the Classroom* with B. Grunwald and F. Pepper (1982). These books are valuable to teachers for their explanations of the motivations behind student behavior.

DREIKURS' MAIN FOCUS

All students want recognition, and most misbehavior occurs from their attempts to get it. When unable to get the recognition they desire, their behavior turns toward four "mistaken goals," which teachers must recognize and deal with.

Dreikurs' Key Ideas

1. Discipline is not punishment. It is teaching students to impose limits on themselves.
2. Democratic teachers provide firm guidance and leadership. They allow students to have a say in establishing rules and consequences.
3. All students want to belong. They want status and recognition. Most of their behaviors indicate efforts to belong.
4. Misbehavior reflects the mistaken belief that it will gain students the recognition they want.
5. Misbehavior is associated with four mistaken goals: attention getting, power seeking, revenge seeking, and displaying inadequacy.
6. Teachers should identify mistaken goals and then act in ways that do not reinforce them.
7. Teachers should strive to encourage students' efforts, but avoid praising their work or character.
8. Teachers should teach students that unpleasant consequences will always follow inappropriate behavior.

THE NATURE OF DISCIPLINE

Discipline is essential to smooth functioning in schools and society. Too often, adults have an either-or concept of discipline—*either* children behave *or* they walk all over you. Most people think of discipline as punishing actions used against children in times of conflict or misbehavior.

Children form stereotyped ideas about discipline, too. Generally, they see it as arbitrary rules set up by adults to show who is in charge. They may view discipline as a complex game with rules they do not understand. Some see it as punishment given without reason. These children soon decide that being punished justifies retaliation, rebellion, and hostility.

Good discipline, however, has little to do with punishment. Punishment is physical pain, humiliation, isolation, and revenge; it is a force imposed on one from an outside source. Dreikurs claims that it teaches what *not to do*, but fails to teach what *to do*.

Discipline requires freedom of choice and the understanding of consequences. It is not imposed by authority figures, but rather on individuals by themselves. By choosing to behave in certain ways individuals learn to gain acceptance from others and, consequently, acceptance of themselves.

Discipline in the classroom means setting limits for students until they are able to set limits for themselves. It involves allowing students freedom to choose their own behavior. They can do this because they understand exactly what consequences will follow any behavior chosen. Good behavior brings rewards. Poor behavior *always* brings undesired consequences. When teachers teach this concept to students, they are teaching students to behave in ways that are acceptable to society. This helps students promote their own welfare in all situations.

Teaching self-discipline requires a positive, accepting atmosphere. Students must feel that the teacher likes and respects them. They must understand that the teacher wants what is best for them. Students must also be allowed input into establishing rules and consequences. They should always understand the reasons for rules because this allows a sense of personal commitment and involvement. It provides recognition of the need for limits.

Dreikurs believes that establishing discipline in the classroom must involve teaching the following concepts:

1. Students are responsible for their own actions.
2. Students must respect themselves and others.
3. Students have the responsibility to influence others to behave appropriately.
4. Students are responsible for knowing what the rules and consequences are in their classrooms.

Dreikurs also believes that teachers who are most effective in establishing discipline are those who teach democratically. Let us explore the qualities of different types of teachers.

TYPES OF TEACHERS

Dreikurs identifies three types of teachers—*autocratic, permissive,* and *democratic*— so categorized on the basis of behavior they show in the classroom.

Autocratic Teachers

Mr. Parrons strides into the classroom in a suit and tie. His back is ramrod straight. He coldly eyes the class, then begins the lesson without a greeting. He thwarts questions by ridiculing the first student who dares to ask.

Such autocratic teachers force their will on students to prove they have control of the class. They motivate students with outside pressure instead of stimulating motivation from within. They need to feel they are powerful and personally superior to their students. This attitude and approach generates more misbehavior than it prevents. Students tend to reject authority figures, seeking instead a democratic atmosphere in which they are treated as human beings.

Permissive Teachers

Mrs. Samuels smiles tentatively as she enters. Several students are not seated but she does not address them. Instead, she says, "You may visit quietly while you are working." Soon a deafening roar fills the classroom, but from her desk Mrs. Samuels seems oblivious.

Such permissive teachers are also ineffective. They, too, generate problem behavior because the atmosphere they allow is not based on everyday reality. Students in a permissive classroom do not learn that living in society requires following rules. They do not learn that failure to follow rules results in consequences. They do not learn that acceptable behavior requires self-discipline. They are confused because they believe that they can do whatever they want, yet when they do, things do not go smoothly for them.

Discipline and control must be present in classrooms if learning is to occur as intended. Students *want* guidance and leadership. They are willing to accept guidance if it is not forced on them and if they believe they are being heard. This does not mean that they want to run the show.

Democratic Teachers

Ms. Tallers enters the room casually, greeting a few students near her. She asks the class to be seated and waits until she has everyone's attention. She asks for student input into certain matters of classroom routines and considers the suggestions carefully. She pauses twice and sends meaningful looks to a pair of students who are visiting in the back of the room.

Democratic teachers like Ms. Tallers are neither permissive nor autocratic. They provide firm guidance and leadership by establishing rules and consequences. They motivate students from within. They maintain order and, at the same time, allow students to participate in decision making. Democratic teachers teach that freedom is tied to responsibility. They allow students freedom to choose their own behavior. They also teach students that they must suffer the consequences if they choose to misbehave. Through this process, students learn to behave in ways that get them what they want.

Students who fail to develop self-discipline limit their choices in life. They choose inappropriate behavior, not understanding that it brings negative consequences to them. Freedom grows from discipline. If students understand that consequences follow behavior, they are more free to choose behavior that will get them what they want. Discipline involves teaching students to establish inner controls that allow them to choose behavior compatible with their best interests. Teaching self-discipline eliminates the need for constant corrective actions by the teacher.

According to Dreikurs, the following conditions foster a democratic classroom:

1. Order.
2. Limits.
3. Firmness and kindness. Firmness from teachers shows they respect themselves. Kindness shows they respect others.
4. Student involvement in establishing and maintaining rules.
5. Leadership from the teacher.
6. Inviting cooperation—eliminating competition between teacher and students.
7. A sense of belonging to a group.
8. Freedom to explore, discover, and choose acceptable behavior through understanding the responsibilities and consequences associated with it.

MISTAKEN GOALS

Dreikurs makes three very strong points in his writings. First, students are social beings who want to belong. All of their actions reflect their attempts to be significant and gain acceptance. Second, students can choose to behave or misbehave. Their behavior is not outside their control. Putting these two beliefs together, Dreikurs makes his third point: Students choose to misbehave because they are under the mistaken belief that it will get them the recognition they seek. Dreikurs calls these beliefs mistaken goals.

All people want to belong, to have a place. They try all kinds of behavior to see if it gets them status and recognition. If they do not receive recognition through socially acceptable means they turn to mistaken goals, which produce antisocial behavior. Antisocial behavior reflects the mistaken belief that misbehavior is the only way to receive recognition.

Dreikurs identified four mistaken goals: *attention getting, power seeking, revenge seeking,* and *displaying inadequacy.* These goals identify the purposes of student misbehavior. They are usually sought in sequential order. If attention getting fails to bring recognition, the student will progress to power seeking. If that is not rewarded the student moves on to seeking revenge, and then to displaying inadequacy. Let's examine each of these mistaken goals more closely.

Attention Getting

When students discover that they are not getting the recognition they desire, they may resort to trying to get attention through misbehavior. These students are trying to seek proof of acceptance through what they can get others to give them, in this case, attention. They want the teacher to pay attention to them and provide them with extra services. They disrupt, ask special favors, continually need help with assignments, refuse to work unless the teacher hovers over them, or they ask irrelevant questions. Some good students can also make unusual bids for attention. They can function only as long as they have the teacher's approval. If that approval is not forthcoming, they may resort to less acceptable ways of getting attention.

Giving attention to misbehaving students does not improve their improper behavior; rather, it reinforces it, increasing their desire for attention. Further, it causes them to be motivated by outside forces, rather than from within.

If attention-getting behavior does not provide students the recognition they seek, they will turn to the next mistaken goal—power.

Power Seeking

Power-seeking students feel that defying adults is the only way they can get what they want. Their mistaken belief is: If you don't let me do what I want, you don't approve of me. A need for power is expressed by arguing, contradicting, lying, having temper tantrums, and exhibiting hostility. If these students can get the teacher to fight with them they *win,* because they succeed in getting the teacher into a power struggle. Whether or not they actually get what they want does not matter. What does matter is that they upset the teacher. Should the teacher win the contest of wills, it only causes the student to believe more firmly that power is what matters in life. If students lose these power struggles, they move on to more severe misbehavior—getting revenge.

Revenge Seeking

Students seeking this goal have failed to gain status through getting attention or establishing power. Their mistaken goal now becomes: I can only feel significant if I have the power to hurt others. Hurting others makes up for being hurt.

Students who seek revenge set themselves up to be punished. They are vicious, cruel, and violent. When adults punish them, revenge-seeking students have renewed cause for action. The more trouble they cause for themselves, the more justified they feel. They consider it a victory to be disliked.

Underneath their bravado these individuals are deeply discouraged. Their behavior only elicits more hurt from others. They feel ever more worthless and unlovable, and these feelings cause them to withdraw to the next mistaken goal—displaying inadequacy.

Displaying Inadequacy

At this level, students feel themselves helpless and see themselves as abject failures. There is no need to try anymore. They withdraw from any situation that can intensify their feeling of failure. They guard what little self-esteem they have left by removing it from social tests. Their mistaken belief is: If others believe I am inadequate, they will leave me alone.

Students with this goal play stupid. They refuse to respond to motivation and passively refuse to participate in classroom activities. They do not interact with anyone. This mistaken goal is very serious and difficult for students and teachers to overcome.

All of the mistaken goals are based on the belief that they provide a way to achieve significance. Most mistaken goals are pursued only one at a time, but some students occasionally switch back and forth from one goal to another.

WHAT CAN TEACHERS DO?

The first thing teachers can do is identify the student's mistaken goal. The easiest way for teachers to do this is to note their own responses to the misbehavior. Their responses indicate what type of expectations the student has. If teachers feel:

- *Annoyed*, it indicates attention-getting behavior
- *Threatened*, it indicates power-seeking behavior
- *Hurt*, it indicates revenge
- *Powerless*, it indicates student displaying inadequacy

Another way to identify mistaken goals is to observe students' reactions to being corrected.

If students:	Then their goal is:
Stop the misbehavior and then repeat it	Attention
Refuse to stop, or increase the misbehavior	Power
Become violent or hostile	Revenge
Refuse to cooperate, participate, or interact	Inadequacy

After the teacher has identified the mistaken goals, the students should be confronted with an explanation of the mistaken goals together with a discussion of the faulty logic involved. By doing this in a friendly, nonthreatening way, teachers can usually get students to examine the purposes behind their behavior.

Dreikurs would have teachers ask students the following questions, in order, and observe reactions that might indicate a mistaken goal.

1. Could it be that you want me to pay attention to you?
2. Could it be that you want to prove that nobody can make you do anything?
3. Could it be that you want to hurt me or others?
4. Could it be that you want me to believe you are not capable?

These questions have three effects. They open up communication between teacher and student; they improve behavior because they remove the fun of provoking the teacher; and they take the initiative away from the student, allowing the teacher to implement actions to change behavior.

When teachers know the mistaken goals that are being aimed at, they can begin to take action that will defeat the student's purposes and initiate new, constructive behavior. Dreikurs recommends teachers take the following steps in each case of mistaken goals.

For Attention Getting

When teachers discover students seeking the mistaken goal of attention getting, they can either agree to go on giving attention, or they can refuse to grant attention or services by ignoring students when they are bidding for attention. Students who seek attention cannot tolerate being ignored. They would rather be punished, belittled, or humiliated, anything as long as they are getting someone to give them something. So, they create misbehavior that cannot be ignored by the teacher. Teachers who fall for this ploy tend to nag, coax, scold, or otherwise reinforce the student's need for attention.

When teachers perceive that students are making undue bids for attention they should consistently and without fail ignore all such behavior. If they do so, the students will not get what they need from their behavior and will be forced to find new ways to gain recognition.

But teachers should strive to give attention to these same students any time they are not demanding it. This encourages students to develop motivation from within instead of depending on attention from without.

Sometimes it is not feasible for teachers to ignore behavior that is disrupting the class. In such cases, teachers need to give attention in ways that are not rewarding to the student. The teacher may call the student's name and make eye contact without any comments. Or the teacher may describe the behavior without any trace of annoyance.

Example: "I see that you are not finishing your assignment."

One technique that has been partially effective is to privately confront the student with his goal and ask, "How many times do you think you will need my attention in the next hour?" The students will usually not know what to say. The teacher might then say, "If I give you attention fifteen times, will that be enough?" This will sound like an exaggeration to the student. Then when the student misbehaves the teacher responds by saying, "Joel, number one," "Joel, number two," and so forth. The teacher does not comment on the behavior or scold, which would give Joel the attention he seeks, but simply lets him know that his misbehavior is being observed.

By encouraging students to seek attention through useful behavior teachers inform students that they can receive recognition through good efforts and accomplishments. This helps students feel pride in themselves. Learning to function for self-satisfaction can be one of the most valuable lessons taught in school.

For Power Seeking

Most teachers react to power struggles by feeling threatened. They fight back, refusing to let students get the best of them. By fighting and winning struggles, teachers only cause students to become more rebellious and hostile and to think about getting revenge. Dreikurs believes that teachers do not have to fight with students or give in. The best thing for them to do is not to get involved in power struggles in the first place. They should withdraw as an authority figure. The student cannot meet a goal of power if there is no one with whom to fight. Teachers may admit to the student and the class that they recognize the need for power. One way is to stop the entire class and have them wait for the disruptive behavior to cease, in which case the student is in conflict with peers and not the teacher.

Teachers can also redirect students' ambitions to be in charge by inviting them to participate in making decisions or by giving them positions of responsibility. A teacher might take a student aside and say, "The language during physical education is very unsportsmanlike. The others look up to you. Do you think you could help out by setting an example?" Or in the same situation the teacher might say, "I have a problem. It concerns the language I am hearing. What do you think I should do?" In this way, teachers admit that the student has power but refuse to be engaged in conflicts.

Teachers may also wish to confront the behavior openly. When a disruption begins they would say, "I cannot continue to teach when you are doing that. Can you think of a way in which you could do what you want and I could still teach?" If students cannot think of any ways, be prepared to suggest some alternatives.

By withdrawing as a power figure, teachers take fuel from a student's fire. Students cannot be involved in a power struggle with themselves. They will not receive status or recognition if they cannot get the best of the teacher. Teachers who withdraw thwart the purpose of power-seeking behavior.

For Revenge Seeking

The goal of revenge is closely related to the goal of power. Some students feel they should be allowed to do whatever they please and should consider anyone who tries to stop them as an enemy. These students are very difficult to deal with because they do not care about consequences. Consequences only give them justification for revenge.

It is difficult for teachers to care for students who are out to hurt them. These students feel the need to hurt others because they have been hurt themselves. What they need most is understanding and acceptance. Teachers can best provide this by calling on the class to support and encourage these students. Sometimes, this is best accomplished by selecting a student with high esteem to befriend the troublemaker and help him or her develop constructive behavior. The teacher also may be able to set up situations that allow revengeful students to exhibit talents or strengths, helping to persuade these students that they can behave in ways that bring acceptance and status.

This is a very difficult thing to ask of a class. Students who seek revenge at first reject efforts made by others. Teachers must encourage their students and persuade them that their efforts will pay off. It is awful for any student to feel unliked by everyone. It takes persistence and patience on everyone's part to change such a situation.

For Displaying Inadequacy

Students who wish to be left alone usually think of themselves as thoroughly inadequate. They want their teacher to believe that they are too hopeless to deal with. Teachers often believe exactly that and promptly give up. After all, the students are not troublemakers—they are not disruptive or hostile. Students who adopt this goal usually do so for one of the following reasons:

1. They are overly ambitious. They cannot do as well as they think they should. If they cannot be the best, they will not put forth any effort at all.
2. They are overly competitive. They cannot do as well as others. They feel that they are not good enough. They withdraw from being compared.
3. They are under too much pressure. They cannot do as well as others want them to. They don't feel good enough as they are. They refuse to live up to anyone's expectations.

In each case, discouraged students feel like failures. They feel worthless and inadequate. They want to keep others from discovering exactly how inadequate they are.

Teachers must *never* give up on these students. They must always offer encouragement and support for even the smallest efforts. Encouragement is especially needed when the student is making mistakes. It is not the achievement but the effort that counts. Every attempt should be made by teachers and peers to make these students feel successful.

Teachers should also be very sensitive to their own reactions to these students. Any indication of defeat or frustration on the teacher's part reinforces the student's conviction of worthlessness and a desire to appear inadequate. One failure does not mean a student is a failure forever, and teachers must help encourage students to see this fact.

FOUR CASES OF MISTAKEN GOALS

Sally

Ms. Morton's class was doing independent seat work. Every few minutes Sally raised her hand to ask for some kind of direction: Should she number the sentences? Should she put her name on the paper? Was this answer right? Ms. Morton became very exasperated. Many times in the past she had to explain things over and over to Sally. Finally, she told Sally she would not help her any more during seat work. She said she would explain the directions to the class once, and if Sally did not understand them she would have to wait and do the assignment at recess. Ms. Morton then ignored all Sally's requests for help. She did, however, immediately encourage Sally when she saw her working without assistance.

Sally's case is an example of attention-getting behavior. The best clue was the teacher's reaction—*annoyance*—to Sally's behavior. But Ms. Morton did the best thing in this instance. She ignored Sally's bids for attention while reinforcing her ability to work independently. She also established logical consequences for Sally's failure to work independently.

Jerry

Jerry and another student were scuffling near dangerous equipment in woodshop class. They knew this was against the rules and would result in their being removed temporarily from the class. Mr. Graves approached them and asked them to leave. Jerry refused. Mr. Graves was tempted to remove him physically. Instead, he walked to the front of the room and told everyone to turn off their machines and put their work down. He explained to the students that woodshop could not continue because Jerry was behaving in a dangerous way around equipment and refused to follow the class rule and leave the room. The class waited, not without directing looks at Jerry. Jerry soon chose to leave the shop.

Jerry's was an example of power-seeking behavior. Mr. Graves's first reaction was to feel his authority *threatened*. He was tempted to get into a power struggle with Jerry. However, he refused to be drawn into a fight. He freely admitted to the class that Jerry had the power to stop them from continuing. Jerry then had no one to struggle against. His power-seeking behavior was thwarted. Later, Mr. Graves asked Jerry to be a member of a group to review the rules for the class. That gave Jerry a position of authority that met his need for power in a constructive manner.

Janette

Shalee was looking at a book that Miss Allen had brought in to read to the class. Janette came over and grabbed it away, saying that she was supposed to get to see it first. Miss Allen gave the book back to Shalee and scolded Janette. When Miss Allen was straightening the room after school, she found the book with pages torn out and cover ripped. She felt certain that Janette had destroyed the book, and was hurt and angered. Miss Allen had punished Janette and Janette had taken revenge. Her revenge hurt Miss Allen, which was what Janette intended.

Miss Allen might have handled the situation better by suggesting that Shalee and Janette sit down and read the book together. Janette would have felt accepted and included, rather than rejected.

Catrina

Mr. Redding gave the class an assignment to write a story. Everyone was soon busily writing, except for Catrina. Mr. Redding walked over to her and said, "Catrina, you can start by writing your name and the date on your paper." Catrina did not pick up her pencil, but continued staring at her paper. Mr. Redding felt frustrated, but he did not feel like coaxing. He felt like saying, fine, if you don't want to work I won't waste my time on you. Instead he said, "Sometimes writers need time to think before they write. I know you'll start writing when you are ready."

Catrina wanted Mr. Redding to see her as inadequate. If she had wanted attention, she would have responded to the teacher. Instead, she acted as though he was not there, hoping he would go away. Mr. Redding did not give up as Catrina wished. He offered encouragement and let her know that he had faith in her ability to do the assignment.

ENCOURAGEMENT VERSUS PRAISE

Teachers have long used a variety of undesirable discipline techniques to deal with disruptive behavior. They have threatened, humiliated, and punished. They have waited for misbehavior to occur and then pounced. The results have been student resentment, rebellion, and hostility. Teachers need better approaches if they are to have effective control. One such approach is *encouragement*. Dreikurs believes that encouragement is a crucial element in the prevention of problem behavior. Through encouragement teachers make learning seem worthwhile and help students develop positive self-concepts.

Encouragement consists of words or actions that convey teacher respect and belief in students' abilities. It tells students that they are accepted as they are. It recognizes efforts, not achievements. It gives students the courage to try, while accepting themselves as less than perfect. Teachers should be continually alert for opportunities to recognize effort, regardless of its results.

Encouragement facilitates feelings of being a contributing and participating member of a group. It helps students accept themselves as they are. It draws on motivation from within and allows them to become aware of their strengths.

Praise is different from encouragement. Praise is given when a task is done well. It promotes the idea that a product is worthless unless it receives praise. Students learn to receive praise from without and fail to learn to work for self-satisfaction. Praise encourages the attitude, "What am I going to get out of it?" Here are some examples showing the differences between praise and encouragement:

Praise	*Encouragement*
You are such a good girl for finishing your assignment.	I can tell that you have been working hard.
I am proud of you for behaving so well in the assembly.	Isn't it nice that we could all enjoy the assembly!
You play the guitar so well!	I can see that you really enjoy playing the guitar.

Dreikurs outlines the following pointers for teachers to use in encouraging students:

1. Always be positive; avoid negative comments.
2. Encourage students to strive for improvement, not perfection.

3. Encourage effort. Results don't matter very much so long as students try hard.
4. Emphasize strengths and minimize weaknesses.
5. Teach students to learn from mistakes. Emphasize that mistakes are not failures.
6. Stimulate motivation from within. Do not exert pressure from without.
7. Encourage independence.
8. Let students know that you have faith in their abilities.
9. Offer to help overcome obstacles.
10. Encourage students to help classmates who are having difficulties. This helps them appreciate their own strengths.
11. Send positive notes home, especially concerning effort.
12. Show pride in students' work. Display the work and invite others to see it.
13. Be optimistic and enthusiastic—it is catching.
14. Try to set up situations that guarantee success for all.
15. Use encouraging remarks often, such as:
    You have improved!
    Can I help you?
    What did you learn from that mistake?
    I know you can.
    Keep trying!
    I know you can solve this, but if you think you need help . . .
    I understand how you feel, but I am sure you can handle it.

Dreikurs points out that there are also pitfalls in using encouragement. He cautions that teachers *should not:*

- Encourage competition or comparison with others.
- Point out how much better the student *could* be.
- Use "but" statements, such as "I'm pleased with your progress, but . . ."
- Use statements such as "It's about time."
- Give up on those who are not responding. Always encourage consistently and constantly.

LOGICAL CONSEQUENCES

No matter how encouraging teachers are, they will still encounter behavior problems. Dreikurs advises setting up "logical consequences" to help deter misbehavior and motivate appropriate behavior. Logical consequences are results that follow certain behaviors; they are arranged by the teacher.

Logical consequences must be differentiated from punishment. Punishment is action taken by the teacher to get back at misbehaving students and show them who is boss. Punishment breeds retaliation and gives students the feeling that they have the

right to punish in return. Logical consequences, on the other hand, are not weapons used by the teacher. They teach students that all behavior produces a corresponding result: Good behavior brings rewards and unacceptable behavior brings unpleasant consequences. If a student throws paper on the floor, that student must pick it up. If a student fails to do work as assigned, that student must make up the work on his or her own time.

Logical consequences must be explained, understood, and agreed to by students. If they are sprung on students at the time of conflict, they will be considered punishment. When applying consequences, teachers should not act as self-appointed authorities. They should simply represent the order required by society and enforce the rules agreed to by the students.

Consequences are effective only when applied consistently. If teachers apply them while in a bad mood, or only to certain students, students will not learn that misbehavior *always* carries unpleasant consequences. They will misbehave and gamble that they can get away with it. Students must be convinced that consequences will be applied each and every time they choose to misbehave. They will have to consider carefully whether misbehaving is worth it. Sometimes it takes time to break old behavior habits, but teachers should never get discouraged and give up on implementing consequences.

Applying consequences allows students to make their own choices about how they will behave. They learn to rely on their own inner discipline to control their actions. They learn that poor choices invariably result in unpleasant consequences. It is nobody's fault but their own. Students also learn that the teacher respects their ability to make their own decisions.

Consequences should relate as closely as possible to the misbehavior, so students can see the connection between them. For example:

1. Students who damage school property would have to replace it.
2. Failure to complete an assignment would mean having to complete it after school.
3. Fighting at recess would result in no recess.
4. Disturbing others would result in isolation from the group.

Teachers should not show anger or triumph when applying consequences. If an assignment is not completed, they should simply say, "You chose to talk instead of doing math, so you must finish your math after school." This shows that when students choose to misbehave, they choose to suffer the consequences.

DREIKURS'S DOS AND DON'TS

Discipline involves ongoing teacher guidance to help students develop inner controls. It should not consist of limits imposed from the outside at times of stress and conflict. Rather, it should be consistent guidance that promotes a feeling of cooperation and team effort. To achieve this feeling, Dreikurs (1982) suggests that teachers do several things, among which are the following:

Teachers Should:

1. Give clear-cut directions for the actions expected of students. Wait until you have the attention of all class members before giving directions.
2. Try to establish a relationship with each individual, built on trust and mutual respect.
3. Use logical consequences instead of traditional punishment. The consequence must bear a direct relationship to the behavior and must be understood by students.
4. See behavior in its proper perspective. In this way, you will avoid making serious issues out of trivial incidents.
5. Let students assume greater responsibility for their own behavior and learning.
6. Treat students as your social equals.
7. Combine kindness and firmness. The student must always sense that you are a friend, but that you will not accept certain kinds of behavior.
8. At all times distinguish between the deed and the doer. This permits respect for the student, even when he or she does something wrong.
9. Set limits from the beginning, but work toward mutual understanding, a sense of responsibility, and consideration for others.
10. Mean what you say, but keep your demands simple, and see that they are carried out.
11. Close an incident quickly and revive good spirits. Let students know that mistakes are corrected, then forgotten.

Teachers Should Not:

1. Nag and scold, since this fortifies a student's mistaken concept of how to get attention.
2. Ask a student to promise anything. Most students will promise to change in order to get out of an uncomfortable situation. It is a sheer waste of time.
3. Find fault with students. It may hurt their self-esteem and discourage them.
4. Adopt double standards—one for yourself and another for the students.
5. Use threats as a method to discipline students. Although some students may become intimidated and conform for the moment, threats have no lasting value since they do not change students' basic attitudes.

COMMENTS ON DREIKURS'S VIEWS

Of all the models of discipline, that of Dreikurs contains the greatest potential for bringing about genuine attitudinal change among students, so that they ultimately behave better because they consider it the proper thing to do. Dreikurs continually refers to his approach as *democratic,* meaning that teachers and students together decide on rules and consequences, and that they take joint responsibility for maintaining a classroom climate conducive to learning.

To bring about democratic discipline, Dreikurs would have teachers spend considerable time talking with students about how their actions, efforts, and results affect themselves and others. This puts teachers into a counseling role far beyond that called for in other models, which can produce very good results for teachers who have counseling skills. Unfortunately, most have never had such training.

For all its strengths, Dreikurs' system produces its valuable results slowly, and must be worked at continually. In addition, it contains a possible defect that worries teachers of hard-to-manage classes—specifically, what do you do when students defy you? Dreikurs says to admit, before the class, that you cannot win a power struggle with misbehaving students. But he seems to suggest that the remainder of the class will side with you and thus coerce the misbehaving student into compliance. Experienced teachers know that defiant behavior is often strongly reinforced by other class members, and that it is sometimes contagious. They feel that such behavior must be stopped at once. Dreikurs supplies no technique for accomplishing that, which causes teachers to consider his model weak in corrective control, though strong in preventive and supportive control.

Despite that shortcoming, Dreikurs' emphasis on mutual respect, encouragement, student effort, and general responsibility finds strong acceptance among teachers who believe their major responsibility is to build desirable character traits in their students. Dreikurs' greatest contribution, they see, lies not in how immediately to suppress undesired behavior, but in how to instill in students an inner sense of responsibility and respect for others.

Application Exercises

Concept Cases: Kris, Sara, Joshua, and Tom.

CASE #1. KRIS WILL NOT WORK:

Kris, a student in Mr. Jake's class, is quite docile. She socializes little with other students and never disrupts the class. But despite Mr. Jake's best efforts, Kris will not do her work. She rarely completes an assignment. She is simply there, like a bump on a log, putting forth no effort.

How would Dreikurs deal with Kris? Dreikurs would suggest that Mr. Jake follow these steps as a means of improving Kris's behavior:

1. Identify Kris's mistaken goal. (Mr. Jake can do this by checking his own reaction to Kris's lethargy and by noting the reactions of other students when he attempts to correct her.)
2. If Kris's mistaken goal is attention-getting, ignore her.
3. If Kris's mistaken goal is power-seeking, admit that Kris has power. "I can't make you do your work. What do you think I should do?"
4. If Kris's goal is revenge, ask other members of the class to be especially encouraging to her.
5. If Kris's goal is inadequacy, encourage her frequently and give her continual support.

6. Confront Kris with her mistaken goal and draw her into a discussion about the goal and her behavior.

CASE #2. SARA CANNOT STOP TALKING:

Sara is a pleasant girl who participates in class activities and does most, though not all, of her assigned work. She cannot seem to refrain from talking to classmates, however. Her teacher, Mr. Gonzales, has to speak to her repeatedly during lessons, to the point that he often becomes exasperated and loses his temper.

What suggestions would Dreikurs give Mr. Gonzales for dealing with Sara?

CASE #3. JOSHUA CLOWNS AND INTIMIDATES:

Joshua, larger and louder than his classmates, always wants to be the center of attention, which he accomplishes through a combination of clowning and intimidation. He makes wise remarks, talks back (smilingly) to the teacher, utters a variety of sound effect noises such as automobile crashes and gunshots, and makes limitless sarcastic comments and put-downs of his classmates. Other students will not stand up to him, apparently fearing his size and verbal aggression. His teacher, Miss Pearl, has come to her wits' end.

What is Joshua's mistaken goal, and how would Dreikurs have you deal with it?

CASE #4. TOM IS HOSTILE AND DEFIANT:

Tom has appeared to be in his usual foul mood ever since arriving in class. He gets up and on his way to sharpen his pencil he bumps into Frank. Frank complains. Tom tells him loudly to shut up. Miss Baines, the teacher, says, "Tom, go back to your seat." Tom wheels around, swears loudly, and says heatedly, "I'll go when I'm damned good and ready!"

What can you find in Dreikurs' work that might help you in this instance?

ACTIVITIES:

For each of the following cases, (a) identify the student's mistaken goal and (b) explain how Dreikurs would have the teacher deal with it.

1. Joe habitually plays with objects on his desk when he should be listening. This causes his teacher to stop instruction frequently and remind him to listen. He usually complies for a few minutes.
2. Lanya seems to have made it her life's goal to taunt and belittle her classmates. If they notify the teacher about her behavior, she harasses them outside the classroom.
3. Maria sits in the back of the classroom. She stares at her desk. She has never turned in an assignment. She does not speak when spoken to.
4. Teresa likes to enter the classroom five minutes late, making enough noise to distract the class. When asked to explain her tardiness, she accuses the teacher of picking on her.

FURTHER ANALYSIS AND APPLICATION:

Examine scenario #2 (secondary) or #1 (elementary) in Chapter 13. Indicate how Dreikurs would advise Mr. Platt or Mrs. Miller to deal with attention-seeking students.

REFERENCES

Dreikurs, R. (1968). *Psychology in the classroom* (2nd ed.). New York: Harper and Row.

Dreikurs, R., & Cassel, P. (1972). *Discipline without tears*. New York: Hawthorn.

Dreikurs, R., Grunwald, B., & Pepper, F. (1982). *Maintaining sanity in the classroom*. New York: Harper and Row.

CHAPTER 6

The Jones Model:

Body Language, Incentive Systems, and Providing Efficient Help

JONES BIOGRAPHICAL SKETCH

Fredric H. Jones, a psychologist, is director of the Classroom Management Training Program, headquartered in Santa Cruz, California. There, for many years, he has worked to develop programs and training procedures for improving teacher effectiveness in motivation, behavior management, and instruction. The procedures he advocates grew initially out of research and development in classroom practices he conducted while on the faculties of the U.C.L.A. Medical Center and the University of Rochester School of Medicine and Dentistry. Now in private practice, he devotes full efforts to the development of his training programs, widely used for staff development in school districts. Teachers receive his ideas enthusiastically, recognizing in them refinements of practices with which they are already familiar but which they have not seen organized into a systematic approach. Jones did not publish a book describing his management system until 1987, several years after full development of his "pyramid" training system, in which teachers are trained to train other teachers with whom they work. Jones's behavior management book, *Positive Classroom Discipline*, is accompanied by a companion volume, *Positive Classroom Instruction*, also published in 1987.

JONES'S MAIN FOCUS

The main focus of Jones's model of discipline is on helping students support their own self control (Jones, 1979). Toward that end he emphasizes effective use of body language, describes how to provide incentives that motivate desired behavior, and details procedures for providing effective and efficient help to students during independent work time.

Jones's Key Ideas

1. Teachers in typical classrooms lose approximately 50% of their instructional time simply because students are off task or otherwise disturbing the teacher or other class members.
2. Practically all of this lost time results from two kinds of student misbehavior—talking without permission (80%) and general goofing off, including making noises, daydreaming, or getting out of one's seat without permission.
3. Most of this lost teaching time can be salvaged if teachers systematically employ three kinds of techniques that strongly assist discipline: (1) effective body language; (2) incentive systems; and (3) efficient individual help.
4. Good classroom discipline results mainly from the first technique—effective body language, which includes posture, eye contact, facial expression, signals, gestures, and physical proximity.
5. Incentive systems, which motivate students to remain on task, complete work, and behave properly, also contribute strongly to good discipline.
6. When teachers are able to provide individual help to students quickly and effectively, the students behave better and complete more work.

JONES'S CONCLUSIONS ABOUT MISBEHAVIOR AND TIME LOSS

During the 1970s, Fredric Jones and his associates conducted thousands of hours of carefully controlled observations in hundreds of elementary and secondary classrooms in various parts of the country. Their concern lay in effective methods of classroom management, especially in how teachers attempted to keep students working on task, how they provided individual help when needed, and how they dealt with misbehavior.

Their observations led them to several important conclusions. Principal among them was that classroom discipline problems are generally quite different from the way they are depicted in the media and perceived by the public. Even though many of the classrooms Jones studied were located in inner-city schools and alternative schools for students with behavior problems, Jones found no terrorism, no bullying attacks on teachers, and very little hostile defiance—the kinds of behavior that teachers fear and that many people believe exist in the schools. Instead, they found what Jones called "massive time wasting," which was comprised almost entirely of students talking, goofing off, and moving about the room without permission. Jones found that in well-managed classrooms, one of those behaviors occurred about every two minutes. In loud, unruly classes the disruptions averaged about 2.5 per minute. In attempting to deal with those misbehaviors, teachers lost almost 50% of the time available for teaching and learning (1987a).

Jones also discovered a critical time for misbehavior during lessons. He found that most lessons go along fairly well until students are asked to work on their own—the well-known "independent practice" portion of many lessons. But it is there, Jones says, that "the chickens come home to roost" (1987b, p. 14). Up until that point, students have seemed to pay attention and have given the impression they have learned perfectly. But when directed to continue work on their own, hands go up, talking begins, students start goofing off, some get out of their seats, and the teacher resorts once more to nagging and admonishment. What is seen, Jones says, is "another day in the life of a typical classroom," with the result that the teacher virtually reteaches the lesson during time set aside for guided practice.

That caused great frustration for teachers, leaving them feeling inept and defeated. Many of them expressed bitterness that they had never received training in how to deal effectively with such misbehavior. New teachers expected that they would quickly learn to maintain order in their classrooms, but most were only partially successful, and many soon resorted to hostility and punitive measures or else threw up their hands in resignation.

Jones concluded that teachers were correct in their contentions that they had not received training in behavior management, and further that many, if not most, were unable to develop needed skills while working on the job. Jones decided to observe and document the methods used by those few teachers who were notably successful with discipline. From those observations, he identified specific clusters of skills that served both to forestall misbehavior and to deal with it quickly when it did occur.

Three such skill clusters emerged—one having to do with *body language,* a second having to do with motivation through the use of *incentive systems,* and a third having to do with *providing help efficiently* to individual students.

Skill Cluster #1: Body Language

Jones maintains that good discipline depends mostly—90%, he says—on effective body language. Therefore, his training program concentrates on helping teachers learn to use their physical mannerisms to set and enforce behavior limits. (These limits are also specified in class rules.) This body language involves eye contact, physical proximity, body carriage, facial expression, and gestures. At its most effective level, it communicates that the teacher is calmly in control, knows what is going on, and means business. The following paragraphs present Jones's views on the various aspects of body language.

Eye Contact. Jacob has stopped paying attention. Miss Remy pauses. The sudden change in her lesson causes Jacob to look at Miss Remy, to find that she is looking directly at his eyes. He straightens up and waits attentively.

Few physical acts are more effective than eye contact for conveying the impression of being in control. Skilled teachers allow their eyes to sweep the room continually, and as they do so they pause directly on the eyes of individual students. Locking eyes makes many people uncomfortable, teachers and students alike, and students often avert their eyes when teachers look directly at them. The effect is not lost, however, for the students realize that the teacher, in looking directly at them, takes continual note of their behavior, both good and bad.

Making eye contact does not seem to be a natural behavior for most beginning teachers and therefore must be practiced before it can be used effectively. Inexperienced teachers tend to look over students' heads, between them, or dart their eyes rapidly without locking onto individuals. Sometimes while teaching, they stare more or less directly ahead, failing to monitor students who are located at the backs and sides of the group, or they find comfort in looking only at the faces of two or three well-behaved, actively responding students, oblivious to others not so attuned to the lesson.

These tendencies are persistent, and it is common to encounter experienced teachers who do not use eye contact effectively. With practice, however, they can learn to focus their eyes directly on the face of each individual student. This in itself sends a message that the teacher is aware and in control. It further serves to inhibit students who are on the verge of misbehaving, and it provides an opportunity to send facial expressions of approval or disapproval.

Physical Proximity. Jacob has stopped working on his assignment and begun talking to Jerry. Suddenly, he sees the shadow of Miss Remy at his side. He immediately gets back to work, without anything being said.

In his classroom observations, Jones noted that most misbehavior occurred some distance away from the teacher. Students near the teacher rarely misbehaved. This phenomenon has long been recognized by experienced teachers, who have learned to move nearer to students who are prone to misbehave, or to seat such students near them.

Jones also noted that teachers who used physical proximity did not need to say anything to the offending students to get them to behave. He therefore concluded that verbalization was not needed, that in fact it sometimes weakened the effect, due possibly to defensive reactions engendered in students when reprimanded verbally. Teachers who need to deal with minor misbehavior are instructed to move near the offending student, establish brief eye contact, and say nothing. The student will usually return immediately to proper behavior.

To use physical proximity effectively, the teacher must be able to step quickly alongside the appropriate student. This is difficult in traditionally arranged classrooms because students are seated in long rows of desks or clusters of tables spread out over most of the floor space. Jones would have teachers seat students in shallow semicircles, no more than three rows deep, with walk space interspersed. The teacher can then operate from within the arc of the semicircle, obtain easy eye contact with students, and move quickly to the side of any student. This arrangement also allows teachers to provide individual help much more quickly, as will be discussed later in the chapter.

Body Carriage. Jones says that body posture and carriage can be quite effective in communicating authority. Students quickly read such body language and are able to tell whether the teacher is ill, tired, disinterested, or intimidated. Good posture and confident carriage suggest strong leadership; a drooping posture and lethargic movements suggest resignation or fearfulness. Effective teachers, even when tired or troubled, tend to hold themselves erect and move with a measure of vigor. One should note here that on those infrequent occasions when the teacher is feeling ill, it is a good idea to inform the students and ask for their assistance and tolerance. Students usually behave with unexpected consideration at such times, although not when the strategy is used insincerely or too frequently.

Facial Expression. Like carriage, facial expression communicates much to students. It can show enthusiasm, seriousness, enjoyment, and appreciation, all of which tend to encourage good behavior; or it can reveal boredom, annoyance, and resignation, which may tend to encourage misbehavior. Perhaps more than anything else, facial expression, through winks, smiles, and contortions, can demonstrate a sense of humor, the trait that students say they like most in teachers.

The face can be put to good use in sending other types of nonverbal signals. Eye contact has been discussed as a prime example. Very slight shakes of the head can stop much misbehavior before it gets under way. Frowns show unmistakable disapproval. A firmed lip line and flashing eyes can indicate powerfully that the limits have been reached. These facial expressions are used instead of words whenever possible. They are as effective as words in showing approval, and for control and disapproval they have the advantage over verbal rebuffs in that they seldom belittle, sting, antagonize, or provoke counterattacks from students.

Gestures. Experienced teachers employ a variety of hand signals that they use to encourage and discourage behavior and to maintain student attention. Examples include palm out *(stop)*, palm up flexing fingers *(continue)*, finger to lips *(quiet)*, finger snap *(attention)*, and thumbs up *(approval)*. These gestures communicate effectively, but do not interfere with necessary instructional verbalization.

A Case of Body Language in Use. The following is an example of body language put to use as suggested by Jones:

1. Sam and Jim are talking and laughing while Mr. Sanchez is explaining the process used to divide fractions. Mr. Sanchez makes eye contact with them, pauses momentarily, and then continues with his explanation. Sam and Jim probably stop talking when Mr. Sanchez looks at them and pauses. But if they continue . . .
2. Mr. Sanchez again pauses, makes eye contact, and shakes his head slightly but emphatically. He may give a fleeting palm-out signal. Sam and Jim probably stop talking when he sends these signals. But if they continue . . .
3. Mr. Sanchez moves calmly and stands beside Sam and Jim. He asks the class, "Who thinks they can go to the board and show us how to divide five-eighths by one-eighth? Tell us what to do, step by step." Sam and Jim will almost certainly stop talking now. But if they continue . . .
4. Mr. Sanchez makes eye contact with them and calmly says, "Jim, Sam, I want you to stop talking right now."

If for any reason they defy Mr. Sanchez' direct order, Mr. Sanchez stops the lesson long enough to separate the boys, or seat them in opposite corners of the room, or as a last resort call the office to inform that they are being sent for detention. In any of these cases, a follow-up conference will be necessary with the boys, and if the defiance continues, it will need to be dealt with by the principal, vice-principal, counselor, and/or the boys' parents.

Note that in all cases except the most severe, Mr. Sanchez used only body language. There was no verbal confrontation and only the slightest slowdowns in the lesson. Instruction continued, students were kept on task, and teaching-learning time was preserved.

Skill Cluster #2: Incentive Systems

Mr. Sharpe tells his class that if all of them complete their work in 45 minutes or less, they can have the last 10 minutes of class time to talk quietly with a friend. Mr. Dulle tells his class that if they promise to work very hard later on, he will allow them to begin the period by discussing their work with a friend. Which teacher is likely to get the best work from his students?

This question has to do with the use of incentives. An incentive is something outside of the individual that prompts the individual to act. It is something that is promised as a consequence for desired behavior, but is held in abeyance, to occur or be provided later. It might be popcorn, a preferred activity, an unspecified surprise, and so forth. It is an effective incentive if students will behave as desired in order to obtain it later.

Jones gives incentives a prominent place in his classroom management program, as a means of motivating students. He found that some of the most effective teachers used incentives systematically, but that most teachers used them ineffectively or not at all. The ineffective teachers typically made use of marks, stars, having work displayed, being dismissed first, and so forth. The problem with such incentives is that they go only to the top achievers; the less able students, once out of contention for the prize, have nothing left for which to work. Moreover, for many students, receiving a badge or being first in line does not compete strongly with the joys of talking or daydreaming.

What, then, are characteristics of effective incentives and their use? Jones implies that teachers should emphasize genuineness, "Grandma's rule," educational value, and ease of implementation. Let us examine these suggestions further.

Genuine Incentives. There is a wide difference between what many teachers *hope* will be incentives (e.g., Let's all work in such a way that we will later be proud of what we do.) and what are genuine incentives from the student's point of view (e.g., If you complete your work on time you can have five minutes of free time to talk with your friends.). This point may seem obvious, but it is often overlooked. Teachers may say, "The first person to complete a perfect paper will receive two bonus points." This works to motivate a handful of students, but most know they have little chance to win so they barely try. Or they may say, "If you really try, you can be the best class I have ever had." This usually sounds better to the teacher than to the students. Although the students might like to think of themselves as the best, that thought will not be strong enough to keep them hard at work.

What, then, are some genuine incentives that can be used in the classroom? Generally, students respond well to the anticipation of preferred activities such as art, viewing a film, or having free time to pursue personal interests or to talk with friends. Such group activities are genuine incentives in that almost all students desire them sufficiently to make extra effort to obtain them. Many teachers use tangible objects, awards, and certificates as incentives. These are less desirable because they may be costly or difficult to dispense and they have little educational value.

Grandma's Rule. Grandma's rule goes like this: First eat your dinner and then you can have your dessert. Applied to the classroom, this rule requires that students first do what they are supposed to do, and then for a while they can do what they want to do. The incentive is the end product of the proposition. In order to obtain it, students must complete designated work while behaving acceptably.

Just as children (and many adults) will ask to have their dessert first, promising to eat all their dinner afterward, students will ask to have their incentive first, pledging on their honor to work feverishly afterward. As we all know, even the best intentions are hard to fulfill once the reason for doing so is gone. Thus, teachers who wish to use effective incentive systems must, despite student urging, delay the rewards until last and make the reward contingent on the students doing required work acceptably. In other words, "If they don't eat their beans and cabbage, they don't get their pudding."

Educational Value. To the extent feasible, every class period should be devoted to activities that have educational value. Work that only keeps students occupied, but teaches them little, can seldom be justified. This principle holds for incentive systems. While few educators would be such Scrooges that they would never allow a moment of innocent frivolity, the opposite extreme of throwing daily or weekly classroom parties as incentives for work and behavior is difficult to condone from an educational standpoint. What then should one do?

There are many educationally valuable activities that students enjoy greatly, both individually and in groups. One of the best for individuals is "free time," in which students may read, work on assignments, do art work, plan with other students, or pursue personal interests. Despite the word "free," students are not left to do just anything, nor do they proceed without rules of guidance. The freedom is that of choosing from a variety of approved activities.

For the total group, activities can be chosen by vote, and all students engage in the same activity during the time allotted. Elementary school students often select physical education, art, music, drama, or construction activities. Frequently, they want the teacher to read to them from a favorite book. Secondary students often choose to watch a film, hold class discussions on special topics, watch demonstrations and performances by class members, or work together on such projects as producing a class magazine.

Group Concern. As mentioned earlier, many classroom incentive systems in normal practice contain a fatal flaw. That flaw is that only a few students—the faster working, higher achieving—have a genuine opportunity to earn the incentive. Most of the others make only perfunctory effort, having learned that they have little chance of success.

Jones teaches a way around this flaw, one that involves every class member and yet remains simple to administer. His plan hinges on causing every student to have a stake in earning the incentive for the entire class. This motivates all students to keep on task, behave well, and complete assigned work. Here is how it works.

The teacher sets aside a period of time in which students can engage in a preferred activity. In keeping with Grandma's rule, this time period must come after a significant amount of work time devoted to the standard curriculum. It can be at the end of the school day for self-contained classes, perhaps 15 to 20 minutes. For departmentalized classes, the time can be set aside at the end of the week, perhaps 30 minutes on Friday. The students can decide on the activity for their "dessert" time, and to earn it they have only to work and behave as expected.

The teacher manages the system by using a stopwatch, preferably a large one with hands that the class can see. When any student begins to misbehave the teacher simply lifts the stopwatch and clicks it on. Every second that ticks off the watch is time deducted from the time originally available for the incentive. The teacher must be dispassionately firm in applying this technique. A burst of perfect behavior cannot be allowed to erase previous misbehavior, since that tells students it is all right to misbehave for a while before settling down. The teacher also must not be talked into canceling time lost on the promise of better behavior in the future. The students know the rules of the game from the beginning, and they know that they can choose through their behavior whether and to what extent they will earn the incentive time.

Teachers often think it unfair to penalize the entire class, through loss of time, for the sins of a few or even a single class member. In practice, this is rarely a problem because the class is made to understand that this is a group not an individual effort. The group is rewarded together and punished together regardless of who might transgress. A strength in this approach is that it brings to bear strong peer pressure against misbehavior. Ordinarily a misbehaving student obtains reinforcement from the group in the form of attention, laughter, or admiration. With the stopwatch system the opposite is true. The class is likely to discourage individual misbehavior because it takes away something the class members want.

Ease of Implementation. Unlike other incentive systems, that advocated by Jones accomplishes two important ends simultaneously: first, it is effective for all students because all are brought into the picture; second, it is easy to implement. Teachers need do only four things:

1. Establish and explain the system.
2. Allow the class to vote from time to time on which teacher-approved activities they wish to enjoy during incentive time.
3. Obtain a stopwatch and use it conscientiously.
4. Be prepared when necessary to conduct the class in low-preference activities for the amount of time that students might have lost from their preferred activity time allotment.

When It Does Not Work. If an incentive system loses effectiveness, it is likely to be for one of the following reasons.

1. The preferred activities might have grown stale. This is cured by allowing the class to discuss the matter and decide on new preferences.
2. The class may temporarily be overly excited by unsettling occurrences such as unusual weather, a holiday, special events at school, or an accident. In such cases the teacher may suspend the incentive program for a time, with explanation and discussion.
3. Individual students may occasionally lose self-control or decide to defy the teacher. In this case, the offending student should be isolated in the room or removed to the office. The teacher can establish a policy wherein the class will not be penalized for these types of actions by individual students.

Skill Cluster #3: Providing Efficient Help

One of the most interesting, important, and useful findings in Jones's research has to do with the way teachers provide individual help to students who are "stuck" during seat work. Suppose that a math lesson is in progress. The teacher introduces the topic, explains the algorithm on the chalkboard, asks a couple of questions to determine whether the students are understanding, and then assigns 10 problems from the textbook to be done by students at their desks. Very soon a hand is raised to signal that a student is stuck and needs help. If only three or four hands are raised during work time, the teacher has no problem. But if 20 students fill the air with waving arms, most of them will sit for several minutes doing nothing while awaiting attention from the teacher. For each student needing help, this time is pure waste and an encouragement to misbehave.

Jones asked teachers how much time they thought they spent on the average when providing help to each student who signaled. The teachers felt that they spent from one to two minutes with each student, but when Jones's researchers timed the episodes they found that teachers actually spent around four minutes with each student. This consumed much time and made it impossible for the teacher to attend to more than a few students during work time. Even if the amount of time spent was only one minute per contact, some students would waste several minutes while waiting.

Jones noted another phenomenon that compounded the problem. He described it as a "dependency syndrome" wherein some students felt so uncomfortable doing independent work that they routinely raised their hands for teacher help even when they did not need it. To have the teacher unfailingly come to their side and give personal attention proved rewarding indeed, and that reinforcement further strengthened the dependency.

From these observations, Jones described independent seat work as having four inherent problems: (1) insufficient time for teachers to answer all requests for help; (2) wasted student time; (3) high potential for misbehavior; and (4) the perpetuation of dependency. Consequently, he gave this matter high priority in his classroom management training program.

Jones determined that all four problems could be solved through teaching teachers how to give help more efficiently. He would have this be accomplished in three steps:

- *Step one:* Organize the classroom seating so that students are within easy reach of the teacher. The shallow concentric semicircles previously described are suggested. Otherwise, the teacher uses too much time and energy dashing from one end of the room to the other.

- *Step two:* Use graphic reminders, such as models or charts, that provide clear examples and instructions. These might show steps in algorithms, proper form for business letters, or simply written directions for the lesson. These reminders are posted and can be consulted by students before they call for teacher help.

- *Step three:* This step is one in which Jones places great stock. It involves learning how to cut to a bare minimum the time used for individual help. To see how it is done, consider that teachers normally give inefficient help in the form of a questioning tutorial as follows:
  "What's the problem?"
  "All right, what did we say was the first thing to do?" (Waits; repeats question.)
  "No, that was the second. You are forgetting the first step. What was it? Think again." (Waits until student finally makes a guess.)
  "No, let me help you with another example. Suppose . . ."

Often, in this helping mode, the teacher virtually reteaches the concept or process to each student who requests help. That is how four minutes can be unexpectedly spent in each interaction. If help is to be provided more quickly, this questioning method must be reconsidered. Jones trains teachers to give help in a very different way, and *he insists that it be done in 20 seconds or less* for each student. Here is what the teacher should do when arriving beside the student:

1. Quickly find anything that the student has done correctly and mention it favorably. ("Your work is very neat" or "Good job up to here.")
2. Give a straightforward hint or suggestion that will get the student going. ("Follow step 2 on the chart" or "Regroup here.")
3. Leave immediately.

In other words, as Jones puts it, be positive, be brief, and be gone.

Help provided in this way solves the major problems that Jones identified. Teachers have time to attend to every student who needs help. Students spend little wasted time waiting for the teacher. Misbehavior is much less likely to occur. The dependency syndrome is broken, especially if the teacher gives attention to students who try to complete their work without calling for assistance. Rapid circulation by the teacher also permits better monitoring of work being done by students who do not raise their hands. When errors are noted in their work, the teacher can provide the same kind of help as that given to the others.

JONES'S REMINDERS FOR TEACHERS

The three skill clusters described in this chapter—body language, incentive systems, and efficient help—comprise the core of Jones's system of discipline. Reminders for teachers were presented in a report by Rardin (1978):

- Catch misbehavior early and deal with it immediately.
- Use body language instead of words. Show you mean business through your posture, eye contact, facial expression, and gestures.
- Use physical proximity in dealing with misbehaving or defiant students.
- Use group incentive systems (following Grandma's rule) to motivate work and good behavior.
- Provide individual help efficiently; aim for 10-second interactions.
- Do not use threats; establish rules and attend to misbehavior.

COMMENTS ON JONES'S MODEL

Jones's model provides strong help in all facets of discipline—preventive, supportive, and corrective—and it does so in a balanced way. Jones has isolated behaviors seen in teachers who are often called "naturals." That is why teachers' heads nod in agreement with his suggestions; they recognize the behaviors he describes and the settings within which they occur. Jones has found that the discipline techniques he advocates are all teachable, though many teachers never learn them well within the pressures of day-to-day teaching. Through specific training episodes, most teachers can acquire the techniques that are usually seen only in the most effective.

But it is unrealistic to think that teachers can read Jones's work and then walk into the classroom the next day transformed. The acts he describes must be practiced repeatedly. Fortunately, teachers do not have to go to expensive, time-consuming training seminars to learn them. They can, instead, assess their own classroom behavior in light of Jones's suggestions and isolate certain behaviors they would like to improve. Then they can take the new learnings into the classroom one by one. That is one of the nice things about Jones's suggestions—they do not have to be utilized as a full-blown total system, but can instead be practiced, perfected, and added incrementally.

Application Exercises

Concept Cases: Kris, Sara, Joshua, and Tom.

CASE #1. KRIS WILL NOT WORK:

Kris, a student in Mr. Jake's class, is quite docile. She socializes little with other students and never disrupts the class. However, Mr. Jake cannot get Kris to do any work. She rarely completes an assignment. She is simply there, like a bump on a log, putting forth no effort at all.

How would Jones deal with Kris? Jones would suggest that Mr. Jake take the following steps to improve Kris's behavior.

1. Make frequent eye contact with her. Even when she looks down, he should make sure to look directly at her. She will be aware of it and it may make her uncomfortable enough that she will begin work.
2. Move close to Kris. Stand beside her while presenting the lesson.
3. Use encouraging facial expressions and hand signals every time eye contact can be made.
4. Give Kris frequent help during seat work. Check on her progress several times during the lesson; give specific suggestions; and move quickly on.
5. Set up a personal incentive system with Kris—a certain amount of work earns something that Kris values.
6. Set up a system in which Kris, by working, can earn rewards for the entire class. This brings added peer support to Kris.

CASE #2. SARA CANNOT STOP TALKING:

Sara is a pleasant girl who participates in class activities and does most, though not all, of her assigned work. She cannot seem to refrain from talking to classmates, however. Her teacher, Mr. Gonzales, has to speak to her repeatedly during lessons, to the point that he often becomes exasperated and loses his temper.

What suggestions would Jones give Mr. Gonzales for dealing with Sara?

CASE #3. JOSHUA CLOWNS AND INTIMIDATES:

Joshua, larger and louder than his classmates, always wants to be the center of attention, which he accomplishes through a combination of clowning and intimidation. He makes wise remarks, talks back (smilingly) to the teacher, utters a variety of sound effect noises such as automobile crashes and gunshots, and makes limitless sarcastic comments and put-downs of his classmates. Other students will not stand up to him, apparently fearing his size and verbal aggression. His teacher, Miss Pearl, has come to her wits' end.

What specifically do you find in Jones's suggestions that would help Miss Pearl with Joshua?

CASE #4. TOM IS HOSTILE AND DEFIANT:

Tom has appeared to be in his usual foul mood ever since arriving in class. He gets up and on his way to sharpen his pencil he bumps into Frank. Frank complains. Tom tells him loudly to shut up. Miss Baines, the teacher, says, "Tom, go back to your seat." Tom wheels around, swears loudly, and says heatedly, "I'll go when I'm damned good and ready!"

How effective do you believe Jones's suggestions would be in dealing with Tom?

ACTIVITIES:

For each of the following scenarios: (a) Identify the problem that underlies the undesired behavior and (b) describe how Jones would have the teacher deal with it.

1. Mr. Anton tries to help all of his students during independent work time but finds himself unable to get around to all who have their hands raised.
2. Ms. Sevier wants to show trust for her class. She accepts their promise to work hard if they can first listen to a few favorite recorded songs. After listening to the songs, the students talk so much that they fail to get their work done.
3. Mr. Gregory wears himself out every day dealing ceaselessly with three class clowns who disrupt his lessons. The other students always laugh at the clowns' antics.

FURTHER ANALYSIS AND APPLICATION:

Examine scenario #10 (elementary) or #2 (secondary) in Chapter 13. What changes would Jones suggest that Denise Thorpe or Mr. Platt make in order to provide a more efficient and satisfactory learning environment?

REFERENCES

Jones, F. (1979). The gentle art of classroom discipline. *National Elementary Principal, 58,* 26–32.

Jones, F. (1987a). *Positive classroom discipline.* New York: McGraw-Hill.

Jones, F. (1987b). *Positive classroom instruction.* New York: McGraw-Hill.

Rardin, R. (1978, September). Classroom management made easy. *Virginia Journal of Education,* 14–17.

CHAPTER 7

The Canter Model
Assertively Taking Charge

CANTER BIOGRAPHICAL SKETCH

Lee Canter is director of Lee Canter & Associates Inc., an organization that provides training in Assertive Discipline and publishes related materials for educators and parents. His wife, Marlene Canter, has collaborated in most of the work. Canter's research into the behaviors of highly successful teachers led to his putting together "Assertive Discipline," a discipline system that helps teachers interact with students in a calm yet forceful manner. Through workshops and graduate courses, Canter has brought Assertive Discipline to hundreds of thousands of teachers and administrators, making his program not only the most popular of all such systems, but also the most discussed and, possibly, the most controversial.

Canter's company also produces quantities of materials on such topics as motivation, homework, dealing with severe behavior problems, and activities for positive reinforcement. All the Canter materials are listed in *The Assertive Educator,* a newsletter available from Canter & Associates Inc., P.O. Box 2113, Dept. A8, Santa Monica, CA 90406.

CANTER'S MAIN FOCUS

The main focus of Canter's model is on teachers' assertively insisting that students behave properly, and on providing teachers a well-organized procedure for following through when students do not. The result is a very effective system of corrective discipline.

Canter's Key Ideas

1. Teachers should insist on decent, responsible behavior from their students. Students benefit from this type of behavior, parents want it, the community at large expects it, and the educational process is ineffective without it.
2. Teacher failure, for all practical purposes, is synonymous with failure to maintain adequate classroom discipline.
3. Many teachers labor under false assumptions about discipline, believing that firm control is stifling and inhumane to students. To the contrary, firm control maintained correctly is humane and liberating. It sets clear limits, which students want and need.
4. Teachers have basic educational rights in their classrooms, including:
   a. The right to establish optimal learning environments.
   b. The right to request and expect appropriate behavior.
   c. The right to receive help from administrators and parents when it is needed.
5. Students have basic rights in the classroom, too, including:
   a. The right to have teachers who help to limit inappropriate, self-destructive behavior.
   b. The right to choose how to behave, with full understanding of the consequences that automatically follow those choices.

6. These needs, rights, and conditions are best met through Assertive Discipline, in which the teacher clearly communicates expectations to students and consistently follows up with appropriate actions but never violates the best interests of the students.

7. Assertive Discipline consists of the following elements, to be followed consistently by teachers:
   a. Identifying expectations clearly.
   b. Willingness to say, "I like that," and "I don't like that."
   c. Persistence in stating expectations and feelings.
   d. Use of firm tone of voice.
   e. Maintenance of eye contact.
   f. Use of nonverbal gestures in support of verbal statements.
   g. Use of hints, questions, and I-messages rather than demands for requesting appropriate behavior.
   h. Follow-through with promises (reasonable consequences, previously established, with emphasis on the positive) rather than with threats.
   i. Assertiveness in confrontations with students, including using statements of expectations, indicating positive and negative consequences that will occur, and noting why action is necessary.

8. To become more assertive in discipline, teachers should do the following:
   a. Practice assertive response styles.
   b. Set clear limits and consequences.
   c. Emphasize the positive.
   d. Follow through consistently.
   e. Make specific Assertive Discipline plans and rehearse them mentally.
   f. Write things down; do not trust the memory.
   g. Practice the broken-record technique for repeating expectations.
   h. Ask school administrators and parents for support in the efforts to help students.

THE BASICS OF ASSERTIVE DISCIPLINE

In 1976, Canter set forth the basic premises and practices of Assertive Discipline. He noted that discipline remains a matter of great concern in schools. Parents and community single it out as greatly in need of improvement, and for teachers it is the overwhelming cause of failure, burn-out, and resignation. The situation has for years been growing worse, possibly because of society's declining respect for authority and parents' failure to require that their children behave acceptably in school. As societal conditions worsen, teachers have become hesitant and unsure in their efforts to control student behavior. This is partly due to the prevalence of mistaken ideas about discipline.

Mistaken Ideas about Discipline

Mistaken ideas about discipline that are frequently heard include:

1. Good teachers can handle discipline problems on their own without any help.
2. Firm discipline causes psychological trauma to students.
3. Discipline problems disappear when students are given activities that meet their needs.
4. Misbehavior results from deep-seated causes that are beyond the influence of the teacher.

Correct Ideas about Discipline

Mistaken ideas about discipline must be replaced by the following correct ideas, if discipline is to be effectively maintained:

1. We all need discipline for psychological security.
2. We all need discipline as a suppressant to acts that we would not be proud of later.
3. We all need discipline as a liberating influence that allows us to build and expand our best traits and abilities.
4. We all need discipline as a necessity to maintain an effective and efficient learning environment.

THE ASSERTIVE TEACHER

Canter maintains that an assertive teacher is one who clearly and firmly communicates needs and requirements to students, follows those words with appropriate actions, responds to students in ways that maximize compliance, but in no way violates the best interests of the students.

He says repeatedly that the basis of this assertive posture is *caring about oneself* to the point of not allowing students to take advantage and *caring about students* to the point of not allowing them to behave in ways that are damaging to themselves (Canter, 1978). This caring is shown by teachers who are positive, firm, and consistent, not wishy-washy, hostile, abusive, or threatening—negative behaviors that are certain to fail.

A climate of care and support rises up from what Canter calls "basic teacher rights" in working with students:

1. The right to establish optimal learning environments for students, consistent with the teacher's strengths and limitations.
2. The right to expect behavior from students that contributes to their optimal growth, while also meeting the special needs of the teacher.
3. The right to ask and receive help and backing from administrators and parents.

When these basic rights of teachers are met, they have the potential for providing a climate of positive support and care. But for that potential to be realized, more is needed. That additional need is training in Assertive Discipline.

FIVE STEPS TO ASSERTIVE DISCIPLINE

Canter emphasizes that teachers can easily incorporate the basics of Assertive Discipline into their own teaching styles. A series of five steps is implied for this implementation:

Step 1. Recognize and Remove Roadblocks to Assertive Discipline

All teachers have within themselves the potential for expressing their educational needs to students and for obtaining student compliance with those needs. Most teachers have difficulty, however, with both the expression and the compliance, due to a group of "roadblocks" that hinder teachers' efforts to be assertive. The first step in learning to use Assertive Discipline is to recognize and remove these roadblocks.

One prominent roadblock is teachers' negative expectations about students. We expect many students to behave badly because of their health, home, personality, or environment. Victor has a history of hyperactivity; Stacy may be a victim of child abuse; no one has ever been able to do a thing with Donald. Therefore we do not expect that they can behave. Such negative expectations must be recognized as false, and they must be supplanted with positive expectations.

Another prominent roadblock is teachers' failure to believe that they can influence in positive ways the behavior of all students under their direction, no matter what the problems. To remove that roadblock teachers should acknowledge the following:

All students need limits, and teachers have a responsibility to set them.

Teachers who fear that students will not like them if they set and enforce limits have not paid attention to human psychology.

We admire and respect teachers who hold high expectations and high standards.

We seldom respect teachers who take a laissez-faire approach to teaching.

A third prominent roadblock is teachers' belief that they function alone, without support. To the contrary, teachers have the right to ask for and receive solid backing from principals, parents, and other school personnel. Teachers who have such support will not be intimidated when students behave defiantly or hostilely.

Step 2. Practice the Use of Assertive Response Styles

Canter differentiates among three styles of responses that characterize teachers' interactions with misbehaving students:

Nonassertive Response Style. The nonassertive response style is typical of teachers who have given in to students or who feel it is wrong to place strong demands on student behavior. Terry and Rick are laughing and engaging in horseplay that has almost ruined the lesson. Miss Jenkins looks up and says, "For the tenth time, would you two *please* stop that?" She continues the lesson. Within a few minutes, the two boys are disrupting again.

Teachers using this nonassertive style are passive. They either do not establish clear standards or else they fail to back up their standards with appropriate actions. They hope their good natures will gain student compliance. They often ask students to "please try" to do their work, or behave themselves, or do better next time. They are not firm or insistent, and they end up resignedly accepting whatever the students decide to do.

Hostile Response Style. Miss Jenkins finally reaches the end of her rope with Terry and Rick. She yells, "All right, you two! That's the last straw! You either pay attention or you are going to regret it!"

The hostile response style is used by teachers who feel that they are barely hanging on to class control. They use aversive techniques such as sarcasm and threats. They often shout. They believe they must rule with an iron fist or else they will be overwhelmed with chaos. Hostile teacher responses produce several bad side effects— they hurt students' feelings; they provoke disrespect and desire to get even; they fail to meet students' needs for warmth and security, and they violate two of the basic student rights described earlier: the right to positive limits on self-destructive behavior and the right to choose their own behavior, with full knowledge of the consequences that will follow.

Assertive Response Style. Terry and Rick are now in Miss Beech's class. They have continued their horseplay. Miss Beech looks directly at them, writes their names on her clipboard, and says, "It is against the rules for you to talk without permission during the lesson." The boys know that they have received a warning, and that if they continue, Miss Beech will take further steps. The lesson resumes and so does their misbehavior. Miss Beech makes a check mark beside each of their names and directs them to take seats elsewhere in the room for a fifteen-minute time-out from the lesson. Miss Beech has shown that she always follows through on enforcing class rules.

The assertive response style, which should be practiced until it becomes natural in dealing with students, protects the rights of both teacher and students. With this style, teachers make their expectations clearly known to students. In a businesslike way, they continually insist that students comply with those expectations. They back up their words with actions. When students choose to comply with teacher guidance, they receive positive benefits. When they choose to behave in unacceptable ways, the teacher follows through with consequences.

The following are some examples of nonassertive, hostile, and assertive responses to misbehavior:

Example: Fighting

Nonassertive: Please try your very best to stop fighting.

Hostile: Your behavior is disgusting!

Assertive: We do not fight. Sit down until you cool off.

Example: Talking Out

Nonassertive: You are talking again without raising your hand.

Hostile: Learn some manners or else you are going to be in big trouble!

Assertive: Don't answer unless you raise your hand and I call on you.

Notice in these examples that the assertive response clearly communicates the teacher's disapproval of the behavior, followed by an indication of what the student is supposed to do. In contrast, the nonassertive response leaves students unconvinced that they are truly expected to behave differently; it suggests that the teacher is afraid or feels powerless. The hostile response is counterproductive in that it wounds students; it smacks of dislike and vengeance and depicts the classroom as a battleground where teacher and students are adversaries. If the threats are not carried out, they quickly lose their effect. But if they are carried out, distrust of the teacher and desire for revenge rapidly grow.

Step 3. Learn to Set Limits

Canter makes this point emphatically: No matter what the activity, in order to be assertive, teachers must be clear about the behaviors they want and need from their students. He would have teachers identify the specific behaviors they expect from students, such as taking turns, not shouting out, starting work on time, and listening quietly while another student is speaking. Following this identification, teachers should then instruct their students very clearly on the behaviors they have identified. It is often helpful to make very succinct lists of dos and don'ts, as well as specific directions and reminders, that can be posted in the room. All of these should refer to setting limits.

Once the specific behaviors are made explicit, the next step in limit-setting is to decide how to follow through for both compliance and noncompliance. Canter repeatedly reminds teachers that positive assertions (approval, rewards) are powerful in maintaining appropriate behavior. Often, facial expressions of approval or verbal acknowledgments are sufficient. At times, special rewards and privileges may be given. Dealing with noncompliance is more difficult, but it is here that assertive discipline is most helpful. When preparing to deal with inappropriate behaviors, teachers should be ready with firm reminders of what students are supposed to be doing. Canter goes into detail in describing verbal limit setting, emphasizing three techniques:

1. *Requesting appropriate behavior,* which is done by means of "Hints" (statements made from time to time to remind students of what they are supposed to be doing (e.g., "Everyone should be reading silently"), "I-messages" (informing students how behavior is affecting the teacher; e.g., "It is getting so noisy I can't do my work"), and "Demands" (statements that direct students on what to do; e.g., "Get back to your reading right now"). Canter warns of the negative effects that demands can have, and here issues his only commandment concerning Assertive Discipline: Thou shalt not make a demand thou art not preparest to follow through on.

2. *Delivering the verbal limit,* which has to do with tone of voice, eye contact,

and gestures. Tone of voice should be firmly neutral and businesslike, not harsh, abusive, sarcastic, or intimidating. Neither should it be mirthful, implying a lack of seriousness. Eye contact should be maintained if messages are to have maximum impact. Teachers should not insist that students look them back in the eye, but even when students look away, teachers should fix them with a direct gaze when verbally setting limits. Gestures add much to verbal messages, especially in Anglo-American society, where few gestures are used. Facial expressions and arm and hand movements accentuate messages, though fingers and fists should not be waved in students' faces. Use of students' names adds further impact to verbal messages, making them more forceful and penetrating. This is especially true for messages delivered across the room or grounds. Physical touch (hand lightly on shoulder) is very effective in conjunction with verbal messages, though some students may pull away abruptly or even thrust back and claim that the teacher has pinched or hurt them.

3. *Using the broken-record technique,* which involves insistent repetition of the original message—especially effective when students seek to divert teachers from their intended message. Here is an example:

> TEACHER: Alex, we do not fight in this room. I will not tolerate fighting. You must not fight again.
>
> STUDENT: It's not my fault. Pete started it. He hit me first.
>
> TEACHER: I understand that might be. I didn't see. But you will not fight in my class.
>
> STUDENT: Well, Pete started it.
>
> TEACHER: That may be. I'll watch. But you may not fight in this class.

The broken-record technique (repetition that we do not fight in this class) was maintained with a firm, positive insistence. Canter gives these reminders concerning its use:

> Use it only when students refuse to listen, persist in responding inappropriately, or refuse to take responsibility for their own behavior.
>
> Preface your repetitions with, "That's not the point . . . " or "I understand, but . . ."
>
> Use it a maximum of three times; after the third time, follow through with an appropriate consequence, if necessary.

Step 4. Learn to Follow Through on Limits

By "limits," Canter means the positive demands you have made on students. By "following through," he means taking the appropriate actions when students comply (the results are then positive) and when they fail to comply (the results are then negative). The students have already been carefully informed that consequences, good or bad, will follow the behavior they choose. Canter presents the following guidelines for following through appropriately:

1. *Make promises, not threats.* A promise is a vow to take appropriate action, positive or negative, when necessary. A threat is a statement that shows intent to harm or punish.

2. *Select appropriate consequences in advance.* Teachers should select several

specific consequences, positive and negative, that can be invoked when appropriate. Gradations of severity are involved for violations of the rules. Examples of positive consequences are reading, preferred activities, talking with a friend, no homework, and special notes and other awards. Examples of negative consequences that teachers have found most effective are time out, loss of privilege, loss of preferred activity, detention, visit to the principal, telephone call to parents, and being sent home from school. All of the consequences, both positive and negative, should indicate that teachers truly care about the students and their behavior and that they are always disposed to influencing behavior in positive directions.

3. *Set up a system of negative consequences that you can easily enforce.* Canter suggests the following, but emphasizes that individual teachers must come up with their own systems with which they feel comfortable. (These suggested consequences are for individual students, starting at the beginning of the day or period. Each new day begins afresh.)

Misbehavior	*Consequence*
First	name written on clipboard and warning issued
Second	check placed by name (10-minute time-out from lesson)
Third	second check by name (15-minute time-out from lesson)
Fourth	third check by name (student phones parents and explains)
Fifth	fourth check (student meets with the principal)

4. *Practice verbal confrontations that call for follow through.* The only way to begin to use assertions and consequences naturally is to practice them in advance, before you have to face them unexpectedly in the classroom. One good way to practice is to follow this sequence:

a. Describe a rule to your imaginary class, such as "No talking out without permission." You briefly explain why the rule is necessary, tell what students should do instead of talking out, and explain what the consequences will be for compliance and noncompliance.
b. Imagine that a student has talked out. Make an assertive response. Suppose the student talks back. Use the broken record technique. Suppose the student still talks back. Assertively state the consequence. Suppose the student defies you. Follow through assertively. (Refer to the suggestions given above.)

Step 5. Implement a System of Positive Consequences

The previous section emphasized negative assertions and consequences, because teachers everywhere are concerned about misbehavior and how to suppress and correct it. Canter insists, however, that positive consequences are more important than negative consequences, because they have the effect of increasing teacher influence over students, decreasing the amount of problem behavior, and making the classroom climate

more positive overall. Here are some of Canter's suggestions for positive consequences.

1   *Personal Attention from the Teacher.* Special, positive, personal attention from the
teacher is one of the most rewarding experiences for students, and most respond
enthusiastically to it. Such attention can be given in the form of greetings, short talks,
compliments, acknowledgments, smiles, and friendly eye contact.

2   *Positive Notes to Parents.* Parents are usually informed about their children only when
they have misbehaved in school. A brief note or phone call, positive and complimen-
tary, can do wonders for both students and parents. They also rally parents to the
support of teachers.

3   *Special Awards.* Students respond well to special awards given for high achievement,
significant improvement, and so forth. Younger students love them. Secondary students' reactions are less predictable, since they are so strongly influenced by peers'
responses to them. This can be discussed with older students before being used.

4   *Special Privileges.* Students of all ages respond well to special privileges, such as
helping take care of classroom animals or equipment, helping with class materials, or
working together with a friend.

5   *Material Rewards.* Many tangible objects are effective rewards. Younger students like
to receive stickers, badges, ribbons, and the like, while older students like such things
as posters, pencils, and rubber stamps.

6   *Home Rewards.* In collaboration with parents, privileges can be extended to the
home. Completing homework can earn extra television time, reading an extra book
can earn a favorite meal, and so forth.

7   *Group Rewards.* Canter discusses methods of rewarding the entire group for good
behavior. He includes suggestions such as: (1) dropping marbles into a jar, as the
entire group remains on task and works hard (when the jar is filled, the class earns
something special); and (2) writing a series of letters of the alphabet on the board that
when completed make up a secret word, such as POPCORN PARTY, which the class
then receives as a reward.

BEGINNING THE YEAR WITH ASSERTIVE DISCIPLINE

Although an assertive discipline program can be implemented at any time, the first
few days of a new school year are an especially good time to introduce the program.
Canter suggests the following:

   1. Decide on behaviors you want from students, together with the positive and
   negative consequences.

2. Take your list to the principal for approval and support.
3. At the first meeting with the new students, discuss the behaviors, consequences, and methods of follow-through you intend to use. Keep the list of behaviors (rules) to six or less.
4. Stress that no student will be allowed to break the rules. Tell the students exactly what will happen each time a rule is broken (first, second, third offense, etc.). Canter suggests that the plan include no more than five different consequences for bad behavior.
5. Ask the students to write the behaviors and consequences on a sheet of paper, take the plan home, have their parents read and sign it, and return it the next day.
6. Emphasize repeatedly that these rules will help the class toward its responsibility of learning and behaving acceptably.
7. Ask students to repeat orally what is expected and what will happen for compliance and for violations.
8. Prepare a short letter concerning the plan to go home to parents, indicating your need for their support and your pleasure in collaborating with them toward the benefit of their child.
9. Implement the assertive discipline plan immediately.

ASSERTIVE DISCIPLINE: PHASE 2 AND BEYOND

The basics of Assertive Discipline described up to this point were set forth in Canter's 1976 book *Assertive Discipline: A Take-Charge Approach for Today's Educators*. As Assertive Discipline grew in popularity, Canter made additions to the program that further increased its effectiveness. These additions are spelled out in materials such as his Phase 2 videotapes and manuals (1986) and the in-service programs designed especially for secondary educators (1989). The skills outlined in the following section are especially noteworthy.

Determining and Teaching Specific Directions

This skill focuses on teaching the students exactly how you want them to follow directions rather than merely telling them. It involves five steps:

Preplanning what you want from students.

Presenting directions students are to follow.

Asking questions to make sure students understand.

Role-playing how students correctly follow directions.

Periodically reviewing the procedures.

Using Positive Repetition to Get Students On-Task

This skill entails repeating directions as positive statements to students who are complying. Example: "Fred raised his hand. Good job."

Using Praise Techniques to Keep Students On-Task

This skill focuses on singling out students who are behaving properly and praising them, keeping the following in mind:

> Practice scanning the room, to identify students who are complying.
>
> Use "proximity praise" (praising properly-behaving students who happen to be near students that are misbehaving).
>
> For secondary students (who do not like to be singled out for public praise), circulate and praise individuals or groups quietly.

Using Special Approaches for Persistent Misbehavior

Teachers frequently encounter students who attempt to manipulate the teacher and control the situation through attention-seeking. When this occurs, the teacher must remain calm and refuse to give attention to the offending student. Once the student behaves properly, the teacher makes sure to give the student attention at that time.

Students also try to manipulate teachers by pretending they are incapable of doing assigned work. When that occurs, the teacher should reassert positive expectations for the student, invoke disciplinary consequences, and provide positive reinforcement when the student makes an effort to do the work.

Using Techniques to Stop Especially Disruptive Behavior

For those times when students become so excitedly disruptive that they do not respond to the normal disciplinary consequences, Canter has added two control skills, "moving-in" and the "freeze technique." The first, moving-in, is used for one or two students and involves stepping into the student's space, as follows:

> Walk directly up to the student.
>
> Use eye contact, touch, and gestures when speaking to the student.
>
> State the directions to be followed.
>
> State the disciplinary consequences already earned ("You have two demerits; you have chosen to stay 30 minutes after school.")
>
> Tell the student what the next consequence will be if the disruptive behavior continues.

The second techniques for very disruptive behavior, the freeze technique, is used when a number of students are out of control:

> Attract the students' attention by stating in a firm voice, "Freeze."
>
> Repeat the directions that students are supposed to be following.
>
> If that does not work, use tougher disciplinary consequences. ("The next student who disrupts will be given a 15-minute detention after school.")

Dealing with Severe Discipline Problems F .

What teachers fear most from students is blatant challenge to teacher authority, where students may be hostilely argumentative and verbally or even physically aggressive. Canter provides a series of steps for the teacher to follow and reminds teachers always to remain calm, yet firm. The steps are:

1. *Assertive Confrontation.* Meet privately with the student. (Another teacher or administrator should be present or nearby.) Do the following:
    a. Confront the student with the misbehavior. ("I will not tolerate your speaking back to me sarcastically in class.")
    b. Communicate your concern. ("I care too much about you to allow . . .")
    c. State your expectations. ("I want you to stop talking back.")
    d. Make sure the student understands. Have the student repeat what you have said.
    e. Avoid arguments. Use the broken record technique. ("I understand, but you are not to talk back to me in class.")
2. *Drop Down.* If after the assertive confrontation the student continues the misbehavior, drop down in the hierarchy of penalties; make them tougher.
3. *Behavior Contracting.* If dropping-down fails to resolve the problem, use a behavior contract with the student. Inform parents and administrators and document the student's misbehavior and improvements.
4. *Involve the Parents.* If efforts have failed up to this point, contact the parents for a conference and solicit their help. Present documentation and assure them that you need their help in working for the benefit of their child.
5. *Use a Tape Recorder.* If parent help is ineffective, place a tape recorder near the offending student and turn it on. Tell the student that you will play the tape for parents and administrators.
6. *Have Parent Come to Class.* Invite the student's parent to sit with the student during class.
7. *Use a Discipline Card.* If the student has different teachers through the day, he or she takes along a discipline card, to be initialed by the various teachers who also mark the card for good and bad behavior. The last teacher of the day sees to it that the student receives the appropriate positive or negative consequences.
8. *In-School Suspension Room.* When students must be banished temporarily from the class, they go to the suspension room where they do academic work, eat alone, and are escorted to and from the restroom.
9. *The Discipline Squad.* This is a group of three or four teachers and/or administrators who can be summoned at once for situations beyond the control of the teacher. The discipline squad sees to it that the offending student is removed from the room.

Evaluating the Discipline Program

Most discipline approaches tend to lose effectiveness over time. When behavior problems seem to become resistant to the usual enforcement procedures, teachers should analyze their discipline programs as follows:

First, they should clarify the nature of the problem, pinpoint the time of day or other circumstances in which the problem is occurring, and identify who is involved.

Second, they should analyze how they are responding to students when the problem occurs. It is a good idea to tape record oneself during those occurrences for later analysis.

Third, they should develop a plan of action for modifying teacher responses for greater effectiveness. They should then explain the changes to the class.

Changing Positive Consequences Throughout the Year

Good discipline programs depend heavily on the use of positive consequences, but consequences lose effectiveness as they become too familiar over time. Therefore, teachers should change consequences from time to time to maintain their effectiveness. Canter has found the following to be effective:

> *Bingo Cards.* Teachers stamp bingo cards on students' desks. When a card is filled, student receives a reward.
>
> *Marbles in Jar.* When students behave, marbles are added to a jar. When the jar is filled, the class receives a reward.
>
> *Class Raffle.* Students receive raffle tickets for good behavior. Periodically, a raffle is held for special prizes.
>
> *Holiday Theme.* Reward programs should be tied in with holiday themes to keep them fresh and interesting.

COMMENTS ON CANTER'S MODEL

You can see that Canter's model of Assertive Discipline integrates ideas and techniques from other models previously presented, such as behavior as choice, logical consequences rather than threats or punishments, positive reinforcement for desired behavior, and addressing the situation rather than the student's character. However, Canter's approach is unique in several ways—in its overall ease of implementation, its insistence on meeting teachers' and students' rights in the classroom, its emphasis on caring enough about students to limit their self-defeating behavior, and its insistence on support from administrators and parents.

A great many teachers are very enthusiastic about Assertive Discipline, because more than any other approach it helps them with strong corrective control (greatly prized) while at the same time enabling them to proceed right ahead with their teaching. It relieves them of the annoyance, or sometimes agony, of verbal confrontations, meanwhile preserving instructional time. It is also effective in preventive control (students know in advance the good and bad consequences of given behaviors) and in supportive control (often a warning is all students need to get back on track).

The popularity of Assertive Discipline is likely to continue, given Canter's efforts in updating his program continually in keeping with emerging needs and trends.

Does Assertive Discipline have shortcomings? Many educators say it does, and that those shortcomings are serious. Among the criticisms are that it is too harsh, too militant, too overpowering for young children, too demeaning to older students, too focused on suppressing bad behavior to the exclusion of building values toward responsible behavior. It is also criticized for its extensive rewards and punishments, which some contend wipe out intrinsic motivation, a major criticism leveled at behavior modification as well (Hill, 1990). Debate continues, too, concerning whether research supports the effectiveness of Assertive Discipline. Some insist that it does (Canter, 1988; McCormack, 1989), while others claim the opposite (Curwin and Mendler, 1989; Render, Padilla, and Krank, 1989). As with anything else, people have different opinions and interpretations. All in all, however, the widespread popularity of Assertive Discipline suggests that it provides teachers and administrators with effective skills that they have been unable to find elsewhere.

Application Exercises

Concept Cases: Kris, Sara, Joshua, and Tom.

CASE #1. KRIS WILL NOT WORK:

Kris, a student in Mr. Jake's class is quite docile. She socializes little with other students and never disrupts lessons. However, despite Mr. Jake's best efforts, Kris will not do her work. She rarely completes an assignment. She is simply there, like a bump on a log, putting forth no effort at all.

How would Canter deal with Kris? Canter would advise Mr. Jake to do the following:

1. Clearly communicate the class expectations to Kris, in assertively unmistakable terms.
2. Use a firm tone of voice and eye contact when reminding Kris of the expectations.
3. Consistently follow through with preestablished consequences. Make the negative consequences more severe and the positive consequences more attractive until finding a level that works for Kris.
4. Contact Kris's parents about her behavior. Explain that it is in Kris's best interest that the parents and Mr. Jake work together to help Kris.

CASE #2. SARA CANNOT STOP TALKING:

Sara is a pleasant girl who participates in class activities and does most, though not all, of her assigned work. She cannot seem to refrain from talking to classmates, however. Her teacher, Mr. Gonzales, has to speak to her repeatedly during lessons, to the point that he often becomes exasperated and loses his temper.

What suggestions would Canter give Mr. Gonzales for dealing with Sara?

CASE #3. JOSHUA CLOWNS AND INTIMIDATES:

Joshua, larger and louder than his classmates, always wants to be the center of attention, which he accomplishes through a combination of clowning and intimidation. He makes wise remarks, talks back (smilingly) to the teacher, utters a variety of sound effect noises such as automobile crashes and gunshots, and makes limitless sarcastic comments and put-downs of his classmates. Other students will not stand up to him, apparently fearing his size and verbal aggression. His teacher, Miss Pearl, has come to her wits' end.

Would Joshua's behavior be likely to improve if Canter's techniques were used in Miss Pearl's classroom? Explain.

CASE #4. TOM IS HOSTILE AND DEFIANT:

Tom has appeared to be in his usual foul mood ever since arriving in class. He gets up and on his way to sharpen his pencil he bumps into Frank. Frank complains. Tom tells him loudly to shut up. Miss Baines, the teacher, says, "Tom, go back to your seat." Tom wheels around, swears loudly and says heatedly, "I'll go when I'm damned good and ready!"

How would Canter have Miss Baines deal with Tom?

ACTIVITIES:

Each of the following exemplifies an important point in Canter's model of discipline. Identify the point illustrated by each.

1. Miss Hatcher, on seeing her class list for the coming year, exclaims, "Oh no! Billy Smythe in my class! There goes my sanity!"
2. "If you talk again during the class, you will have to stay an extra five minutes."
3. "I understand what you are saying, but you may not curse in this room."
4. "How many times do I have to tell you not to talk?"
5. If a student receives a third check, he or she must go to the office and call his or her parent to explain what has happened.
6. If the class is especially attentive and hardworking, they earn five minutes for visiting at the end of the period.
7. "If you talk again during the class, I guarantee you will regret it!"

For a grade level and/or subject you select, outline an Assertive Discipline plan that includes:

1. Four rules.
2. Positive and negative consequences associated with the rules.
3. The people you will inform about your system, and how you will inform them.

Examine scenario #3 (library) or #4 (elementary). How could assertive discipline be used to improve behavior in Mrs. Daniels' library or Mrs. Desmond's second grade?

REFERENCES

Canter, L. (1976). *Assertive Discipline: A take-charge approach for today's educator.* Seal Beach, CA: Canter and Associates.

Canter, L. (1978). Be an assertive teacher. *Instructor, 88,* 60.

Canter, L. (1988). Let the educator beware: A response to Curwin and Mendler. *Educational Leadership, 46*(2), 71–73.

Canter, L., & Canter, M. (1986). *Assertive Discipline Phase 2 in-service media package [videotapes and manuals].* Santa Monica, CA: Lee Canter and Associates.

Canter, L., & Canter, M. (1989). *Assertive Discipline for secondary school educators: In-service video package and leader's manual.* Santa Monica, CA: Lee Canter and Associates.

Curwin, R., & Mendler, A. (1988). Packaged discipline programs: Let the buyer beware. *Educational Leadership, 46*(2), 68–71.

Curwin, R., & Mendler, A. (1989). We repeat, let the buyer beware: A response to Canter. *Educational Leadership, 46*(6), 83.

Hill, D. (1990). Order in the classroom. *Teacher Magazine, 1*(7), 70–77.

McCormack, S. (1989). Response to Render, Padilla, and Krank: But practitioners say it works! *Educational Leadership, 46*(6), 77–79.

Render, G., Padilla, J., & Krank, H. (1989). What research really shows about assertive discipline. *Educational Leadership 46*(6), 72–75.

CHAPTER 8

The Glasser Model:

Good Behavior Comes from Meeting Needs Without Coercion

GLASSER BIOGRAPHICAL SKETCH

William Glasser (1925–) is a Los Angeles psychiatrist who for many years has consulted and spoken extensively on issues related to quality education. Born in Cleveland, Ohio, he first trained to be a chemical engineer, but later turned to psychology and then to psychiatry. Glasser first achieved national acclaim in psychiatry for the theories expressed in his book *Reality Therapy: A New Approach to Psychiatry* (1965), which shifted a long-standing focus in treating behavior problems. Instead of seeking to uncover the conditions in one's past that contributed to inappropriate behavior (the traditional approach in psychoanalysis), Glasser directed attention to the present, to the reality of the situation, contending that it is what one does in the present to work out problems that matters.

Glasser soon extended his ideas from reality therapy to the school arena. His work with juvenile offenders further convinced him that teachers could help students make better choices about their school behavior. Glasser insisted that teachers should never excuse bad student behavior. Poor background or undesirable living conditions do not exempt students from their responsibility to learn and to behave properly in school. This point of view, together with practical advice for carrying it out, was set forth in Glasser's book *Schools Without Failure* (1969), acknowledged to be one of the century's most influential books in education.

In 1985, Glasser published a book entitled *Control Theory in the Classroom*, in which he gave a new emphasis to his contentions concerning discipline, encapsulated in the following pronouncement: If students are to continue working and behaving properly, they must "believe that if they do some work, they will be able to satisfy their needs enough so that it makes sense to keep working." Glasser thus has put much greater emphasis than before on the school's role in meeting basic student needs, as a prime factor in discipline and work output. This theme is furthered in Glasser's 1990 book, *The Quality School: Managing Students Without Coercion*. Because of the different emphases in Glasser's earlier and later works, together with the historical importance of his earlier work, his model of discipline is presented in two parts—pre-1985 and post-1985. The pre-1985 model, as it does not represent Glasser's current thinking, is presented in condensed form.

GLASSER: PRE-1985

Main Focus

Prior to 1985, Glasser's focus was on helping students make good behavioral choices that led ultimately to personal success.

Key Ideas

1. Students are rational beings. They can control their behavior. They choose to act the way they do.
2. Good choices produce good behavior. Bad choices produce bad behavior.

C **3.** Teachers must always try to help students make good choices.

D **4.** Teachers who truly care about their students accept no excuses for bad behavior.

E **5.** Reasonable consequences should always follow student behavior, good or bad.

F **6.** Class rules are essential and they must be enforced.

G **7.** Classroom meetings are effective vehicles for attending to matters of class rules, behavior, and discipline.

[**Note:** You have seen many of these points incorporated into the Jones and Canter models of discipline.]

WHAT SCHOOL OFFERS

Prior to 1985, Glasser contended that schools offer students a good chance to be successful and to be recognized. Indeed, for many students schools offered the only opportunities to meet those needs. Success in school produces a sense of self-worth and a success identity, which mitigate deviant behavior. The road to a success identity begins with a good relationship with people who care. For students who come from atrocious backgrounds, school may be the only place to find a person genuinely interested in them.

Yet students often resist entering into quality relationships with their teachers. They may fear teachers, distrust adults in general, or obtain peer rewards by disdaining teachers. Teachers must therefore be very persistent, never waning in their efforts to help students. Glasser maintains that students cannot begin to make better, more responsible choices until they become deeply involved emotionally with people who can make such choices, people such as teachers.

WHAT TEACHERS SHOULD DO II

Glasser has always maintained that teachers hold the key to good discipline. In 1978 he described their responsibilities as follows:

A **1.** Stress student responsibility in making good choices, showing that they must live with the choices they make. Keep this in the forefront.

B **2.** Establish class rules that lead to success. Glasser considered class rules essential and wrote disparagingly of teachers who tried to function without them, in the mistaken belief that rules stifle initiative, self-direction, and responsibility. Rules were to be formulated jointly by teachers and students, always reinforcing the point that students are in school to study and learn.

C **3.** Accept no excuses. Glasser used the "no excuse" dictum with regard both to conditions outside the school and to students' failure to live up to commitments. Conditions outside the school, however bad, do not excuse misbehavior in school. Glasser also said teachers should accept no excuses when students fail to live up to commitments they have made. A teacher who accepts an excuse says, in effect, that it is all right to break a commitment, that it is all right for students to harm themselves. Teachers who care about their students accept no excuses.

4. **Call for value judgments.** When students misbehave, they should make value judgments about it. Glasser (1977) suggested the following procedure:

TEACHER: What are you doing? (Asked in nonthreatening tone of voice.)
STUDENT: (Will usually give an honest answer if not threatened.)
TEACHER: Is that helping you or the class?
STUDENT: No.
TEACHER: What could you do that would help?
STUDENT: (Names better behavior; if student can think of none, teacher suggests appropriate alternatives and lets student choose.)

5. **Suggest suitable alternatives.** When students misbehave, teachers should call on students to identify suitable alternatives. If unable to think of any, two or three should be suggested to them, from which they are expected to select.

6. **Invoke reasonable consequences.** Glasser stressed that reasonable consequences should follow any behavior the student chooses—desirable consequences when good behavior is chosen and undesirable when poor behavior is chosen. Teachers must see to it consistently. The knowledge that behavior always brings consequences and that individuals can largely choose behavior that brings pleasant as opposed to unpleasant consequences builds the sense that people are in charge of their own lives and in control of their own behavior.

7. **Be persistent.** Caring teachers work toward one major goal—getting students to commit themselves to desirable courses of behavior. They must always help students make choices and have them make value judgments about their bad choices.

8. **Carry out continual review.** Glasser insisted that any discipline system be reviewed periodically and revised as necessary. This was to involve students and be done through classroom meetings, which as mentioned earlier were not for the purpose of finding fault, but of finding solutions to problems.

The classroom meeting was to be conducted with teacher and students sitting together in a closed circle, an arrangement that came to be known as the Glasser Circle.

Sometimes the student does not respond in an acceptable way, but instead replies hostilely or caustically. For that eventuality, Glasser presents the following scenario:

1. **Student is misbehaving.**

TEACHER: What are you doing? Is it against the rules? What should you be doing?
STUDENT: (Responds negatively, unacceptably.)
TEACHER: I would like to talk with you privately at (specifies time).

2. **Private conference between teacher and student.**

TEACHER: What were you doing? Was it against the rules? What should you have been doing?

STUDENT: (Agrees to proper course of behavior.)

3. Student later repeats the misbehavior. Teacher calls for another private conference.

TEACHER: We have to work this out. What kind of plan can you make so you can follow the rules?
STUDENT: I'll stop doing it.
TEACHER: No, we need a plan that says exactly what you *will do*. Let's make a simple plan you can follow. I'll help you.

4. Student later repeats misbehavior; does not abide by own plan. Teacher assigns "time out." This is isolation from the group. Student is not allowed to participate with the group again until making a commitment to the teacher to adhere to the plan. If student disrupts during time out, he is excluded from the classroom. (A contingency plan should be set up in advance with the principal.)
5. Student, after returning to the group, disrupts again.

TEACHER: Things are not working out here for you and me. We have tried hard. You must leave the class. As soon as you have a plan you are sure will allow you to follow the rules of the class, let me know. We can try again. But for now, please report to the principal's office. (Principal was informed in advance of this possibility.)

6. If student is out of control, principal notifies parents and asks them to pick up student at school immediately.
7. Students who are repeatedly sent home are referred to a special school or class, or to a different community agency.

By following this procedure consistently, teachers can cause students to doubt the value of their misbehavior, make responsible and better choices, and thus gradually make a commitment to choosing behaviors that bring personal success instead of failure.

COMMENTS ON GLASSER: PRE-1985

In Glasser's earlier work, he depicted the school in a positive light. While acknowledging that problems existed for some students, he steadfastly maintained that schools afforded students the best—often the *only*—opportunity to associate with quality adults who genuinely cared about them. Schools therefore offered students the best opportunity many would ever have for finding belonging, success, and positive self-identity. In order to take advantage of this crucial opportunity, students were continually asked to make value judgments about their misbehavior and urged to make good choices and plans that improved the chances for good choices. Meanwhile, they were consistently made to confront the consequences of whatever behavior they chose, good or bad.

GLASSER: POST-1985

Major Focus

If schools are to survive, they must be refocused to emphasize quality in all student work. They must no longer attempt to coerce students, but must lead them deeply into learning activities that meet basic needs for belonging, power, fun, and freedom.

Key Ideas

1. All of our behavior is our best attempt to control ourselves to meet five basic needs—survival, belonging, power, fun, and freedom. The school experience is intimately associated with all but survival.
2. We feel pleasure when these needs are met, frustration when they are not.
3. Today's schools must create quality conditions in which fewer students and teachers are frustrated. Students must feel they belong, have some power, have fun in learning, and enjoy a sense of freedom in the process.
4. Few students in today's schools do their best work. The overwhelming majority is apathetic. Many do no school work at all.
5. What is needed is a commitment to quality education, brought about through quality schools, in which students are encouraged, supported, and helped by the teacher.
6. In quality teaching, teachers do not scold, punish, or coerce. Instead they befriend students, provide encouragement and stimulation, and show an unending willingness to help.

THE REFOCUS ON STUDENT NEEDS

For one who long and staunchly maintained that it was a student's responsibility to make choices that brought success, Glasser has taken an interesting new tack. What could have prompted so important a redirecting, a refocusing on the nexus of classroom discipline?

Glasser's newer views have grown from his conclusions that the majority of students are quite satisfied to do low quality work or even no work at all. He maintains that "no more than half of our secondary school students are willing to make an effort to learn, and therefore cannot be taught" (1985, p. 3), and further, "I believe (in light of student apathy) that we have gone as far as we can go with the traditional structure of our secondary schools"(1985, p. 6).

What we must find, he says, is a way to improve instruction which now sees no more than 15% of high school students doing quality work (1990, p. 5). This can be done by managing students "so that a substantial majority do high-quality schoolwork: Nothing less will solve the problems of our schools" (1990, p. 1). The solution he proposes involves stimulating students to work while providing encouragement and assistance, done so as to meet students' needs. This would require little change in curricula, materials, or physical facilities, but a significant change in the way teachers work with students.

Glasser contends that teaching effectively is the hardest job in the world (1990, p. 14) and expresses sympathy for beleaguered secondary teachers who yearn to work with dedicated, high-achieving students, but who are continually frustrated by the majority who make little effort to learn. Those teachers report that their main discipline problems are not defiance or disruption, but students' overwhelming apathy and benign unwillingness to participate in classroom activities and assignments. Students, for their part, tell Glasser that the problem with school work is not its difficulty; the problem is that it is too boring (1990, p. 7). For Glasser, this means that school work does not meet students' primary psychological needs.

He has a remedy for this problem, which he puts forth in three fundamental propositions:

1. Schools must be organized to meet students' needs for belonging, power, fun, and freedom.
2. Quality school work and self-evaluation (of quality) by students must replace the fragmented and boring requirements on which students are typically tested and evaluated.
3. Teachers must stop functioning as "boss-managers" (who dictate) and begin functioning as "lead-managers" (who stimulate and help).

Let us examine what Glasser means by these three points.

Students' Needs

Glasser is very plain about needs. Students, like all of us, have genetic needs for (1) survival (food, shelter, freedom from harm), (2) belonging (security, comfort, legitimate membership in the group), (3) power (sense of importance, of stature, of being considered by others), (4) fun (having a good time, emotionally and intellectually), and (5) freedom (exercise in choice, self-direction, and responsibility).

Glasser is adamant in his contention that education that does not give those needs top priority is bound to fail.

Quality Work

Glasser says that present-day education is defined in terms of how many fragments of information students can retain long enough to be measured on standardized achievement tests (1990, p. 22). Students agree, and they resist education of that sort. Most critics of education want to change the curriculum, but Glasser finds little fault with curriculum contents. He finds much fault, however, with the way material is presented and learning evaluated. School, he says, should be a place where students learn interesting things well. Plenty of interesting topics are in the curriculum. Glasser suggests that teachers discuss the curriculum contents with students and ask them to identify what they would like to explore in depth. Adequate time should then be spent on those topics, and students should regularly do written self-evaluations concerning the quality of their own work.

Boss-Teachers and Lead-Teachers

Teachers typically function as bosses, Glasser contends, not realizing that motivation cannot be furnished to students; it must come from within. Boss-teachers, as Glasser describes them, do the following:

1. Set the task and standards.
2. Talk rather than demonstrate, rarely asking for student input.
3. Grade the work without involving students in evaluation.
4. Use coercion when students resist.

To illustrate how a boss-teacher functions, consider the example of Mr. Marquez, who introduces his unit of study on South American geography in this way:

> Class, today we are going to begin our study of the geography of South America. You are expected to do the following things:
>
> 1. Learn the names of the South American countries.
> 2. Be able to locate those countries on a blank map.
> 3. Describe the types of terrain typical of each country.
> 4. Name two products associated with each country.
> 5. Describe the population of each country in terms of ethnic origin and economic well being.
> 6. Name and locate the most important rivers that drain to the north, east, and southeast.
>
> We will learn this information from our textbooks plus encyclopedias.
> You will have two tests, one at . . . [and so forth].

Mr. Marquez's boss approach limits both productivity and quality of work. Most students will probably find the work boring and will do only enough, and only well enough, to get by.

Glasser would have teachers forego Mr. Marquez' style and function not as boss-teachers but as lead-teachers. Lead-teachers realize that genuine motivation to learn must arise within students. They also realize that their task in teaching is to help students learn, in any way they can. Glasser says teachers should spend most of their time on two things: organizing interesting activities and providing assistance to students. Such lead teachers would:

1. Discuss the curriculum with the class in such a way that many topics of interest are identified.
2. Encourage students to identify topics they would like to explore in depth.
3. Discuss with students the nature of the school work that might ensue, emphasizing quality and asking for input on criteria of quality.

4. Explore with students resources that might be needed for quality work and the amount of time such work might require.
5. Demonstrate ways in which the work can be done, with models that reflect quality.
6. Emphasize the importance of students' continually inspecting and evaluating their own work in terms of quality.
7. Make evident to students that everything possible will be done to provide them with good tools and a good workplace that is noncoercive and nonadversarial.

To illustrate how lead-teaching might proceed, consider the example of Mr. Garcia's introduction to a unit of study on the geography of South America:

Class, have any of you ever lived in South America? You did, Samuel? Which country? Peru? Fantastic! What an interesting country! I used to live in Brazil. I traveled in the Amazon quite a bit and lived for a while with Indians. Supposedly they were head hunters at one time. But not now. Tomorrow I'll show you a bow and arrow I brought from that tribe. Samuel, did you ever taste monkey? I think Peru and Brazil are very alike in some ways, but very different in others. What was Peru like compared to here? Did you get up into the Andes? They have fabulous ruins all over Peru, I hear, and those fantastic "Chariots of the Gods" lines and drawings on the landscape. Do you have any photographs or slides you could bring for us to see? What a resource you could be for us! You could teach us a lot!

Class, Samuel lived in Peru and traveled in the Andes. If we could get him to teach us about that country, what do you think you would most like to learn?

[Class discusses, identifies topics]

We have the opportunity in our class to learn a great deal about South America, its mountains and grasslands and dense rain forests and huge rivers and interesting people and strange animals. Did you know there were colonies of English and Welsh and Italians and Germans living in many parts of South America, especially in Argentina? Did you know there are still thought to be tribes of Indians in the jungles that have no contact with the outside world? Did you know that almost half of all the river water in the world is in the Amazon basin, that in some places the Amazon river is so wide that from the middle you can't see either shore?

Speaking of the Amazon, I swam in a lake there that contained piranhas, and look, I still have my legs and arms. Surprised about that? If you wanted to learn more about living in the Amazon jungle, what would you be interested in knowing?

[Discuss]

How about people of the high Andes? Those Incas for example, who in some mysterious way cut and placed enormous boulders into gigantic, perfectly fitting fortress walls? Samuel knows about them. They were very civilized and powerful, with an empire that stretched for three thousand miles. Yet they were conquered by a few Spaniards on horseback. How in the world could that have happened? If you could learn more about those amazing people, what would you like to know?

[Discussion continues in this manner, identifying topics about which students would be willing to make an effort to learn]

Now let me see what you think of this idea: I have written down the topics you said you were interested in, and I can help you with resources and materials. I have lots of my own, including slides, South American music, and many artifacts I have collected. I know two other people who lived in Argentina and Colombia that we could invite to talk with us. We can concentrate on what you have said you would like to learn about. But if we decide to do so, I want to see if we can make this deal: We explore what interests you; I help you all I can; and you, for your part, agree to do quality work—to do some of the best work you are capable of. We would need to discuss that, to get some ideas of what you might do that would show the quality of your learning. In addition, I would want each of you regularly to evaluate yourselves as to how well you believe you are doing. Understand, this would not be me evaluating you—it would be you evaluating yourself, not for a grade, but for you to decide what you are doing very well and what you think you might be able to do better.

What do you think of that idea? Want to give it a try?

HOW DOES THIS RELATE TO DISCIPLINE?

Glasser believes that teachers who learn to function as lead-managers will avoid the trap of becoming adversaries of their students, a trap that destroys both incentive to learn and pleasure in teaching. If they can stay out of that trap, teachers will not only foster quality learning but in so doing will reduce discipline problems to a minimum.

That notion, whether correct or not, appeals to teachers, at least at first glance. However, Glasser has found that when it comes time to change their style of teaching, teachers become nervous and reticent. Glasser maintains that the change is not nearly so difficult as one might imagine.

Glasser does admit that no approach to teaching can eliminate all behavior problems. He continues to say that it is, therefore, necessary to work with students to establish standards of conduct in the classroom. He makes the following suggestions.

Rules

The teacher should begin with a discussion of the importance of quality work, which is to be given priority in the class, and of how the teacher will do all possible to help students while not forcing them. That discussion should lead naturally into asking students about class rules they believe will help them get their work done, truly help them learn. Glasser says that if teachers can get students to see the importance of courtesy, no other rules may be necessary.

Mrs. Bentley's second graders decided they needed only two rules in order to do their work well:

1. Be kind to others.
2. Do our best work.

Mr. Jason's physical education class decided on these:

1. Be on time.
2. Play safely.

3. Show good sportsmanship.

4. Take care of the equipment.

Teachers should also solicit student advice on what should happen when rules are _broken_. Glasser says students will suggest punishment, though they know punishment is not effective. If asked further, they will agree that behavior problems are best solved by looking for ways to remedy whatever is causing the rule to be broken. Glasser urges teachers to ask, "What could I do to help?"

Once the rules and consequences are agreed to, they should be written down. All students sign, attesting that they understand the rules and that, if they break them, they will try—with the teacher's help—to correct the underlying problem.

Rules established and dealt with in this way, says Glasser, show that the teacher's main concern lies in quality, not power, recognizing that power struggles are the main enemy of quality education.

When Rules Are Broken

Every teacher knows that rules will invariably be broken, even in the best classes. Glasser acknowledges that fact and provides specific guidance for teacher intervention—nonpunitive intervention that will stop the misbehavior and refocus the student's mind on class work (1990, p. 138). Applied to angry Jonathan, Glasser's advice would suggest the following:

Jonathan has come into the room angry. As the lesson begins, he turns heatedly and throws something at Michael.

> TEACHER: It looks like you have a problem, Jonathan. How can I help you solve it? (Jonathan frowns, still obviously upset).
> TEACHER: If you will calm down, I will discuss it with you in a little while. I think we can work something out.

Glasser says you should make it clear that you will not help Jonathan until he calms down. You are to speak without emotion, recognizing that your anger will only put Jonathan on the defensive.

If Jonathan doesn't calm down, there is no good way to deal with the problem. Glasser says to allow him 20 seconds, and if he isn't calm by then, admit that there is no way to solve the problem at that time. Give Jonathan "time out" from the lesson, but don't threaten or warn:

> YOU: Jonathan, I want to help you work this out. I am not interested in punishing you. Whatever the problem is, let's solve it. But for now you must go sit at the table. When you are calm, come back to your seat.

Later, at an opportune time, you discuss the situation with Jonathan, approximately as follows (1990, p. 141):

> YOU: What were you doing when the problem started? Was it against the rules? Can we work things out so it won't happen again? What could you and I do to keep it from happening?

If the problem involves hostilities between Jonathan and Michael, the discussion should involve both boys and proceed along these lines (1990, p. 141):

> YOU: What were you doing, Jonathan? What were you doing, Michael? How can the three of us work things out so this won't happen any more?

It is important to note that *no blame* is assigned to either Jonathan or Michael. No time is spent on trying to find out whose fault it was. You remind the boys that all you are looking for is a solution, so that the problem won't occur again.

Glasser contends that if you treat Jonathan and Michael with respect and courtesy, if you show you don't want to punish them or throw your weight around, and if you talk to them as a problem solver, both their classroom behavior and the quality of their work will gradually improve.

COMMENTS ON GLASSER'S MODEL

In the preceeding illustration, teachers are advised to talk with misbehaving students "at an appropriate time," meaning later in the period or day. Arranging times and places for these talks can be awkward. Here is how it is done by Maureen Lewnes, who teaches a fourth- and fifth-grade combination class:

> For conferencing with students I use a "consultation corner," which in my room is not a corner at all but rather four feet of wall space to the rear of my desk between a table and file cabinet. A small kindergarten chair is there for students to sit in, which they love to do as I bend down low to converse with them, out of sight of the rest of the class, which creates an impression of closeness between the two of us.
>
> I introduce the consultation corner at the beginning of the year, telling my students I may request them to join me there to discuss matters of class work or behavior, or to tell them how much I appreciate their help and good work, which I make sure to emphasize.
>
> Several benefits have come from use of the corner. When the need arises, I say to the student, "May I see you in the consultation corner at study time?" The chat there gives me insights into matters that might be troubling the students and it encourages shy students to share feelings, interests, and problems.
>
> Most students react well to the talks, appreciating the privacy, and I find that problems of misbehavior are more easily resolved there. When I ask their opinions, my students say that every room should have a consultation corner because it makes them more comfortable about talking with the teacher.

As you have seen, Glasser no longer blames students for poor classroom behavior, pointing out that schools expect students to do boring work while sitting and waiting, against which their inherent natures rebel. In his eloquent way, Glasser in 1985 wrote that what we expect students to do in school "... *is like asking someone who is sitting on a hot stove to sit still and stop complaining*" (1985, p. 53, italics added).

At that time, he insisted that "teachers should not depend on any discipline program that demands that they do something *to* or *for* students to get them to stop behaving badly in unsatisfying classes. Only a discipline program that is also concerned with classroom satisfaction will work" (1985, p. 56).

Glasser expanded on that theme in his 1990 work, *The Quality School*, by describing how schools can emphasize quality work. This depends on teachers functioning as "lead-managers" who provide great support and encouragement but who do not coerce, throw their weight around, or punish. In such schools, students find their genetic needs met sufficiently that they will stay in school and do better quality work.

In changing his emphasis, Glasser now gives discipline, our main concern here, much less attention than before, insisting that if schools and classes are conducted in keeping with his "quality" concept, discipline problems will be few and relatively easily resolved.

The difficulty for teachers is that schools are not likely to make a sudden transition to the scheme Glasser proposes. Though such a change may well occur over time, for the present it is certain that most classes will continue to emphasize fragmented information of the type that enables students to perform better on achievement tests.

Can teachers, then, make any use of Glasser's newest model of discipline? The answer is yes. Like Jones's model, Glasser's does not have to be taken as a total system and set into place lock, stock, and barrel. His suggestions for teachers' acting as problem solvers without arguing or punishing should be seriously considered by all teachers. His procedures can be practiced, allowing teachers to evaluate for themselves the effect on classroom climate and morale. Let's remember too that Glasser didn't imply that his quality school would forestall all discipline problems. Students are human beings, and even the best-intentioned sometimes violate rules, short-change work assignments, and have conflict with others, including teachers. When such behavior occurs, any teacher can calmly try to identify the problem and then, without assigning blame, enlist the help of everyone in correcting its cause.

In the commentary on Dreikurs' model, Chapter 5, it was suggested that Dreikurs' approach, while time-consuming and requiring counseling skills, offered teachers a good procedure for helping students become genuinely self-directing and responsible. Glasser's 1990 model, less time-consuming than Dreikurs' and less dependent on special skills, may well possess the same potential.

Application Exercises

Concept Cases: Kris, Sara, Joshua, and Tom.

CASE #1. KRIS WILL NOT WORK:

Kris, a student in Mr. Jake's class, is quite docile. She socializes little with other students and never disrupts class. However, despite Mr. Jake's best efforts, Kris never does her work. She rarely completes an assignment. She is simply there, like a bump on a log, putting forth no effort.

How would Glasser deal with Kris? Glasser would first suggest that Mr. Jake think carefully about the classroom and the program to try to determine whether they contain obstacles that prevent Kris from meeting her needs for belonging, power, fun, and freedom. He would then have Mr. Jake discuss the matter with Kris, not blaming her, but noting the problem of nonproductivity asking what the problem is and what he might be able to do to help. In that discussion, Mr. Jake might ask Kris questions such as:

- You have a problem with this work, don't you? Is there anything I can do to help you with it?
- Is there anything I could do to make the class more interesting for you?
- Is there anything in this class that you enjoy doing?
- Do you think that, for a while, you might like to do only those things?
- Is there anything we have discussed that you would like to learn very, very well?
- How could I help you do that?
- What could I do differently that would help you want to learn?

Mr. Jake would not punish Kris nor would he use a disapproving tone of voice. Meanwhile, every day he would make a point of talking with her in a friendly and courteous way about non-school matters—trips, pets, movies, and so forth—casually, but often, showing he is interested in her, willing to be her friend.

Glasser would remind Mr. Jake that there is no magic formula for success with all students. Mr. Jake can only encourage and support Kris. Scolding and coercion are likely to make matters worse, but as Mr. Jake befriends Kris she is likely to begin to do more work, of better quality.

CASE #2. SARA CANNOT STOP TALKING:

Sara is a pleasant girl who participates in class activities and does most, though not all, of her assigned work. She cannot seem to refrain from talking to classmates, however. Her teacher, Mr. Gonzales, has to speak to her repeatedly during lessons, to the point that he often becomes exasperated and loses his temper.

What suggestions would Glasser give Mr. Gonzales for dealing with Sara?

CASE #3. JOSHUA CLOWNS AND INTIMIDATES:

Joshua, larger and louder than his classmates, always wants to be the center of attention, which he accomplishes through a combination of clowning and intimidation. He makes wise remarks, talks back (smilingly) to the teacher, utters a variety of sound effect noises such as automobile crashes and gunshots, and makes limitless sarcastic comments and put-downs of his classmates. Other students will not stand up to him, apparently fearing his size and verbal aggression. His teacher, Miss Pearl, has come to her wits' end.

How do you think Glasser would have Miss Pearl deal with Joshua?

CASE #4. TOM IS HOSTILE AND DEFIANT:

Tom has appeared to be in his usual foul mood ever since arriving in class. He gets up and on his way to sharpen his pencil he bumps into Frank. Frank complains. Tom tells him loudly to shut up. Miss Baines, the teacher, says, "Tom, go back to your seat." Tom wheels around, swears loudly and says heatedly, "I'll go when I'm damned good and ready!"

How would Glasser have Miss Baines deal with Tom?

ACTIVITIES:

1. Select a preferred grade level and/or subject. As the teacher, outline what you would consider and do, along the lines of Glasser's suggestions, concerning:
   a) Organizing the classroom, class, curriculum, and activities so as better to meet your students' needs for belonging, fun, power, and freedom.
   b) Your continual efforts to help students improve the quality of their work.
2. Do a comparative analysis of Glasser's and Canter's systems of discipline, in terms of:
   a) Effectiveness in suppressing inappropriate behavior;
   b) Effectiveness in improving long-term behavior;
   c) Ease of implementation;
   d) Effect on student self-concept;
   e) Effect on bonds of trust between teacher and student.
   f) The degree to which each model accurately depicts realities of student attitude and behavior.

FURTHER ANALYSIS AND APPLICATION:

Examine scenario #9 (secondary) or #10 (elementary) in Chapter 13. What advice would Glasser give Mr. Wong or Miss Thorpe in order to improve learning conditions in the classroom?

REFERENCES

Glasser, W. (1965). *Reality therapy: A new approach to psychiatry.* New York: Harper and Row.

Glasser W. (1969). *Schools without failure.* New York: Harper and Row.

Glasser, W. (1977). 10 steps to good discipline, *Today's Education, 66,* 60–63.

Glasser, W. (1978). Disorders in our schools: Causes and remedies. *Phi Delta Kappan, 59,* 331–333.

Glasser, W. (1985). *Control theory in the classroom.* New York: Perennial Library.

Glasser, W. (1990). *The quality school: Managing students without coercion.* New York: Harper and Row.

PART II

From Models
to Classroom Practice

CHAPTER 9

Classrooms That Encourage Good Behavior

In classroom discipline, an ounce of prevention is worth much more than a pound of cure, for once misbehavior has occurred even the best corrective techniques (despite what the various proponent-experts might say) disrupt teaching and take their toll on feelings and relationships. It is clearly to teachers' advantage to do whatever they can to reduce student misbehavior while still providing quality educational programs.

This does not suggest that misbehavior can be eliminated entirely. The best teaching in the world cannot accomplish that, and never will. Yet there are many provisions teachers can make to encourage good behavior. Those provisions fall into three broad categories, referred to here as the *person component*, the *management component*, and the *teaching component*.

THE PERSON COMPONENT

The person component centers on students' sense of self, individually and as members of the group. Students with good self-esteem who feel secure within the group do not normally cause much trouble aside from talking and laughing. Teachers can do much to enhance students' sense of self-worth and belonging, and by a happy coincidence those efforts earn for teachers the respect of their students. If you learn nothing else from this book, commit this great truth to memory and put it into action.

Strengthening Student Self-Concept

Self-concept, the overall opinion each of us holds about our self, is strengthened through success and acceptance, while weakened through failure and rejection. It affects all behavior, including learning. Thus, as teachers enhance student self-concept they simultaneously facilitate learning while reducing misbehavior.

Teachers can routinely do three things to strengthen student self-concept—(1) give each student personal attention regularly, (2) ensure that each student experiences success in learning, and (3) make sure that students receive recognition for the accomplishments they make.

Personal Attention from the Teacher

Most of us, when thinking back on the teachers we liked and admired, realize that those teachers gave us much personal attention. They acknowledged us, spoke with us, encouraged us, sometimes pushed us, and enjoyed the improvements we made. In so doing, they made us see ourselves as worthwhile. We felt we belonged, were capable, and that someone important cared about us. They helped us believe in ourselves.

What they did was not difficult. They merely treated us as all good teachers treat their students—as human beings who can be talked with and who need encouragement and support. At the same time, however, such teachers get across the message that second-rate is not good enough.

Providing Genuine Success

People can be made to think they are successful when honestly they are not. Students can be told they are "really learning" or "behaving great" when the opposite is true. Teachers sometimes do this to try to keep their students excited and in a good mood. But any resultant sense of success is fleeting, for sooner or later students will recognize it as false.

That is why "genuine success" is necessary, comprised of true accomplishments, significant improvements, and tasks well done. Genuine success can be made available to every student, though it may be difficult to get some to take advantage of it. One of teachers' most important tasks is to arrange instruction so that a maximum number of students experience genuine success regularly.

This task is accomplished by (1) setting realistic goals and using them as clear targets, (2) employing a curriculum that builds competence, (3) providing good direction, urging, and help, (4) using effective instructional materials, and (5) developing esprit de corps. Let us see what is involved in each.

Clear Goals as Targets. Goals (call them objectives if you prefer) indicate what students are to accomplish. In order to be effective in promoting success the goals must be attainable, clearly understood, and seen as worthwhile by the students. Discussions should be held to make sure these criteria are met. Timelines and progress checkpoints can be established to monitor long-range goals, thereby helping students know whether they are progressing as expected.

Curriculum for Competence. When students are involved in a curriculum that leads toward goal attainment (as opposed to hit and miss activities used only to fill time), they have frequent opportunities for success. Such a curriculum often builds new learnings atop old ones, which allows students to see that they are becoming steadily more competent. Their progress should be acknowledged frequently.

Direction, Urging, and Help. Many students are neither self-directed nor self-controlled, and they will not work well on their own for long even in the best activities. In such cases teachers must guide, exhort, help, monitor, provide feedback, entertain, and otherwise encourage students to do quality work. This role is traditional in teaching and its importance should not be slighted. Let's be realistic: Most of us need a taskmaster, preferably a positive one, if we are to learn well in school.

Effective Instructional Materials. Good instructional materials enliven learning by making the subject interesting and understandable. They provide extensions, examples, illustrations, problems, and entertainment. They allow students to explore far afield and permit easier application of new learnings. There is no way that most of us can visit the Amazon jungle, the Pyramids, Antarctica, or the Laplanders of Finland. There is no way we can see molecules, solar systems, or the inner workings of nuclear reactors. But students deal with such topics daily. Instructional materials allow them to do so with much greater likelihood of understanding and success.

Esprit de Corps. Success depends in large measure on morale, which in turn is related to the phenomenon called *esprit de corps*—group spirit. Esprit de corps strengthens the class through stimulation, direction, sense of purpose, enjoyment, and desire to work for the group.

Regrettably, the recipes we have for building esprit de corps don't always work, though we know they consist of portions of teacher enthusiasm, personal attention to students, golden-rule concern, enjoyable curriculum, and sense of group purpose. Often, classes with esprit de corps have a mountain to conquer—a contest to win or a performance to stage. But such is not always the case. Sometimes personalities simply mesh so that the class members take genuine delight in each other.

This is not to say, however, that esprit de corps occurs entirely spontaneously. Teachers can do several things to encourage it, as indicated in the following paragraphs.

A Sense of Togetherness

A first step is to work toward an understanding that the class is a unit that lives and works together, that all members are striving toward a common goal, that all face similar obstacles, that all benefit from helping each other, that all lose something when any member is unsuccessful, and that all can take justifiable pride in the accomplishments of the class.

Contrast that group view with an individualistic view, where the successful student is prized and rewarded while the unsuccessful is slighted and disparaged. The unsuccessful begins to behave in one of two ways: either gives up and stops participating (which produces an uncomfortable sense of failure for the teacher), or else becomes actively disruptive (which hinders class learning and makes the teacher's life miserable).

To foster a sense of togetherness, the teacher should continually talk with the class about what they can accomplish *as a group,* how they will deal with the problems they encounter as a group, how they will work together to get the best achievement possible for every individual. In order to bring this about, responsibilities are given and shared, students are encouraged to speak of their concerns while the class attempts to find solutions, and the teacher takes special steps to incorporate every student into the ongoing work of the class.

Purpose in Class Activities

Sense of purpose grows with students' understanding of what they are expected to Effective classroom management, which improves both learning and behavior, refers to how teachers *organize, deliver, monitor,* and *communicate* their instructional programs. Poorly managed classes are frequently in turmoil. Unproductive noise test, or even getting the six math problems completed by the end of the class period are much preferable to long-range goals such as (later) enjoying life more, making a better living, or passing the final test at the end of the year.

It should be noted that a sense of purposefulness is not dependent on activities' being fun or creative. Rather, it is dependent on students'—at least those beyond primary grades—having a fairly good idea of the reasons behind what they are asked to do. Students resent busy work, which after a while they learn to detect instantly.

Public Recognition

Purposeful group behavior is greatly motivated though anticipation of public exposition. The kindergarten class puts on its annual Thanksgiving feast, to which parents are invited. The children wear paper costumes they have helped make and display artwork and sing songs about Thanksgiving. The sixth grade holds its semiannual science fair, which features displays of every student's work. The physical education department presents its recreational sports night for the invited public, with entire classes demonstrating rhythmic exercises, collaborative games, and tumbling. The graphics arts class presents its annual multimedia display in a city shopping mall, with large photographs of the students at work on their projects.

Events such as these are often reported in the local newspapers and occasionally on television. When students work on projects such as these and receive public recognition, their sense of purposeful, responsible behavior improves dramatically. Most of us have a general idea of whether or not we are being successful in our work or studies, but we are never quite sure without feedback from others. Just as our self-concept grows from what others think of us, so does our sense of success. For that reason it is important that teachers take pains to ensure that student success is recognized by others. The following are suggestions for providing such recognition.

Chart Group Gains. Gains and other improvements shown by the class as a whole can be depicted graphically. Many elementary classes demonstrate progress through timelines, made of string or paper and placed high along the walls. Some make murals that illustrate activities and accomplishments. These are popular for display at open houses and other school events. Elementary and secondary classes can keep class diaries, with students taking turns making entries decided on by the class. This provides a documented history of class activities and accomplishments, which students very much enjoy reading later in the year.

Chart Personal Gains. Charts showing individual progress are also motivating. They are not to be displayed in the classroom if they show any student in a derogatory light, but all students may keep them in personal folders they share with their teacher and parents. Such charts can indicate attainment of objectives, amount of work attempted and completed, percentage of correct responses, and so forth. Parents react well to such documentation, which shows the teacher's specific plans for students.

Inform Parents. Parents should be regularly informed about their child's success (not just the lack thereof). This information can be provided through student reports to parents, teacher communication with parents, and other materials that show student progress. In order to help students better report success to parents, at the end of the day for elementary students and the end of the week for secondary students, teachers should take a few minutes to review what students have accomplished, so they can relay this information to their parents.

Systematic communication from teacher to parents is also excellent for publicizing group and individual success. It takes time, but pays good dividends. Teachers can send notes home with students, send weekly newsletters, and make very brief telephone calls. In all cases, the purpose is to convey accomplishment and success, not to speak of problems. (Of course problems must be dealt with too, but in separate communications.)

Parents are always eager to see samples of their child's work. Worksheets, assignments, and test results can be shared with parents, but teachers are well-advised to be very careful that such work has been checked correctly. Any errors made by the teacher are almost certain to be noticed by parents, and one tiny mistake can undo the good will that may have taken weeks to build.

Share in the Classroom. Students need to receive attention from their peers, to have their classmates recognize their efforts and their accomplishments. Such attention comes naturally with oral presentations, demonstrations, and displays of work. Some shy students are hesitant at first to participate, but with gentle encouragement, most soon overcome their reticence.

Produce a Class Newsletter. Most classes can produce a monthly or quarterly newsletter that explains projects, contains samples of student work, and presents announcements of displays and performances. The tone of the newsletter should be businesslike (not silly or gossipy) and it should include all the students' names in one place or another.

The newsletter is delivered to administrators, parents, other community members, and even at times to organizations and businesses. Local newspapers usually show interest in them. Few avenues can so well publicize the efforts and achievements of students, and the positive attention that results does much for everyone concerned.

THE MANAGEMENT COMPONENT

Effective classroom management, which improves both learning and behavior, refers to how teachers *organize, deliver, monitor,* and *communicate* their instructional programs. Poorly managed classes are frequently in turmoil. Unproductive noise abounds. Students become dissatisfied and their misbehavior increases. Teacher stress builds, and teaching becomes less and less enjoyable.

A different picture is seen in well-managed classrooms. Students work as intended, without teacher nagging. Disruptions are minimal. Little conflict occurs. Teachers feel successful, even rewarded, and enjoy their work. When such classrooms are examined carefully, it can be seen that special effort has been put into judicious management of climate and routines.

Managing the Classroom Climate

Climate refers to the *feeling tone* that prevails in the classroom. This feeling tone is a composite of attitudes, emotions, values, and relationships. All teachers are aware of its existence, and can almost always tell whether it is good or bad. Climate probably has as much to do with learning, productive work, and self-concept as does anything else in the educational program.

A poor classroom climate is characterized as either chaotic and disorganized or as cold, unfriendly, and threatening. In the latter case, good humor is absent, replaced by sarcasm and animosity. Such climates depress learning, although threatening environments may cause students to work under duress (which then makes them dislike both teacher and school). Students, when coldly and rigidly controlled, fear making errors. They obey the rules only to prevent teachers' taking reprisal against them.

In contrast, a good classroom climate is characterized as warm, supportive, and pleasant. It is friendly and filled with good nature and acceptance. It is encouraging, helpful, and low on threat. Such a climate encourages productive work and promotes a sense of enjoyment and accomplishment.

Cynthia, a second-grade teacher, describes how she attempts to set the tone in her classroom:

> I begin the year with a discussion about my expectations for the year. I tell the children that I consider them my "school family." I explain that just as in any family we might not always agree on everything, but that I will always care about them. I say that each and every one of them is very special and important to me, and that I want them to have the best possible school year. Because they are so important to me, I will not tolerate any cruelty or unkindness to each other. I expect them to be the best behaved and well-mannered class in the entire school, both in the classroom and on the playground. I tell them that good behavior is really just good manners, because it shows respect for others, whether children or adults. I also go over the golden rule, and I make a bulletin board on that theme. I refer to the golden rule as our class motto. That is the only rule we have in

the class, and I discuss with them how it covers everything. If you don't want to be called names, then don't call other people names. If you want people to listen to you, then be sure to listen to others. And most important, if you want to have friends, then be a friend. The children seem to understand and accept all of this very well. They see it as a fair and sensible way to do things, and I think it helps them know they have a teacher who cares about them.

Human Relations Skills and Classroom Climate

Human relations skills improve the quality of classroom interactions, thereby contributing to a positive atmosphere. In particular, three aspects of human relations skills merit understanding and implementation: general human relations skills; relations between teacher and students; and relations between teacher and parents.

General Human Relations Skills. Four general skills of human relations serve us well in almost all situations. They are friendliness, positive attitude, ability to listen, and ability to compliment genuinely.

Friendliness is a trait everyone admires, yet many of us have difficulty in displaying it, especially when threatened or in the company of people we dislike. Yet with small effort we can show friendliness even toward people who displease us, by smiling, speaking gently, addressing them by name, asking how they are, asking about their family and work, and so on. When we behave in this way, we find that others begin to respond similarly.

A *positive attitude* means that we focus on the brighter side of things. When dealing with problems, we look for solutions rather than lamenting obstacles or blaming others. We refrain from complaining, backbiting, and gossiping. When we speak positively, others begin to do so as well.

Ability to listen is a trait we admire in others but often find lacking in ourselves, as most of us would rather talk than listen. Yet, listening produces so many desirable outcomes that it behooves teachers to cultivate the habit. Listening communicates genuine interest in the other person, an essential first step in establishing good relationships. It shows that we value the other person's opinions, and it improves the quality of communication by permitting a true exchange of ideas.

Ability to *compliment genuinely* is a behavior that receives relatively little attention in human relations but has, nevertheless, considerable power. Many of us are reluctant to compliment others, having seen how some people use compliments falsely in hopes of currying favor. Still, it is obvious that we all like to receive compliments. Weigh your attitude toward people who compliment you against those who do not (or who give you unsolicited "constructive criticism"). With which of the two would you rather work and socialize?

As you learn to give compliments, however, you must make sure they are genuine and that the other person sees them as such. It helps if you make your compliment explicit: rather than saying, "Your ideas are brilliant," you might say, "Your explanation of the Persian viewpoint is the most understandable I have heard." On a more personal level, rather than saying, "Hey, looking great today!" you might say, "That color surely suits you."

Human Relations with Students. The general skills of human relations apply to everyone in all situations. When working with students, however, there are additional relations skills that teachers should employ. They are regular attention, using reinforcement, showing continual willingness help, and modeling courtesy and good manners.

Giving *regular attention* to students was discussed earlier in the chapter. Let us note here that it does much to build bonds of trust and cooperation. It should be given to all students equally, not just to the favorites and to those who misbehave.

Reinforcement. In human relations, reinforcements are given verbally and behaviorally to show support, encouragement, understanding, and approval, with the result that student attention and work output increase. Examples of verbal reinforcers are: "You are showing improvement in your handwriting every day," "I can see you put a great deal of thought into preparing your essay," "Thanks a lot for being so helpful today." Examples of behavioral reinforcers are nods, smiles, winks, thumbs-up, and other expressions and gestures that show approval.

Continual willingness to help is a trait much admired in teachers. Students gravitate to helpful teachers, tend to admire them, and usually remember them with respect years later. You hear them say, "Yeah, Miss Smith expected a lot, but she really tried to help every one of us."

Modeling Courtesy and Good Manners. You should make a point to demonstrate through your own behavior the best of what you would like to see in your students. Even when they are boorish, you should be genteel. When they forget their manners, you should make a special point of remembering yours. This behavior is catching. If you want your students to live by the golden rule, your behavior must be a prime example of what that rule means when put into practice.

Human Relations with Parents. Teachers have a responsibility to communicate with their students' parents. Many teachers use this responsibility to advantage while others avoid it, believing that parents don't care, or else that such communication is more trouble than it is worth. Yet, good communication usually brings increased support from parents.

For building stronger relationships with parents teachers should employ the general skills of human relations, described earlier. In addition, they should communicate regularly, communicate clearly, describe expectations, and emphasize the child's progress while downplaying the child's shortcomings.

Regular communication with parents is accomplished through notes, telephone calls, and newsletters. This communication shows respect for parents and interest in their children, and it causes parents to think more highly of teachers. Any communication should be very clear. Remember that most parents do not understand educational jargon such as "critical thinking" or "cognitive levels," nor do they recognize acronyms such as SAT, IEP, or GATE. It is also wise to avoid involved sentence structure and the use of big words where little ones suffice. In short, make sure your messages to parents are clear, simple, and to the point.

In communicating with parents, *clearly describe your expectations.* Most parents like to know about your program, what their child is supposed to do, how you will evaluate, what you require concerning homework, and what role at home is to be, if any. Always remember one thing: parents don't like to hear their child criticized. Criticism is a sure way to alienate parents at once. So what you want to do is emphasize the child's progress, and where shortcomings exist, indicate them in terms of new learnings that you and the child are working on.

Conferencing with Parents

All teachers must conference with parents, either as a routine procedure or because of trouble with a particular student. Such conferences typically produce great anxiety on both sides. Teachers fear criticism of their program, judgment, ways of teaching, or means of dealing with students. Parents fear hearing faults in their children, which they internalize as faults in themselves.

However, the purpose of parent conferencing is to improve the overall success of the child. If you can keep that essential point in mind, and if you prepare adequately for the conference, you will find most meetings with parents pleasant and productive.

Preparing for the Parent Conference. Careful preparation is highly desirable. Remember to do these things:

1. Have the student's strengths and weaknesses clearly in mind.
2. Prepare an attractive folder with the student's name on it.
3. Include in the folder a summary of your program, showing work completed and work yet to be done.
4. Include samples of the student's work.
5. Have available grades and tests that back up your evaluation.
6. Anticipate questions parents are most likely to ask:
   How does my child get along with others?
   Does my child cause problems?
   Is my child progressing as well as expected?
   What are my child's specific needs?
   Is there anything you want me to do to help?

Once you have made your preparation, free your mind to concentrate on conducting the conference professionally:

1. Think of yourself in the parent's place. Be tactful and polite.
2. Greet the parent in a friendly, relaxed manner.
3. Sit side by side with the parent at a table, rather than on opposite sides of a desk.
4. Begin by chatting about the student as a worthwhile person. Mention good traits. This reassures the parent.
5. Guide the parent through the student's file, commenting on samples of work included. Refer to tests and grades if appropriate.
6. Encourage the parent to talk. Listen carefully and be accepting. Do not argue

or criticize; this causes resentment. Parents cannot be objective about their child.

7. Throughout the conference, make sure the parent sees that you want the best education for the child.

8. End the conference by describing your plans for the student's future progress. Earnestly request the parent's support. Thank the parent for meeting with you to talk about the child.

On Giving Advice to Parents

Teachers should be careful about giving parents advice on matters where they lack qualifications. They should limit themselves to academic matters and normal behaviors that affect learning. If parents ask about matters outside normal teacher expertise, refer them to the school nurse, psychologist, or other trained expert. If they ask you about study time at home, suggest that they stipulate a specific place for doing homework with no distractions (such as television), and that they talk with the child about school work. If they ask about how to control misbehavior at home, tell them only what you insist on in school: a few important rules that you stick to, reasonable consequences when the rules are followed and broken, maintaining open communication, and showing the child that he or she is wanted, loved, and respected.

Managing Classroom Routines

Generally speaking, teachers rated as most effective have put into place classroom routines that minimize disruption while maximizing productive work time. Keith, a secondary math teacher, describes an opening routine he uses to good advantage, and shares some of his related views:

> It is important to me for things to run smoothly. I begin the period with a one-minute timed exercise. The students know I will quickly say "go," and if they don't have their pencils, scratch paper, and test sheet ready they are out of luck—they can try again the next day.
>
> The subject matter is very important to me. Assignments are to be completed. If they are not, a note goes home, filled out by the student, stating what was not completed and why. The work must be made up on their own time. I go over all the assignments ahead of time so students know exactly what is expected. They know the schedule of tests and what they have to do to earn their grades. This makes them responsible for their own grades. Occasionally, I receive a call from a parent whose child has received a failing grade for the first time ever. Their anger quickly subsides when I remind them that the child knew exactly what work was required for a good grade, and I explain how little the child did.
>
> This may sound harsh, but I treat the students with great respect and courtesy. I always say "please" and "thank you" and "excuse me." I admit my mistakes and tell the students I am sorry. They reflect my example. We are courteous, we are considerate, we have an enjoyable time, and best of all we get our work done.

Routines, the commonplace procedures and chores of day-to-day activities, are far more important to discipline than is generally recognized. Well-managed routines permit students to know exactly what they are supposed to do, thus reducing dead time that fosters misbehavior. Teachers should establish routines for opening and ending class activities, use of materials, disposition of completed work, the duties of student helpers, and the procedures in assisting students at work.

Opening and Closing Activities. In many classrooms the students waste several minutes before getting started on their work. They come into the classroom talking, are slow to take their seats, continue talking once seated, and do not stop until the teacher's insistent voice is heard above the noise. This situation is corrected by establishing routine procedures for the students to follow upon entering the room. Generally, it is best to have them begin work immediately. This can be established as one of the class rules. Secondary teachers may write an assignment on the board. Students enter, sit down, and begin work within one minute after the bell. Elementary teachers may have students write in journals, read silently from library books, or do math or vocabulary exercises while roll is taken. Very young children may begin by playing with instructional toys or sitting quietly while the teacher or aide reads a story. In all cases, the point is to cause students to begin schoolwork at once, rather than talking and fooling around.

It is equally important to establish routine procedures for ending the class activity. For classes such as art, shop, and physical education, a cleanup time is required. In practically all classes, materials are to be re-stored, completed work is to be filed, and everything is to be readied for dismissal. Students should automatically follow established routines, on cue.

Materials Usage. Inefficient classrooms waste time while students obtain materials and replace them after use. Procedures should be established that allow students to obtain or receive needed materials very quickly. If materials are to be distributed, several students should help, each obtaining and distributing materials to five or six other students. If students are to obtain their own materials, they should be able to go to convenient shelves or cupboards without crowding or waiting in line. Pencil sharpening can be especially distracting. Many teachers permit pencil sharpening only before class begins. Others keep containers of sharpened pencils; students can exchange their dull pencils for sharp ones when necessary.

At the end of the period, the materials should be replaced as efficiently as they were obtained. Students are taught exactly what to do and are allowed a minimum of time to replace the materials.

What to Do with Completed Work. Clear procedures should be established concerning what students are to do with work they have completed. If students are allowed to come individually to the teacher and hand in their work, there is likelihood of noise, wasted time, and disturbance to students still working. For that reason, many teachers use more efficient procedures such as having students place completed work on the corner of their desks or tables, or in conveniently-located baskets. The work is then collected by a teacher, aide, or student assistant.

The Use of Student Assistants. It is strongly recommended that students in the class be assigned duties to help with routine procedures. Not only does this help teachers, but it also tends to improve student attitude. At the secondary level, student assistants are most useful for distributing and collecting materials and for replenishing and taking care of supplies. They are frequently used, as well, for simple grading of papers, record keeping, typing, and duplicating materials. At the elementary level, teachers often assign tasks to every student in the class—president, flag salute leader, lights monitor, window monitor, news and weather reporters, messenger, line monitors, group or table leaders, plant and pet caretakers, materials monitor, audiovisual assistants, visitor greeter, and so on. There are plenty of jobs for all students, and all should participate.

Providing Assistance to Students at Work. As you recall from the Fredric Jones model, teachers tend to be inefficient in providing help to students doing seatwork. In particular, they spend too much time with each student who raises a hand, letting other students sit for several minutes, doing nothing or getting into trouble. Jones provided excellent advice on how to give help efficiently. As you probably remember, his suggestions included:

1. Make sure students know what they are supposed to do and how they are supposed to do it.
2. Provide a written model to which students can refer.
3. Circulate among students to check for progress and errors.
4. When students raise their hands, give them direct help and then move away quickly, preferably in 20 seconds or less. Do not let students become psychologically dependent on your presence before they will do their work. Reinforce those who work well on their own.
5. Do not succumb to the temptation to reteach individual students or take them through question and answer tutorials. If several students are having the same difficulty, reteach the concept or process to the entire class.

THE TEACHING COMPONENT

While all teachers can acquire good discipline techniques, some do so only through effort. Others seem to give discipline little attention, yet their classes run smoothly, with few difficulties. Such teachers are often called "naturals," though they may vary considerably in the way they teach. One thing they have in common is that they seem to anticipate problems and take steps to prevent them.

It is on these teachers with good preventive discipline that we now focus. They seem to be of three rather distinct types, which we will call *well-liked teachers,* *efficient teachers,* and *master teachers.* Keep in mind that the three types are not exclusive. Not only is there overlap, but some teachers vacillate between types from day to day, especially as concerns efficiency.

The *well-liked* teacher is sought out by students because of the classroom conditions they provide: individual attention, interesting activities, relaxed atmosphere, and prevalent sense of humor. Good academic learning can occur in those classes, but it can also be mediocre to poor. Students behave well because they want to please the teacher they like, and they want the teacher to like them in return.

The *efficient teacher* plans, organizes, instructs, and manages well, with nothing left to chance. Achievement tends to be high in their classrooms, but those teachers are not necessarily well-liked, especially when efficiency comes at the expense of stimulation and caring. As students are often uncomfortable in classrooms with little personal warmth, they do not enjoy their educational experience. They usually behave well because there is little opportunity to do otherwise in tightly structured programs backed by strong systems of rules and consequences.

The *master teacher* displays the best qualities of the other two types. Master teachers are efficient, yet flexible. They show that they care about their students. They do what they can to make learning interesting, exciting, and satisfying. Their students learn well, admire and respect them, and usually like them personally. Good behavior occurs because of the teacher's reasonable standards and personal concern for the students, which makes students want to please them in return.

How to Become a Master Teacher

If you see yourself as well-liked but feel you need to be more efficient, work on procedures and routines that keep students on task. Add more structure to your lessons, concentrate on corrective feedback, and keep your teaching as free from disruptions as possible. But remember that while master teachers organize well, they are not slaves to efficiency. They remain flexible in accord with circumstances.

As much as anything else, master teachers provide stimulating lessons. They add the flair of mystery, suspense, and drama to their teaching. They draw students in by providing for active involvement. Meanwhile, good communication continues to build human relations, resulting in a growing sense of esprit de corps.

Application Exercises

1. Examine this contribution from teacher Colleen Meagher and identify management that has to do with physical environment, classroom climate, and routines:

   "I arrange things so that the daily schedule flows more smoothly and I don't have to give unnecessary directions. Transitions are timed with a kitchen timer and the class is challenged to see if they can quietly clean up and prepare for the next activity before it rings. I allow the students to work in cooperative groups and at times allow them to talk quietly and move about the room. Traffic patterns are clearly defined. Desks are arranged in a U-shape facing the chalkboard, so I have eye contact and easy access to all students."

2. Mr. Tales has prepared the following note to send to parents describing his goals for the class:

   "We will be working to maximize self-image through both traditional and newer affective approaches. Intended learnings will be stated in terms of experiences rather than behaviorally. Assessment of progress will be accomplished observationally. Your input into this process will be valued."

Application Exercises (continued)

Mr. Tales asks you to look over the note and make suggestions before he sends it out. What do you suggest to him?

3. For a grade, subject, and topic you select, describe how you would manage materials distribution and collection, work routines, and assistance for students during independent or group work.

4. For a grade or subject you select, describe what you would want to communicate to parents at the beginning of school and how you would communicate with them. Be realistic in terms of time required.

5. You are preparing for a conference with the father of James, a delightfully humorous and well-intentioned boy who is barely passing his course work. His study habits are poor in school and, you suspect, nonexistent at home. The principal has informed you that James's father requires that James work in their upholstery shop after school hours. What will you say to the father, and how will you proceed?

FURTHER ANALYSIS AND APPLICATION:

Examine scenario #1 (elementary) or #2 (secondary) in Chapter 13. From what you can see in the scenario you select, what changes would you make so that better behavior might be encouraged (as opposed to enforced)?

RECOMMENDED READINGS

Cangelosi, J. (1988). *Classroom management strategies: Gaining and maintaining students' cooperation*. White Plains, NY: Longman.

Charles, C. (1983). *Elementary classroom management*. New York: Longman.

Emmer, E., Evertson, C., Clements, B., & Worsham, M. (1984). *Classroom for secondary teachers*. Englewood Cliffs, NJ: Prentice-Hall.

Evertson, C. (1986). Training teachers in classroom management: An experimental study in secondary school classrooms. *Journal of Educational Research, 79,* 51–58.

Evertson, C., & Emmer, E. (1982). Effective management at the beginning of the school year in junior high classes. *Journal of Educational Psychology, 74,* 485–498.

Evertson, C., Emmer, E., Clements, B., Sanford, J., Worsham, M., & Williams, E. (1981). *Organizing and managing the elementary school classroom*. (Report No. 6060). Austin: University of Texas, Research and Development Center for Teacher Education.

Fifer, F. (1986). Effective classroom management. *Academic Therapy, 21,* 401–410.

Gordon, T. (1989). *Teaching children self-discipline—At home and at school*. New York: Times Books.

Lemlich, J. (1988). *Classroom management: Methods and techniques for elementary and secondary teachers* (2nd ed.). White Plains, NY: Longman.

Maurer, R. (1988). *Special educator's discipline handbook*. West Nyack, NY: The Center for Applied Research in Education.

CHAPTER 10

The Management
of Students at Risk

Judith Schulman reports a teaching experience related by Michael, a new inner-city teacher with a master's degree in marine biology:

> My descent from innocence was swift and brutal.
>
> I was faced with classes populated by unruly students, gang members, and other children with only rudimentary scholastic skills.
>
> Convinced that with kindness and patience I could help them all if only the students saw my concern for them, and eager to disseminate my knowledge to the masses, I launched into my lessons.
>
> I typed up lab sheets (on a metric unit) explaining in detail what should be measured and in what units I wanted the measurements. The students were then assigned lab tables, paired off, and provided with metric sticks. What next ensued can only be described as pandemonium.
>
> My intention had been to visit with each group of students and answer any questions they might have. I also figured this would provide an excellent opportunity for me to get to know some of the students. Unfortunately, as I have found to occur with alarming frequency, intentions and reality often have nothing whatsoever to do with one another (Schulman, 1989, p. 4).

Students at Risk

Michael's class contained many *students at risk*, a label applied to those whose likelihood of success in school is questionable. The situation he described is experienced by thousands of teachers every day, leaving them frustrated and insecure. Those teachers will admit, albeit reluctantly, that they are at a loss as to how to motivate such students and manage their unruly behavior.

The number of students at risk is increasing yearly, for reasons hardly mysterious. This is a time of rapid social change. Drug usage has devastated a significant portion of the population. Poverty is increasing, now affecting one child in every four. The homeless are seen in almost every city. Thousands of children live in single-parent homes, often with no parental supervision during the day. Inadequate nutrition and lack of health care are common.

Grant and Sleeter (1989, pp. 1–2) report the following characteristics of students now entering public schools in the United States:

- 25% are from families living in poverty.
- 14% are children of teenage mothers.
- 15% are non-English-speaking immigrants.
- almost 30% are of color.
- 40% will live in a single-parent home before age 18.
- 25%–30% are latchkey children.
- 15% are in special education.

Trends indicate that by the year 2020 one person of every three in the United States will be what we now call a minority (Sobol, 1990). Most of that group will have cultural, social, and linguistic traits that seem to contribute to lower school achievement, producing the "achievement gap" that exists between Anglos and certain minority groups (Hernandez, 1989). Poverty, with yet more depressing effects on school achievement, exists in differing degrees according to group. In 1987, 48% of African-Americans lived in poverty, compared to 42% for Latinos, 29% for other nonwhite groups, and 13% for whites (Slavin, Karweit, and Madden, 1989). On a numerical basis, twice as many white children live in poverty as all nonwhite groups combined (Hernandez, 1989, p. 15).

Along with such changes in social conditions comes the distressing fact that Americans no longer place as much value on education as they once did. Parental support for schools has declined, as has parental insistence that children do well in school. Students now drop out of high school in alarming numbers, while many of those who remain make little effort to learn.

The resultant damage to education is substantial and difficult to correct. Educators report little headway in reducing the achievement gap, which by high school amounts to three full grade levels for Latino and African-American students (Slavin, Karweit, and Madden, 1989). Teachers warn that student motivation for school success is on the decline, while problem behavior is rising. Unacceptable behavior is hardly restricted to the classroom. Over 50,000 juveniles are now being held in detention, correctional, and shelter facilities. Among them a disproportionately high percentage is nonwhite (Williams, 1989).

Who Specifically Are the Students at Risk?

As noted, the term "at risk" is used without precise definition, but in general it refers to students who are unlikely to graduate from high school because of one or more "risk factors"—low achievement, lack of motivation, bilingualism, learning disabilities, or severe behavioral problems. The term is also applied to students who remain in school but fail to acquire adequate skills in reading and writing.

What Are Schools Doing for At-Risk Students?

For the most part, schools are attempting to save at-risk students by providing programs of "equity education." Rothman and Wilson (1988) describe equity education as providing those conditions in which:

- All pupils have access to educational resources and processes commensurate with their needs.
- No pupil is adversely discriminated against, but is instead treated with respect.
- All pupils are prepared to determine their own destiny regardless of socioeconomic status, race, or ethnic background.

Rothman and Wilson suggest that schools, in implementing equity education, must accomplish certain critical tasks, including (p. 50):

- decrease in racial isolation of pupils
- equal treatment of minority pupils in disciplinary referrals
- increase in cross-sectional student participation in school activities
- implementation of human relations programs that facilitate group cooperation in school.

In keeping with the intent of equity education, students identified as at-risk are usually given special help in school through compensatory education, which is federally funded and targeted at students with special needs. Included are Head Start, Chapter 1, special education, and bilingual education, all intended to produce more rapid and more appropriate learning.

Chapter 1 is heavily funded to provide remedial instruction in reading, mathematics, and language. Approximately one out of every nine students in the United States receives Chapter 1 assistance. *Special education*, also heavily funded and overseen by Public Law 94-142, provides assistance to students with one or more categories of handicap. One of nine American students receives specific assistance in special education. *Head Start* is provided in half-day preschool sessions for children from low-income families, for the purpose of improving early social and cognitive development. *Bilingual education* is provided to many students with limited English proficiency.

THE CULTURALLY DIVERSE

The United States is a nation comprised of a great many racial, ethnic, and linguistic groups. The two largest minority groups, African-Americans and Latinos, have traditionally received most of the attention in multicultural educational programs, though programs for Native Americans have long existed. Specific attention is now being given to numerous other groups that have recently immigrated into the United States. Many large city school districts enroll students from fifty or more different language groups.

Beginning teachers, including most of those who are nonwhite, when anticipating their new classes still visualize rows of happy students who are predisposed to learning and willing to behave, needing only a compassionate, understanding teacher. Occasionally, new teachers do in fact find approximately what they expect, but for the vast majority conditions are far different—students with minimal English language skills, poor reading ability, and lack of interest in school. Some of those students are apathetic, some delightful personally but unmotivated to learn, some overtly resistant to teachers. Many have had experiences that could bring richness to the class, but they can't seem to find a niche or a way to participate and contribute. Many respect their teachers but simply see little point in attending school.

Teachers of such students know that education is not doing what it should for the culturally diverse, yet they feel powerless, unable to make needed modifications or even to identify changes that should be made. Those teachers wrack their brains for better ways to teach, but are timid about asking experienced teachers for help and very reluctant to approach administrators, fearing they will be considered incompetent (Huling-Austin, 1986). They struggle on in the hope that somewhere, somehow, the secret of success will reveal itself.

The Nonmagic Formula

It must be understood that there is no magic formula for motivating resistant learners, for improving everyone's achievement overnight, or for making reluctant students behave angelically in school. If there were, every teacher would hear of it and have it committed to memory by the next day.

Nevertheless, teachers can find help from three sources. The first has to do with the management of classroom behavior. The fundamental principles of behavior management, together with the best schemes for putting them into practice, were presented in the preceeding chapters of this book. As has been stated throughout this book, every teacher must ultimately organize his or her own system of discipline. The same is true when it comes to developing strategies for motivation and instruction.

The second source of help comes with the understanding of how one meets fundamental student needs. The needs for belonging, power, fun, and freedom exist in students from all backgrounds. As those needs are met, students become more willing to learn and behave acceptably.

The third source of help comes from an increased awareness of why multicultural education is needed and how it can be implemented. What is advocated in such programs ties directly into meeting student needs, as is evident in the following goal-expectations held for teachers in multicultural education (Hernandez, 1989, pp. 13–14):

- An understanding of how sociocultural factors influence learning and teaching, and the application of that understanding in maximizing students' academic and social development.

- An understanding of bilingualism and its implications for the education of students with limited English proficiency.
- The ability to use instructional procedures that are culturally appropriate for diverse student populations.
- The adaptation of teaching to meet specific needs of individual learners of diverse backgrounds and ability levels.
- The ability to evaluate, develop, and modify curricular materials with specific attention to sociocultural content.

Hernandez goes on to describe multicultural education as valuable in preparing students for the realities of life in a pluralistic nation, emphasizing that it must be sensitive to the academic and social needs of all students, attempt to serve all students equally, and build the understanding that multicultural education is important for everyone.

The Abandonment of Stereotype

Teachers, whether they work in multicultural, bilingual, or traditional classrooms, want their students to be orderly, eager to learn, patient, hardworking, and compliant. Unfortunately, they often find just the opposite—students who are rowdy, uninterested in learning, and unwilling to do the work provided them. Teachers, operating with middle-class Anglo values, may conclude that African-American students are hyperactively irreverent and careless in their work, that Latino students are unmotivated and only waiting to drop out of school, that Native American students are always stoically unproductive, or that Asian-American students are so diligent they need no special attention or help.

Such stereotyped notions should be discarded and replaced with sincere efforts to understand and work with students on an individual basis, keeping foremost in mind that students from various cultural groups show a diversity of values and behave in ways not always immediately understood. Many cultural groups in the United States have not wished to melt into Anglo-American culture, but rather to maintain their own separate identities. In some cases school-age members of those groups have not worked hard in school because to do so is to "act white." Mydans (1990) reports that some segments of the black population see school achievement in such a light, considering academic success the prerogative of white Americans.

Facts such as these suggest ever more strongly that schools and teachers must understand the realities of the students they teach, and then attempt from that basis to provide every opportunity for quality education.

Basic Needs the Same for All

It is true that typical patterns of behavior may differ somewhat among ethnic groups, but there is no evidence that those behaviors arise from differences in basic psychological needs. All students seem to function from the same needs described earlier in the works of Dreikurs and Glasser. Dreikurs, you remember, asserted that all students have *belonging* as their prime need, and that much of their classroom behavior can be seen as an attempt to meet that need. If unsuccessful, they turn to the mistaken goals of attention, power, revenge, and withdrawal. Glasser maintained that students are motivated not only by the need for belonging, but by three additional needs—power, fun, and freedom.

The meeting of such needs seems to take on greater importance each day, while the opportunities for many students decline. Schaps and Solomon (1990) point out that today's children often have few if any close relationships with caring adults, and that schools would do well to reorient themselves into something like caring, supportive communities. They report that such efforts in the Child Development Program in California have increased students' motivation to learn and their willingness to help each other and resolve interpersonal problems.

Teachers must also understand that while all students are struggling to meet the same needs, cultural variations will be evident in the efforts made to meet those needs. Understanding the nuances of those differences—understanding that diverse students are likely to behave somewhat differently from the typical Anglo-American—enables teachers to work more effectively with all students.

Behavior Management Based on Cultural Understanding

Understanding of culturally diverse students means little unless it gives teachers the power to teach more effectively. It was stressed earlier that no magic formula exists for removing all behavior problems from the classroom. But the recognition that behavioral diversity is a natural phenomenon can help teachers greatly in *reducing* the occurrence of discipline problems in the classroom. Such understanding empowers the teacher to do the following:

1. Accept the fact that neither individual students nor groups of students behave in exactly the same ways, nor do they need to do so.
2. Help all students find a sense of belonging in the class—as valued members—while recognizing and accepting that differences will sometimes be seen in how students try to meet that need.
3. Treat all students with courtesy and respect, regardless of whether they are boisterous, compliant, meek, or withdrawn, and insist that students treat each other with that same respect.
4. Show unending commitment to helping students be successful in school, regardless of how individual students may behave.
5. Provide for extensive interaction among members of the class, as a means of building togetherness and pride in the classroom. Invite to the class adult members of the community who provide positive role models.
6. Increase the amount of cooperative classroom work, recognizing that most students prefer cooperation and behave better in that mode.
7. Stress the importance of students' helping each other and learning from each other.
8. Recognize the importance of taking time to discuss class problems and explain the reasons for work provided.

9. Give students a greater role in classroom governance, especially in deciding on rules of conduct and procedures for resolving conflict. The resultant rules and consequences should then be clearly stated and discussed.
10. Stay out of power struggles that pit teacher against student, by learning not to take personal offense when misbehavior occurs, but rather to behave sensitively in resolving the cause of the problem. For teacher sanity, this point is crucial. Teachers expend enormous amounts of psychic energy struggling against students—against apathy, disrespectful behavior, and failure to do assigned work. It is that struggle that frustrates teachers and burns them out. Glasser's admonition to avoid such adversarial relationships is nowhere more appropriate than in working with diverse students.

New Directions

To date, compensatory and remedial programs have not produced the results envisioned. According to Anderson and Pellicer (1990), Chapter 1 programs frequently impede student learning and are especially ineffective for students with severe learning problems. Knapp, Turnbull, and Shields (1990) conclude that programs for at-risk students typically expect too little of students, that higher academic performance can and should be demanded. Clifford (1990) insists that the "easy success" endemic to programs for at-risk students produces negative results, and should be restructured to provide moderate success probability (better for motivation), prompt specific feedback (enhances learning), and moderate risk-taking (provides the tonic of challenge), all of which emphasize error tolerance and the importance of error correction.

Concerns such as these are being addressed in isolated programs in various locales. Typical of such programs is Workshop Way, described and taught by Grace H. Pilon (1988). Merrill Harmin (1990) analyzed Workshop Way in practice in a New Orleans inner-city school. He reported that teachers do not try to motivate students but, rather, involve them, catch them up in the activity. They never use humiliation, sarcasm, teasing, ignoring, or negative judgments. Instead, they work at showing students how to live as fully dignified, intelligent human beings who need the opportunity to learn to manage their own time and energy.

Harmin (1990, p. 46) summarized Workshop Way as consisting of seven elements:

1. Specific teacher guidance.
2. High student involvement, with dead time relentlessly avoided.
3. Intelligent involvement, with students challenged to think and create.
4. Daily student-teacher contact.
5. Meeting diverse needs, especially for those students who are insecure, belligerent, or slow to accept responsibility.
6. Promoting learning-living truths (e.g., "Everyone has a right to time to think"; "It's intelligent to ask for help.")
7. Respecting dignity at all costs, by keeping attention on the good in people.

DISCIPLINE AND STUDENTS IN SPECIAL EDUCATION

More than five million elementary and secondary students now receive some kind of special education service. The vast majority of those students, about 86%, are in the categories of learning disabled, speech impaired, or mentally retarded. Another 5% suffer from hearing, visual, orthopedic, or other health impairments. Students in these particular groups offer no unusual discipline problems. To the contrary, they are often rather well-behaved.

Such is not the case, however, for America's four to five hundred thousand emotionally disturbed children. A great many of those students display behaviors that seriously disrupt teaching and learning, behaviors such as acting out, making noise, moving hyperactively, crying, and throwing tantrums. Others, not disruptive, may be withdrawn and unresponsive in normal learning activities.

In the past, regular teachers did not have to deal with very many such students, most of whom were taught in special education classes. With the advent in 1975 of Public Law 94-142, however, large numbers of emotionally disturbed students entered regular classrooms for at least part of the day.

These students have presented especially difficult behavior management problems for regular classroom teachers. Traditional systems of discipline are based on the assumption that misbehavior is willful, that students can behave well if they want to. Such is not always the case for emotionally disturbed students. Much of their behavior comes from causes outside their conscious control. That makes most of the behavior management techniques suggested in the eight models of discipline relatively ineffective in suppressing misbehavior and giving it positive redirection.

Discipline for Handicapped Students: Special Techniques

Most authorities who write on mainstreaming give attention to matters of instruction while largely ignoring teachers' main concern, behavior management. Those authorities say that the emotionally handicapped respond to "good teaching" just as other students do, requiring little more than a positive, supportive learning environment. They do acknowledge that for very difficult-to-manage students special techniques of behavior modification may be required. They are correct that behavior modification can produce good results, but they seldom point out that behavior modification is very time-consuming when used with difficult individual behaviors. Regular classroom teachers do not enjoy the luxury of small classes. They too frequently deal with thirty-five or more in each class.

A refreshingly realistic view is presented by Richard E. Maurer in his book, *Special Educator's Discipline Handbook* (1988). There he suggests many discipline techniques for the special student that can be used in the regular classroom. The techniques Maurer describes vary from the familiar "time out" to "behavior contracting" and on to techniques for changing students' ways of thinking about themselves. Teachers will appreciate his practical advice on such specific matters as "how to avoid being hit by an assaultive student" (which he says to do by reflecting back the student's feelings, nonjudgmentally, rather than confronting them head-on).

While most of Maurer's points are already familiar to you, having come from authorities whose ideas were presented in the eight models of discipline, some of his suggestions add new twists. For example, he instructs on how to deliver effective reprimands through a "Don't Then Do" paradigm, which is intended first to stop the misbehavior (the don't), then give the student positive direction (the do). Maurer gives this example (1988, p. 69):

> A student, Patti, is swearing at Mike.
>> (The DON'T): Teacher says, "Patti, stop swearing at Mike."
>> Patti stops swearing, leaving herself in a neutral position.
>> (The DO): Teacher now says, "Patti, pick up your pencil and and copy these letters."
>> These teacher statements are supported by eye contact, physical proximity, and a few seconds' wait-time for the message to sink in. (If Patti does not comply, Maurer would have the teacher discuss with her the need for the swearing to stop, with mention of the consequences that will follow.)

Maurer suggests that this procedure, if Patti's misbehavior is chronic, be supported by keeping a private personal chart on which the frequency of her misbehavior is graphed. The chart is used in discussions with her, and possibly with her parents, concerning her misbehavior.

The Difficult-to-Manage Student in the Regular Classroom

Curwin and Mendler (1988) also provide helpful suggestions for the prevention of discipline problems among difficult-to-manage students. A few of their suggestions are:

1. *For the hyperactive:* Seat them close to you. Place masking tape on the floor around their desks to show the limits of their movements during seatwork time.
2. *For the easily distracted:* Place their desks facing the wall or provide study carrels to block out visual distractions.
3. *For resistant workers:* Make lists of specific activities to be done, with time limits. Tape the lists on students' desks and check off activities as they are completed.
4. *For students with poor memory and sequencing:* Break tasks down into components. Give instructions in two—or at most, three—steps, pausing between each.
5. *For unmotivated students:* Find ways to show visible evidence of progress, such as graphing on a chart. Keep running records of new learnings.

Behavior Contracting

When misbehavior is chronic, behavior contracting can produce good results. Introduced in Chapter 3, behavior contracting is a powerful means for improving behavior in the difficult-to-manage. It is done as follows:

1. Decide what behavior you want the student to exhibit instead of the misbehavior being shown. For example, if Shawn continually disrupts lessons by yelling out, you decide what you want him to do instead, which in this case is simple—you want him to sit quietly without yelling. You need to realize that Shawn's chronic misbehavior will probably change only slowly, so you begin with short periods of time that can be lengthened as Shawn improves.

2. Inform Shawn frankly and honestly of his misbehavior and the change that is needed.

3. Negotiate a reward system. For example, for each five minutes that Shawn does not yell out, he receives something he wants—a star, sticker, bonus point, or the like. The reward must be something he likes so much that he will avoid yelling out in order to get it.

4. Draw up on paper an official-looking contract that states what Shawn agrees to do and what he will receive for doing so. Teacher and Shawn both sign and date the document. Parents sometimes sign as well, to show consent, approval, and participation.

5. Begin the behavior contract. Make sure Shawn can succeed. As he does so, lengthen the time he must go without yelling in order to receive the reward.

6. Modify the contract as appropriate. Give Shawn regular feedback on his behavior and progress. Discuss with him and explain any changes that are warranted in the contract.

At times, behavior contracts may be used so that the individual earns rewards for the entire class. That is, if Shawn refrains from yelling out during a lesson, the entire class is rewarded, perhaps through a few minutes of preferred activity. The attention Shawn receives may be highly motivating. Use this with care, however, for Shawn's behavior may become worse if other students become antagonistic toward him. As another caution, when you use behavior contracts with only a few students, discuss with the class what you are doing so there will be no concern about what appears to be preferential treatment.

Discipline in New Programs

When new programs—such as multicultural education or mainstreaming—are put into effect, teachers often fear they will be overwhelmed with behavior problems. This is especially common as teachers encounter larger numbers of students at risk, leaving those teachers feeling helpless and hopeless. Rather than withdrawing into themselves, they should realize that they are not alone, that innumerable fellow teachers are in similar situations, and that many of those colleagues have found ways to do their work effectively. With a bit of effort, they will find considerable good counsel, such as:

1. Make it plain that you expect all your students to learn and behave well in school and that you will do all you can to help them.

2. Provide learning activities that are as interesting as you can make them. As Grant and Sleeter (1989, p. 16) say, "If it's boring or demeaning, avoid it!"

3. Remember that powerful discipline systems exist that can dramatically improve student behavior. Moreover, schools that devote themselves to excellence in learning and behavior often bring about significant improvements quickly. Many schools, in collaboration with parents and concerned communities, are increasingly moving in this direction.

4. You don't get anywhere fighting against students. They will ultimately win out (meaning that even if you can somehow force them to do what you want, their disrespect and hostility will make your life miserable).

5. Most students can be reached on a personal level. This personal relationship will be the most important thing you can give most of them, and when you are successful it makes teaching all worthwhile. But it takes time, often a great deal of time, and disappointment is part of the process.

6. Personal relationships grow as you show your students—sincerely and courteously—that you care about them, are interested, want to help, and will not work against their best interests. Once again, it takes a while for this to work, but it's worth the effort.

7. The more you know about your students, the better your chances of reaching them personally. This means you need to know their life styles, typical behaviors, cultural traits and values, personal abilities and inabilities, and hopes and aspirations.

8. Allow yourself to be patient. Teach yourself how to enjoy small successes whenever you find them (they will occur). But while showing patience, never become complacent and never give up.

Application Exercise

Review scenarios #7 and #8 in Chapter 13. In scenario #7, identify specific areas where cultural understanding is needed. In scenario #8, what discipline techniques would you consider most appropriate for controlling misbehavior and increasing work output? For both groups, what specifically would you try to keep in mind when working with the class?

REFERENCES

Anderson, L., & Pellicer, L. (1990). Synthesis of research on compensatory and remedial education. *Educational Leadership, 48*(1), 10–16.

Clifford, M. (1990). Students need challenge, not easy success. *Educational Leadership, 48*(1), 22–26.

Curwin, R., & Mendler, A. (1988). *Discipline with dignity.* Alexandria, VA: Association for Supervision and Curriculum Development.

Grant, C., & Sleeter, C. (1989). *Turning on learning: Five approaches for multicultural teaching plans for race, class, gender, and disability.* Columbus, OH: Merrill Publishing.

Harmin, M. (1990). The Workshop Way to student success. *Educational Leadership, 48*(1), 43–47.

Hernandez, H. (1989). *Multicultural education: A teacher's guide to content and process.* Columbus, OH: Merrill Publishing.

Huling-Austin, L. (1986). What can reasonably be expected from teacher induction programs. *Journal of Teacher Education, 37*(1), 12–15.

Knapp, M., Turnbull, B., & Shields, P. (1990). New directions for educating the children of poverty. *Educational Leadership, 48*(1), 4–8.

Maurer, R. (1988). *Special educator's discipline handbook.* West Nyack, NY: The Center for Applied Research in Education.

Mydans, S. (1990, April 25). Black identity vs. success and seeming "white." *New York Times*, sec. B, p. 9, col. 3.

Pilon, G. (1988). *Workshop Way.* New Orleans: The Workshop Way.

Rothman, J., & Wilson, C. (1988). A conceptual framework for achieving equity-based education through desegregation, innovation, and planned change. *Equity and Excellence, 24*(1), 44–53.

Schaps, E., & Solomon, D. (1990). Schools and classrooms as caring communities. *Educational Leadership, 48*(3), 38–42.

Schulman, J. (1989). Blue freeways: Traveling the alternate route with big-city teacher trainees. *Journal of Teacher Education, 40*(5), 2–8.

Slavin, R., Karweit, N., & Madden, N. (1989). Effective programs for students at risk. Boston: Allyn & Bacon.

Sobol, T. (1990). Understanding diversity. *Educational Leadership, 48*(3), 27–30.

Williams, J. (1989). Reducing the disproportionately high frequency of disciplinary actions against minority students. *Equity and Excellence, 24*(2), 31–37.

CHAPTER 11

Building a Personal System
of Discipline

The purpose of this book has been to help you build and implement an effective system of discipline—one that takes into account the ages and personalities of the students you teach as well as your own philosophy and personal preferences. Teachers have always attempted to develop personal systems of discipline, but until recently did not have access to all the elements needed for truly efficient systems. They would set up reasonable requirements only to find that they had no positive ways to enforce them. When they tried to be friendly and gentle, students would take advantage, so in order to be successful, teachers found it necessary to fall back on stern treatment, backed by threat of punishment.

That picture still holds true in many classrooms, where teachers and students face each other in stand-offs more adversarial than cooperative. But as the preceding chapters have shown, teachers no longer need waste energy and instructional time in dealing with misbehavior under such circumstances. They have at their disposal proven methods of guiding student behavior; the information is there for the taking.

The major question for teachers today is not whether they can have discipline but, rather, how they can organize what is known into systems that meet their needs. You might think that the simplest approach would be to examine existing models of discipline and select the best of them. That solution proves illusory. Take behavior modification as an example: it may work wonderfully well with young and some handicapped students, but not so well with older students and those inclined to rowdiness. Or consider assertive discipline: while effective in controlling misbehavior at all levels, it may be too cumbersome for primary grades and unsatisfactory to teachers trying to help students learn to value proper behavior. And so it is with the other models, all of which have special strengths, but also limitations.

Thus, despite having at hand so much information and proven technique, teachers

155

still have the necessity (or might one say the opportunity?) to build their own personal systems of discipline tailored to their preferences and the needs of their students. They can do this by selecting from among the various models those elements that suit them best and recombining them into the kind of system they want.

PART 1. BACKGROUND FOR BUILDING YOUR SYSTEM OF DISCIPLINE

What Teachers Want

Teachers want a system of discipline that:

1. Prevents misbehavior.
2. Controls misbehavior positively.
3. Promotes trusting relationships between teacher and students.
4. Engenders parental support and assistance.

Review this list to see if it describes what you would like to get with your system of discipline. Modify the list as needed so you can use it as a starting place in building your own personal system.

What Teachers Know About Students

Satisfactory systems of discipline must be shaped in accord with the traits typical of the students being taught. Some of the obvious sociocultural traits were discussed in Chapter 9. But more pervasive are human traits that cut across cultural groups, as indicated in the following paragraphs.

Primary Grades (Ages 4 to 9). Kindergarten children come to school at the age of 4 or 5, still babies in many ways. They parallel play, talk to themselves, tire easily, get fussy, cry, and require frequent rest. They fall, sprawl, and crawl about the floor. They make little distinction between work and play, and they require close supervision. Some play well together; others are spoiled and expect to have their own way.

Teachers at this level usually establish two or three rules for behavior and know those rules will be broken regularly. They spend much time reminding students of rules and proper behavior. This pattern continues into grades 1 and 2, with students gradually becoming socialized to school, learning to raise hands, stand in lines, and wait patiently.

At the primary level students accept adult authority without question though they often try to circumvent it. They respond well to praise, affection, and personal attention.

Intermediate Grades (Ages 9 to 12). As students move into grade 4 they are becoming much more independent, though they still like attention and affection from their teachers. Hugging may no longer be eagerly sought; holding hands with the teacher may take its place.

These students now recognize the logic of rules, their necessity, and the need for enforcement. They recognize and accept sensible consequences for breaking rules, especially where others are concerned. They can help establish rules and consequences and are usually eager to discuss transgressions and procedures of enforcement.

No longer is teacher authority blindly accepted. Students may argue, talk back, and drag their heels. But they are sure to fuss if rules and consequences are not administered consistently and impartially.

Junior High or Middle School Grades (Ages 12 to 14). Discipline is difficult for students at the junior high or middle school level, and their teachers must have exceptional skill if they are to maintain control, teach well, build supportive relationships, and maintain their own sanity.

Teaching these students is difficult because so many changes are taking place within them. Bodily changes worry, perplex, excite, and dismay their minds. New realities of an opposite sex stir and baffle them. The students begin psychological weaning from parents, which leaves them feeling lost and cut off. On top of those concerns comes adjustment to a new kind of school organization, a new curriculum, and new teaching styles.

These factors provide devastating competition against the learning of English, math, and history. Moreover, students are showing increasing rebelliousness, poking defiantly at outer boundaries of rules and customs. Their awe of the teacher has waned, but can be replaced with respect and affection for teachers of good humor who provide encouragement and support.

High School Grades (Ages 15 to 18). The high school years mark a time of settling down, as most students begin to find themselves and reach a truce with their bodily and emotional changes. Some get a positive fix on the future. Others, lamentably, become further alienated from the educational mainstream.

A new level of relationship with adults becomes evident. For most, the love-hate syndrome of earlier years fades, while respect for adults grows a bit as students recognize their interdependence with the larger community.

Teachers should now deal with students on an adult-adult basis. This does not imply equal authority. The teacher is still in charge, but students assume greater responsibility for their own learning and behavior, while looking upon teachers as guides and role models.

What Teachers Can Expect Regarding Students and Parents

The Positive Side. This book has made continual reference to misbehavior, since its focus has been on helping teachers deal with that problem. But we should recognize that most students have positive attitudes that outweigh the negative. We need to acknowledge that the majority of students want to learn. Those students recognize that they need an adult in charge of their learning, and they appreciate and like kind teachers who try to help them. They also want a humane learning environment with fair rules of behavior that are impartially enforced.

With regard to parents, we need to remember that all of them want their children to learn. Most support teachers' efforts. Most believe fairly strict discipline is needed. And a large majority think teachers are doing a good job.

And yet . . .

Teachers must be realists. They have to accept that *students are going to misbehave in school.* Though beginning teachers hope they will encounter no misbehavior—and some even believe they will not—misbehavior is a fact of classroom life.

At the same time, teachers must recognize that *students need discipline.* Most of us would rather goof-off than work, rather talk than keep quiet, rather interact humorously (or naughtily) with others than sit immobile. That is well and good, but does not change the fact that most school work depends on paying attention and making diligent effort. Most of all, teachers must recognize that *all students seek acceptance, belonging, success, and enjoyment.* Most social behavior in the classroom, the bad as well as the good, can be understood as students' attempts to meet these needs.

Persistent Annoyances

Fredric Jones, in his model of discipline, revealed that teachers spend most of their discipline time dealing with the innocuous behaviors of talking or moving about without permission. Relatively rare are the instances of open defiance or hostility that teachers fear. Still, teachers must deal with a cluster of persistent problems that sometimes drive them to distraction, such as:

1. *Tattling.* This is the elementary teacher's great exasperation. It makes teachers want to yell at students, but they do better to say something like:
   "We have a rule against tattling," or
   "Would you tell me about it at recess please?" or
   "Would you write it out for me so I can read it later?"
2. *The "cool" syndrome.* An extremely annoying form of attention-seeking, this behavior emerges in preadolescence and blossoms during adolescence. It pushes at limits without producing overt confrontation. It is shown in slight tardiness to class, a bit of back-talk with a pleasant face, facial signals to other students, fringely-unacceptable articles of clothing worn, intentionally misspoken answers to teacher questions, and the like. All of this is reinforced by other students who admire the cool behavior but are not daring enough to try it themselves. Wise teachers, instead of getting sucked into controversy (from which the cool student backs off smilingly), deal with this problem through class discussions, personal talks with offending students, and requests of help from parents.
3. *Cliques.* Endemic though by no means limited to preadolescent girls, student cliques can be devastating to class morale. They exclude and demean, cause jealousy and anger, and pit student against student. Cliques reach their height during years when emotions are fragile, so their effects can be terribly hurtful. This damanges academic learning as well. Wise teachers make this prob-

lem the topic of class discussions, soliciting student input concerning its avoidance. They also form and change work groups so that the members of cliques associate and work with others.

4. *Refusal to do or complete work.* This is seen at all grade levels but becomes chronic in late junior high and high school. It may be part of the cool syndrome or simple disengagement from school. Teachers have tried to correct this through punishments such as bad grades, only to conclude finally that adolescents can't be forced into what they are unwilling to do. William Glasser has provided the freshest insight into dealing with this problem, which is to find topics or cooperative work groups sufficiently interesting to motivate students to work.

Your Final Pep Talk

By now, you probably see discipline as an onerous task and fervently wish you never had to deal with it. This is certainly understandable, but you can ease the burden by taking cognizance of the following truths, which summarize the points previously made. Keep them in mind as you build your system of discipline:

Students require discipline. They must have it for positive social development and for adequate educational progress.

You are the most important figure in establishing class discipline. The process depends on you, although you will be wise to involve students in its development. You will want to communicate your plan to parents as well. You may not enjoy doing this, but remember that it is one of the most important things you can ever do for your students. They will respect you for it.

As you implement your plan, keep in mind that *the best way to teach good behavior is through example.* Your personal standards of quality will be imitated to a surprising degree. If you are kind and respectful, students will tend to follow your lead, but if you are negative and sarcastic, they will follow that lead as well.

Not only do students need discipline, but equally importantly *you cannot teach well without it.* More than anything else, you will want to be able to teach the contents of the curriculum to students who are attentive, cooperative, and appreciative. Your system of discipline is the ticket to your being able to teach this way. Remember Lee Canter's insistence on two basic rights in the classroom—the students' right to learn in a caring atmosphere, and your right to teach without disruptions.

PART 2. BUILDING YOUR SYSTEM OF DISCIPLINE

Three Faces of Discipline

It is helpful to think of discipline as having three faces: (1) *preventive discipline,* (2) *supportive discipline,* and (3) *corrective discipline.* The labels suggest the different, equally-important aspects of classroom discipline to which you must give attention.

Preventive Discipline. Teachers have found that preventing misbehavior is much better for all concerned than having to deal with trouble after it has occurred. It used to be said that the best way to prevent misbehavior is to make sure you provide a very interesting curriculum, where students become so involved in learning that it never occurs to them to misbehave. In case that failed, teachers were advised to get their bluff in from the start so students won't dare to cross them. While there is truth in both those adages, especially concerning good, interesting curriculum, more is required if classroom discipline is to remain sound over time.

There are a number of specific things you can do to reduce the likelihood of misbehavior. Each presented here has the additional advantage of building good relationships and fing a more positive attitude toward school.

1. *Make your curriculum as worthwhile and enjoyable as possible.* Select valuable learnings and provide enjoyable activities. Keep in mind students' basic needs for fun, belonging, freedom, and power.
2. *Take charge in your classroom.* Every authority on discipline agrees that teachers must maintain ultimate authority in the classroom. As they do so they should be pleasant and helpful. They ask for student input, but make the final decisions.
3. *With your students make good rules for class conduct.* Keep the rules short, clear, and few in number (no more than five). Discuss each rule thoroughly with students, thest the list in the room for reference and review.
4. *Continually emphasize good manners and living by the golden rule.* Make it plain from the outset that you care enough about your students to expect the highest standards of behavior from them, that you expect them to use good manners and never be sarcastic or cruel to each other. Be the best model you can, by showing concern, manners, courtesy, and helpfulness. Discuss this point frequently and call attention to improvements.

Supportive Discipline. Misbehavior seldom starts with bad intentions. All students at times become restive, inclined to squabbles and difficulties with others. Often they fall under the charismatic spell of misbehaving peers. Sometimes for unknown reasons they simply can't seem to resist misbehaving.

It is when these kinds of behaviors first appear that supportive discipline is brought into play. As the label indicates, this type of discipline simply helps students maintain self-control, mainly through subtle techniques that help students get back to work. Often, only the student toward whom the technique is directed knws it has been used. The following strategies are suggested for supportive discipline:

1. *Use signals directed to a student needing support.* Learn to catch students' eyes and use head shakes, frowns, and hand signals to direct them back to work.
2. *Use physical proximity when signals are ineffective.* Simply moving nearer the student is usually more than enough to revive interest in the work at hand.
3. *Show interest in student work.* Move alongside students who show signs of restlessness, look at their work, ask cheerful questions or make favorable

comments. Sometimes give a light challenge: "You have done a great deal of this already. I bet you can't get five more done before we stop."

4. *Restructure difficult work or help with it.* Quickly spot students who seem to be having difficulties. Give a hint, clue, or direct suggestion that solves their problem. At times you may need to restructure an activity—change it in midstream, add excitement, or reduce the level of difficulty.

5. *Interject humor into lessons that have become tiring.* Students place high value on humor, as it provides a lift and a respite from tension. A momentary break is all that is needed. You must be careful, though, that the humor does not provoke joking and horseplay that ruins the lesson before work is completed.

6. *Remove seductive objects.* A great variety of nonschool objects regularly appears in the classroom—toys, comics, rubber bands, animals, notes, and numerous unmentionables. They intrigue students and divert them from the lesson. Ask students to put such objects away. If they do not, take possession of them without fuss, then return them to the owners (accompanied by a few pointed comments) at the end of the period or day.

7. *Reinforce good behavior, in appropriate ways at appropriate times.* This should be done informally, with nods, smiles, and words such as "Thanks," "Good," "Keep it up." Compliment students when they show good effort, but be careful not to single out individuals for praise in front of their peers. Reinforce them as a group as much as possible.

8. *Request good behavior.* Use suggestions, hints, and I-messages as students begin to drift toward misbehavior. Show that you recognize trying situations: "You have worked so hard, and we are all getting tired. Please give me five more minutes of your best attention and we will be able to finish."

Corrective Discipline. You will find that despite your best efforts at preventive and supportive discipline, some misbehavior will occur. When students violate rules, it becomes your unpleasant duty to stop the misbehavior and redirect it, though not in the manner envisioned by most people when they think of classroom discipline—students acting awful and teacher reacting with scowl and sharp tongue.

Your corrective techniques should be neither intimidating nor harshly punitive, but instead only what is necessary to stop the misbehavior and redirect it positively. Consider the following corrective strategies:

1. *Assertively insist on the two basic rights in the classroom—your right to teach without disruptions and the students' right to learn.* Explain what these ideas mean and give hypothetical examples of violations. When students begin to misbehave, reassert the rights.

2. *Stop the misbehavior.* It is best to put an immediate end to the misbehavior rather than ignore it and hope it will go away. If the behavior is a gross violation of rules or decorum—fighting or loud swearing, for example—it must be squelched immediately: "Johnny, there is no swearing in this class!" Or, "Boys, sit down at once!" Milder misbehavior can be stopped by using

names and checks as Canter suggests or by a number of other techniques described in the various models.

3. *Invoke the consequences tied to the misbehavior.* Since you have thoroughly discussed class rules and consequences, your students understand that when they choose to misbehave they simultaneously choose the consequences that accompany the misbehavior. You need not get upset, but simply say, "Susan, you are not living up to our agreement, so you will have to sit at that table and complete your work by yourself."

4. *Follow through consistently.* Make sure you invoke consequences the same way day after day. Being stern one day and lax the next leaves students confused and encourages them to test your rules. Don't let students talk you out of the consequences they have chosen; if you do, they will be sure to test you again.

5. *Redirect misbehavior in positive directions.* Ask students who have misbehaved to return to work as agreed. Talk with them when you have time about their behavior. Ask how you can help so they can get the most out of school while not interfering with others.

Seventeen Steps to Personalized Discipline

The ideas you have considered in this book show that it is possible for you to build a system of discipline that will meet your students' needs as well as your own. The three faces of preventive, supportive, and corrective discipline, when combined, give you a balanced system with which you and your students can live comfortably. What remains is to tailor your system so that it allows your personality to function naturally. You can accomplish this final task through the following seventeen steps:

To Plan and Initiate Your System

1. *Clarify needs and tentatively set limits.* Make a list of your students' predominant traits and needs, then make a list of your own traits and needs. Envision behavior limits that permit both sets of needs to be met. Be sure to consider matters such as talk, movement, noise, self-control, beginning and completing work, and personal manners. If you have a particular need, such as for quiet or order, be up front about it and willing to ask for cooperation.

2. *Make a tentative list of what you think you will do for prevention, support, and correction.*

3. *If you have a class of students, discuss discipline with them the very first day.* From upper elementary to high school levels, ask the students how they would prefer to work, so they can learn well under pleasant circumstances. Share with them your needs and explore procedures that would be comfortable for all. Show that you are flexible and willing to compromise, but retain the right to veto suggestions that are not in the students' best interest.

4. *With your students, write out rules for governing behavior in your classroom.* Discuss the rules for verification and support.

5. *Now write out a revised, complete list of what you intend to do for preventive, supportive, and corrective discipline.*

6. *Give thought to how you can build a positive classroom climate that will help students' self-control while allowing personalities (including your own) to be evident.* Discuss these ideas with students.
7. *Establish your support system.* Inform the principal in detail about your discipline plan and ask for his or her support. Ask one or more fellow teachers if you can turn to them for help or counsel, should it be needed. Write out a description of your system to share with parents. Ask for their support in providing the best education possible for their children.

To Test Your System

8. *Put into effect the system to which you and your students have agreed.*
9. During the first week *assess your system* in terms of: its contribution to a positive, enjoyable climate, its ease of operation, and its effectiveness in controlling misbehavior.
10. For third grade and higher, *discuss your assessment with the students.* Give attention to their input as you consider changes.
11. *Modify your system if necessary.* Make sure students are involved and understand the need for the changes.

To Maintain and Strengthen Your System

12. *Work to enliven your curriculum.* Provide work that is worthwhile and interesting. Include topics in which you are especially interested or about which you are knowledgeable or excited.
13. *Establish classroom procedures that produce smooth flow, without dead spots or confusion.*
14. *Be the best possible model for your students.* Act as you want them to act; speak as you want them to speak.
15. *Interact with students on a personal level.* Talk with them. Show interest and help with difficulties.
16. *When students misbehave, discuss the problem with them.* Ask for their suggestions about how you can help.
17. *Never give up,* even when the going gets tough, even when you are demoralized, even when students don't seem to appreciate your efforts. Remain secure in the knowledge that you are providing a quality opportunity for your students to learn.

A Model System

How might a system look when prepared according to these guidelines? Wide variations are possible, of course, because of the differences in needs, philosophies, and situations among students and teachers. One example is shown in the following model, prepared by Deborah Sund for use in her third-grade class and presented here with her permission. (Six additional discipline plans of actual teachers at other levels and subjects are presented in Chapter 12.)

THE SUND MODEL

My Needs, Likes, and Dislikes

My Needs

1. Orderly classroom appearance—good room arrangement, materials neatly stored, interesting, well-thought-out displays.
2. Structure and routines—set schedule, with flexibility, allowing for improvisation when needed.
3. Transitions—smooth between activities, with no wasted time.
4. Attention—student attention for directions and given to all speakers and instructional activities.
5. Situational-appropriate behaviors—quietly attentive during instruction, considerate interaction during group activities, and so forth.

My Likes

1. Enthusiasm—from me and my students.
2. Warmth—as reflected in mutual regard among all individuals in the class.
3. Positive, relaxed classroom environment—reflecting self-control, mutual helpfulness, assumption of responsibility.

My Dislikes

1. Inattention to speaker, teacher, other adult, or class member.
2. Excessive noise—loud voices, inappropriate talking, and laughing.
3. Distractions in the form of toys, unnecessary movement, poking, teasing, etc.
4. Misusing, wasting, or destroying instructional materials.
5. Unkind behavior—verbal or physical abuse of others in the classroom.
6. Rude conduct—ridicule, sarcasm, bad manners.
7. Tattling.

My Classroom Rules

The following are my classroom rules, together with indications of how I discuss and explain them to my students.

1. Be considerate of others at all times. (Speak kindly, be helpful, don't bother others.)
2. Do your best work. (Get as much done as you can. Do your work neatly, so you can be proud of it. Don't waste time.)
3. Use quiet voices in the classroom. (Use regular speaking voices during class discussions. Speak quietly during cooperative work groups. Whisper at other times if you need help.)
4. Use signals to request permission or receive help. (Explain the signal systems for assistance, movement, restroom pass.)

The rules are discussed and agreed to by the students on the first day of school. After the students have familiarized themselves with the rules and routines, I continue to give them prompts, cues, hints, and other assistance in practicing adherence to the rules.

Positive Consequences

As students follow the rules, they know they will routinely receive the following positive consequences:

1. Positive verbal feedback.
2. Positive nonverbal feedback (smiles, winks, nods, pats).
3. Occasional tangible and privilege awards (stickers, marks, favorite activities).
4. Positive reports to parents (notes, phone calls).

Negative Consequences

When students do not abide by the rules, they know they will routinely receive the following negative consequences:

1. "Pirate eyes"—a stern glance, accompanied by a disappointed and puzzled expression.
2. Unapproving general comments—"I hear noise." "Some people are not listening."
3. Direct negative verbal feedback—"Gordon, you did not use the signal. Please use the signal."
4. Unfavorable reports to parents (note, call, school conference).
5. In-class isolation—student separated from group but still in sight of teacher.
6. Student sent to principal or counselor or removed from the class.

My Preventive Discipline Measures

I take the following steps to minimize the occurrence of behavior problems in my classroom:

1. Involve students in establishing class rules and assuming responsibility. In discussions I ask questions such as:
   "What do you think happens when everyone tries to talk at the same time?"
   "How do you like other people to speak to you?"
2. Make contact with parents. I do the following:
   Send letters outlining expectations and discipline system.
   Make short, positive phone calls to parents.
   Send notes with children concerning good work and behavior.
3. Organize a classroom environment for best temperature, light, and comfort, with traffic patterns for efficient movement within the room.
4. Stress, model, and hold practice sessions on good manners, courtesy, and responsibility.
5. Provide a varied, active curriculum with opportunities for physical movement, singing, interaction, and so forth.
6. Provide a sense of consistency, familiarity, and security, through structure and routines.

My Supportive Discipline Measures

In order to help my students support their own self-control when I see them beginning to drift, I use the following supportive measures:

1. Eye contact; facial expressions.
2. Physical proximity.
3. Reference to classroom rules.
4. Interest in individual students' work.
5. Modification of the lesson or routine if needed to increase interest or reduce anxiety.
6. Behavior modification—rewards for perseverance.

My Corrective Discipline Measures

When my students misbehave, I use the following corrective measures:

1. Comment on misbehavior. "I hear talking. I don't like it. Everyone should be listening."
2. Emphatic verbot. "Stop that now!"
3. Isolation of the student from the group.
4. Removal of the student to the principal or counselor's office.
5. Parental contacts by telephone.

My Way of Maintaining a Positive Classroom Climate

I have found that a positive climate results in better feelings, more enjoyment, and ultimately better self-control for both the students and myself. The following are some of the things I do to maintain such a climate:

1. Respect each child as an individual who is entitled to a good education.
2. Look for the good or likable qualities in each child.
3. Acknowledge appropriate behavior, good work, effort, and improvement.
4. Take time to get to know students better.
5. Give out as many nonverbal positive responses as possible—winks, nods, smiles.
6. Take time each day to assess student feelings.
7. Talk with students in ways that imply their own competence—e.g., "OK, you know what to do next."
8. Provide interesting and fun activities that are challenging, but at which students can succeed.
9. End each day on a positive note, with a fond goodbye and hope for a happy and productive tomorrow.

Regarding Schoolwide Systems of Discipline

Today a great many schools across the country have established schoolwide discipline programs, where all teachers in the school use the same system of discipline. This movement, intended to make discipline more consistent and effective, began to gain momentum in the middle 1980s, fueled by the nationwide push for "effective schools" that would provide:

- A safe and orderly environment for learning.
- High standards and expectations.
- Opportunities for student involvement and responsibility.
- Emphasis on positive behavior and preventive discipline.

If you should teach in such a school, you would be expected to follow the schoolwide discipline plan. You would be certain, however, to find yourself using techniques advocated in the models presented in this book. While it would be impossible to present here the varieties of discipline systems that schools have developed, it is possible to categorize them into three general types—single power systems (secondary), single power systems (elementary), and combination systems (elementary).

Single Power Systems: Secondary Level. A power system is one that contains procedures for firmly stopping misbehavior and consistently invoking consequences. Assertive discipline is an example of a power system. Power systems may be distinguished from "softer" systems, such as behavior modification, that provide influence through more subtle means such as modeling and persuasion.

Most schoolwide systems at the secondary level are single power systems, that is, one strong system is used by all teachers and other personnel in the school. The system has three main components: (1) a policy concerning discipline that is established by the school board and then disseminated to the school and community, (2) rules for student conduct, and (3) enforcement procedures, consequences, and follow through.

Component one, the *school board policy,* describes: (1) the district's philosophy concerning the relationship of discipline to education, (2) the student responsibilities at school and in the educational program, (3) the teachers' responsibilities for communicating clear standards and consequences and consistently implementing them, (4) the administrators' responsibilities in communicating and enforcing discipline, (5) a list of prohibited behaviors, such as use of drugs and alcohol, destruction of property, fighting, and so forth, and (6) the consequences that will be invoked for violations of the rules.

Component two in the power system is *rules of student conduct.* Rules have been discussed repeatedly in previous chapters. For secondary schools, schoolwide rules are usually similar to the following list:

1. Always be on time and ready to work.
2. Treat all people and property with respect.
3. Cooperate with those in positions of authority.
4. Leave nuisance objects at home.
5. Do not disrupt the teaching-learning process.

In some schools, all school personnel, including librarians, secretaries, bus drivers, cafeteria workers, custodians, and so forth are empowered to enforce the rules.

Component three, *enforcement, consequences, and follow through,* includes measures similar to the following:

1. All students are carefully made aware of the rules, consequences, and enforcement procedures. Charts displaying the rules are posted in classrooms and elsewhere in the school.
2. When a student violates a rule, a verbal warning is given. This warning carries no penalty. If the student misbehaves again, the person in authority

makes a notation on a special form in triplicate—one copy goes to the student, a second to the office, and the third is kept by the person writing the complaint.

3. School counselors keep a conduct card for all students assigned to them. When the counselor receives a note indicating misbehavior, that infraction is entered on the student's conduct card.

4. Consequences are imposed on the student, beginning with restitutions and progressing on to detention, conferences with the teacher, referral to the counselor, calling the parent, referral to the vice principal, and loss of normal privileges such as attendance at dances, taking a class trip, or participation in athletic events. Always in effect is a "severe clause," which allows immediate referral to the principal and suspension from school for such acts as fighting and using drugs.

Single Power Systems: Elementary Level. Single power systems are occasionally used at the elementary level. A widely-used example is Canter's Assertive Discipline, which is very effective in suppressing misbehavior. Many primary teachers do not approve of single power systems, however, considering them too harsh and too focused on punishing misbehavior rather than teaching proper behavior. Teachers who believe in assertive discipline counter that argument by insisting that such programs give students a feeling of consistency. They add that nothing prevents teachers from teaching good behavior along with the system.

Combination Systems: Elementary Level. Often favored in elementary schools are combinations of power systems and persuasive systems. Typically, persuasive and redirective techniques are used with primary grade children who are still in the process of learning what are and are not acceptable behaviors. This learning occurs best through good example combined with reinforcement and reteaching.

By the end of the primary grades students have become fully aware of the difference between acceptable and unacceptable behavior. At the same time, they fall progressively more under the influence of peers. Therefore, many schools use a stronger system of discipline for students in fourth grade and higher.

Rules at the elementary level tend to be more specific than those at the secondary level. They usually name specific behaviors such as staying in one's seat, raising hands before speaking, and so forth.

The power aspect of the combination system differs somewhat from that described as typical for high schools. At these earlier grades, strong emphasis remains on positive reinforcement for good behavior. Parents are often asked to assist at home in reinforcing good behavior and work and study habits. Enforcement procedures for misbehavior are carried out mainly by the classroom teacher. Counselors are seldom used.

Disagreements About Schoolwide Systems. While most teachers acknowledge the benefits of schoolwide systems, many claim that overall student behavior is no better than when teachers take care of the problems on their own. This is especially true for teachers who have been successful with discipline. They resent giving up their effective approaches to turn to a system about which they are unsure.

Teachers complain too of weariness of years of administrative press for solutions to school problems, only to see after much work and effort that conditions are no better than before. This feeling must be addressed when schools attempt to put new discipline systems into place. One way of handling this concern is to allow teachers to visit other schools where such systems are used effectively and talk with teachers and students about their reactions.

Finally, there is the old "still more extra work" bugaboo that has become an almost insupportable burden for teachers. Teachers already suffer from very high levels of stress, much of which is brought about by too much to do and too little time in which to get it done. They automatically equate new plans with more work, taking a stance of rejection until proven wrong. Yet it is evident that teachers will willingly work on new systems that bring benefits to their students or themselves. Once persuaded that schoolwide systems of discipline are effective without requiring extra work, they tend to endorse them wholeheartedly.

Comment on Schoolwide Systems

Schoolwide systems of discipline do not improve class control for stronger teachers, but they do seem to improve student behavior in classrooms of teachers who have difficulty with control, as well as in other areas of the school such as library, shops, cafeteria, grounds, buses, and so forth. Moreover, the community tends to stand strongly behind schoolwide systems, appreciating school's attempt to provide positive learning climates and the consistency the program brings.

Application Exercises

1. Clarify what you as a teacher consider acceptable with regard to noise, talk, movement, and courtesy. Formulate your ideas into questions or topics that you could discuss with your class.
2. Outline your personal system of discipline to include as many of the 17 steps to personalized discipline as possible.
3. Select, from the classroom scenarios presented in Chapter 13, one that is most similar to the grade, subject, or type of students that most interests you. Test your system against what you see described in the scenario. Will your system:
   - Stop the misbehavior?
   - Keep students working productively?
   - Reduce the cause(s) of misbehavior?
   - Help build self-esteem and positive relationships?
   - Engender support from parents and administrators?

CHAPTER 12

Exemplars: Personal Systems of Discipline

Chapter 11 presented guidelines to help you build your own personal system of discipline. To provide you with further insights and assistance, this chapter presents samples of personal discipline systems that were developed using those same guidelines. These systems were all composed and used by real teachers who have been kind enough to allow their work to be included here. Presented are two systems used at high school level, two at intermediate grade level, two at primary grade level, and two "specialty systems."

TWO HIGH SCHOOL SYSTEMS

High School System #1:

Teacher: Leslie Hays
Subject: Physical Science

My personal belief is that every one of my students can behave appropriately in my classroom every day. My personal goal is to be an effective teacher for them. I try to accomplish this through clarity, firmness, and a human touch. It is very important to me to establish a sense of class belonging and unity, with shared objectives and goals. Toward that end I try to inject humor and fun, and I find that student participation follows naturally.

At the same time I concentrate on preventive and supportive discipline by doing extensive planning and by constantly monitoring each of my students. This frees me from having to deal continually with misbehavior. I communicate with parents by note and telephone, and most of them are so thankful that I have called them to talk about their child, they become my allies in class control.

My students range from remedial (almost always considered behavior problems) to advanced. With all levels, my discipline plan works best for me with a very structured approach that communicates my standards and requirements.

My plan goes into effect within the first five minutes of class each September. Each individual is given a class behavior contract, which must be taken home, signed by their parents, and returned to me the next day. If they bring it back when due, I give them points. If they are a day late, they get no points, and if it doesn't come back the third day I call the parents at home. The contract outlines my philosophy and behavior guidelines:

Dear Student and Parent:

In order to guarantee all the students in my classroom the excellent learning climate they deserve, I am utilizing the following discipline plan.

Attendance: Attendance is essential to the learning process. You cannot expect to succeed if you do not participate in the daily activity of the classroom. Therefore, after a student's fourth absence, the parent will be notified. After 15 absences, the student will be subject to failure in the class.

Tardies: Students are expected to be in their assigned seat and ready to begin work when the final bell rings. A student/parent warning is issued after two tardies. After four tardies a letter will be sent home. Following the seventh tardy, you are subject to being dropped from the class with an F. Citizenship grades will be lowered one grade for every two tardies.

Class Behavior: I believe that all my students can behave appropriately in my classroom. I will not tolerate a student stopping me from teaching or preventing any other student from learning.

Class Rules:
1. Bring your science book, notebook, and pencil every day. I DON'T LEND ANYTHING.
2. Be attentive while the teacher, or a student who is called on, is talking.
3. Bring no food, drink, candy, gum, hats, or sunglasses to the class.
4. Handle all equipment properly.
5. Profanity and verbal abuse are not tolerated.
6. Remain in your seat at the end of the period until dismissed by the teacher.

Consequences: High citizenship and conduct grades will be awarded to those students who contribute positively to the daily activities of the classroom.

If, on the other hand, a student chooses to interfere with learning process, the following consequences will be invoked:

• First time: Warning: mark on discipline card.
• Second time: Notify parent of behavior problem.
• Third time: Referral to counselor.
• Fourth time: Referral to vice principal for disciplinary action.
• Students who write on desks or throw trash around the room will be assigned immediate after-school detention to clean *all* of the desk tops and *all* of the trash.
• **Note:** More serious problems such as defiance, fighting, theft, abuse of equip-

ment, or violation of laboratory safety rules will result in immediate referral to the vice principal.

It is in the student's best interest that the student, teacher, and parent work together. I will therefore be in close contact with parents regarding students' progress. Parents, please sign the tear off and have the student return it to me tomorrow. If you have any questions or comments, please call me or write them on the tear off.

After reviewing the rules with the students, I have them fill out a behavior card that becomes part of my system for recording behavior problems. This is yet another way of telling the students that discipline is an important part of my classroom organization. I begin by seating students according to a seating chart, then explain procedures concerning homework, grading, and required materials. Textbooks are distributed and we go over the plans for the semester. After that, we begin the first lesson. By the end of the first class, all students have the feeling that I am in control, with a well-organized plan.

Gradually over the years of trying various discipline approaches, I have found that students react positively to my system. As the year progresses, occasional gentle reminders are usually enough to maintain good behavior. I also use eye contact, hand signals, and physical proximity to assist. When more serious disruptions do occasionally occur, students know the rules and consequences and it thus becomes easier to invoke the consequences without emotional upheavals and confrontations that I find personally offensive.

High School System #2:

Teacher.: Elaine Maltz
Subject.: Math Basic Skills

At my first class meeting, I distribute a copy of my class rules to each student. These are signed by parent and student and returned to me the next day. A copy of the rules is then kept in each student's math notebook. The rules are as follows:

1. Come to class on time and be in your seat when the bell rings.
2. Bring your textbook, math notebook with paper, and a sharpened pencil every day.
3. Work quietly at your seat unless you have permission to do otherwise.
4. Food and drink are not allowed in the classroom.

Consequences: (all shown in citizenship grades)

- For tardiness:
  0–3 tardies = G (good)
    4 tardies = S (satisfactory)
    5 tardies = N (needs improvement)
    6 tardies = U (unsatisfactory)

- For truancy: Two truancies lower citizenship grade. Four truancies lower academic grade.
- Infractions of other rules:
  - 0–4 infractions = G
  - 5–6 infractions = S
  - 7–8 infractions = N
  - 9–10 infractions = U

When I present the rules, I discuss my expectations and explain the rules fully. I mention that in addition to my consequences, the school maintains a system by which students get referred to the counselor or vice principal. If necessary, the parents are contacted for assistance.

In teaching, I feel that an essential element of classes in math is the use of humor. It combats boredom as well as "math phobia." The tone has to be set at the beginning of the class, as a part of an overall atmosphere of acceptance and encouragement where each student is treated with respect. At the same time, the best is clearly expected of each student. I work hard to avoid sarcasm and try never to attack the students personally.

I find it also helps to provide occasional changes of pace. Reviewing homework, introducing new material, and starting corresponding homework are the nuts and bolts of my class, but I try to intersperse visual problems with abstract ones and include real problem solving at least once each class as a respite from routine work.

To help with behavior, I also stay active while my students are working at their seats, constantly circulating and helping. This not only allows me to help students with their work, but it permits me to deal subtly with incipient misbehavior without drawing the attention of other class members. I use eye contact, facial expressions, and light touches to help students control their own behavior.

I admit there are times when I use nagging, or the broken record technique, to remind students of standards and expectations. I do this to help my students give high priority to academics and to proper social behavior. At the same time, I remember to smile when dealing with my students. I think teenagers, more than others, need concrete proof of their teacher's feelings. Other ways I try to give this proof are to be as helpful as possible, get work corrected and back to students quickly, and provide unending encouragement, especially to reluctant students. I work hard at all this. Being a consistent disciplinarian has not come naturally to me.

TWO INTERMEDIATE GRADE SYSTEMS

Intermediate Grade System #1:

Teacher: Nancy Natale

I believe a positive atmosphere is most conducive to learning, so I set up my discipline system so it will be fun and rewarding for my students. My system is based on points; the points have value that can later be used to buy items such as toys, games, and books.

Earning Points. Each student is able to earn points all during the week. I assign points for a number of different behaviors. For example, when I begin an activity I give points to those students who begin work immediately. First, I give them verbal praise: "Thank you, Jennifer; Good going, Shawn," and as I do this I give them each a point on a master chart I keep near my desk. This provides immediate reinforcement and also influences other students positively, reminding them that they too can earn points.

As an extra work incentive, I assign points to students who bring into class something that is pertinent to what we are studying. For example, one day I was teaching about diagrams. The next day a girl brought in a diagram of a house her parents were building and a boy brought in a diagram of a model airplane he was putting together.

I use discretion in offering numbers of points. For example, my class was writing autobiographies to be bound and displayed at an open house but they just weren't using their time well. I decided to offer five points to each student who completed his or her work to my satisfaction by noon of the day of the open house. This motivated students to high work output.

I also give out points at unexpected times. In a recent geometry lesson we were discussing the number of faces, edges, and vertices that various shapes have. After we had examined about 10 different shapes, a girl pointed out to me that on every pyramid the number of faces was always equal to the number of vertices, regardless of whether the pyramid had a triangular, square, hexagonal, or other-shaped base. We tested her observation and found it to be true. I gave her a point for an excellent observation.

Class Rules. I use only four class rules. They are:

1. Pay attention during class.
2. Keep hands and feet to yourself.
3. Do not prevent others from learning.
4. Follow directions and complete your work.

Misbehavior. Even with all the attention I give to keeping a positive atmosphere, my students still misbehave sometimes. When they do, I have them fill out a "See Me" card. On this card, the student must answer these four questions:

1. What was I doing?
2. Why was I doing it?
3. What should I have been doing?
4. What class rule was broken?

After the card is filled out, the student must bring it to me and we have a discussion about it. If any student accumulates three See Me cards in one week, that student has to write a letter to his or her parents stating why they received the cards. This procedure helps me document misbehaviors in my classroom, but, better yet, it makes the student take ownership of the misbehavior. If a student receives even one

See Me card in a week, he or she may not participate in the week's spending of earned points, but must do homework instead.

Intermediate Grade System #2:

Teacher: Micheal Brus

I base my discipline system on the golden rule and find I need to spell out only three rules, which I prepare calligraphically in gold, Gothic lettering and display prominently in the room. My rules read as follows:

- Teachers have a right to teach;
- Students have a right to learn!

Therefore:

1. We agree to treat fellow students and teachers as we ourselves would like to be treated.
2. We agree to be on time, prepared to work, and to stay on task.
3. We agree to have no unauthorized food, gum, or drink.

I believe in treating my students very much like adults, letting them know they are responsible for how they behave. I define the behavior boundaries within my three rules and discuss gray areas around them. I invite my students to add a fourth rule, if there is one in which they believe strongly.

I use much positive reinforcement. Whenever I see a student behaving especially well, I ask him or her to go to the master list of student names (displayed on a wall chart) and make a vertical stroke beside the name with my gold marker. The student receiving the most marks in a month is named citizen of the month. Having been a professional portrait artist, I honor the student by drawing a color pastel portrait of him or her.

The points accumulated by other students may be used at an end-of-the-month auction to bid for prizes I furnish, such as inexpensive toys, books, erasers, pieces of chalk, and stickers. In order to emphasize good group behavior I keep a separate tally of points earned by the class as a whole for being quiet and orderly at lunch, library, auditorium, and especially for helping us all have an unusually pleasant day at school. These points accumulate toward free minutes on Fridays, extra physical education, or time for playing with computers and games.

By my own demeanor in the classroom, I try to show my sincere belief that there is much good in every person. I try to find in all my students something they do especially well and help instill in them a sense of pride and achievement.

When my students break class rules, I have them go to the master chart and make a black tally mark beneath their name. The consequences associated with the black marks are as follows:

- First mark—I verbally reinforce the opposite behavior in another student.

- Second mark—I give a short verbal desist, referring to the rule that is broken.
- Third mark—I send the student to a fellow teacher's room, with an assignment to complete (this is arranged in advance, reciprocally, with the other teacher).
- Fourth mark—The student is sent to the principal's office. The principal knows and supports my system and takes further appropriate action.

When the consequences for more serious misbehavior are invoked, I follow up with the student, insisting that a plan for proper behavior be made that is acceptable to both the student and me. At appropriately private times, I talk openly and honestly with the student about his or her success in living up to the plan, and what must be done next when the plan does not work.

TWO PRIMARY LEVEL DISCIPLINE SYSTEMS

Primary System #1:

Teacher: Virginia Villalpando

The old proverb about an ounce of prevention being worth a pound of cure serves as the foundation for my discipline program. I arrange the environment so as to discourage misbehavior by arranging tables and chairs to allow easy access to instructional areas and provide clear lines of vision to all parts of the room. Supplies are placed in conveniently accessible locations. Special interest areas are separated from work areas so as not to distract students. I do not seat students closely together, and I make sure the seating allows me to reach every student in the room quickly when necessary.

I make my expectations known clearly on the first day. I emphasize that I want my students to have a learning environment that is free from disruptions, and that I will expect the students' help in keeping it friendly and pleasant. I let them know that I want to know their feelings, but that my decisions will be final. I go over the classroom rules, discuss what they mean, and explain the consequences for following and breaking them. I continually emphasize that behavior is their choice, as are the consequences of that behavior. I go over the rules, explain them with examples, and describe the consequences, as follows:

Rule	Explanation	Consequence
Respect others.	No hitting, tattling, name-calling. Let others work. Speak quietly, be kind.	Negative: time out, isolation, note to parents, stay in at recess. Positive: rewards.
Raise hand.	Do this before speaking, getting drink, asking for help, etc.	Negative: ignore, deny request, frown. Positive: praise, special reward, thanks.

Rule	Explanation	Consequence
Work quietly.	No loud noise; don't disturb others.	Negative: move to other area. Positive: stars, smiley faces, thank-yous.
Be orderly.	Don't run; enter room quietly; stay in line.	Negative: frown; checkmark by name on board. Positive: smile; praise.
Respect property.	Take care of things; keep them clean.	Negative: note home. Positive: note home; thanks.

I keep the basic rules (but not the explanations and consequences) posted on a chart at the front of the room. When students break the rules I invoke the consequences and often refer to the rules chart. If the infractions are minor or infrequent, I merely use eye contact or shakes of the head to get students back on track. I make a point of thanking them when they behave well. I smile and say, "Good, keep it up, that's the way." I want them to feel good about behaving well.

Primary Level System #2:

Teacher: Thomas F. Bolz

Two years ago I moved from teaching a fifth grade to a kindergarten-first grade combination. I soon learned a far different approach to discipline was required. Primary children get more excited about praise and correction—in fact, they get more excited about almost everything. At my school, we have a discipline plan that everyone uses, but into that plan I weave much of my own philosophy and personality. The rules we all use are the following:

1. I will listen and follow directions.
2. I will respect and use kind words toward others. Profanity is not permitted.
3. I will keep hands, feet, and objects to myself. Fighting is prohibited.
4. I will complete all assigned work on time.
5. I will respect school property and the property of others.

These rules apply to the playground as well as to the classroom and school environment.

We have a hierarchy of consequences set up for students who break the rules. They are:

- Step 1. Verbal warning. Additional consequence if apology is necessary or if there is damage to property.
- Step 2. Conference with teacher, with one or more of the following results: repair of damage, time out, loss of recess, loss of a privilege.
- Step 3. Child remains after school and calls to notify parents of reason.

- Step 4. Teacher contacts parents to inform them of behavior and discuss consequences for the child. Teacher may set up conference with parents.
- Step 5. If all else fails and the child's behavior has not improved, teacher contacts the principal who decides on further consequences and sets up conference with parents.

Personally, I invest much time and energy into preventive and supportive discipline. When I want students to get in their seats, sitting up with hands folded, I give the direction and then start a nursery rhyme: "One, two, buckle my shoe . . . " Soon the whole class is reciting the rhyme, and by the time we get to "a big fat hen"—usually about 10 seconds—the whole class is attentive with their eyes on me.

Another preventive technique I use is the "good walker" tickets. Whenever we are walking down the hallway I hand out two or three tickets to students who are walking nicely. In class they put them in an oatmeal container and when we line up to go outside, I draw a ticket out. That person gets to be first in line.

The major breakthrough for the year has been the Happy Face Chart. Our day usually begins like this: "Elsie, Josh, and Aaron, boom! Sign the Happy Face. Notice how they came in quietly and sat up straight and tall." A tide of good behavior ripples out from that. At the end of the week, I read off the names for each day. The names are put on slips of paper for a drawing. Whoever wins gets a coupon for a bag of french fries.

When it comes to corrective discipline, I want it to be short, simple, clearly understood, and unpleasant for the child. When individual children are noisy or not doing their work I have them put their head down at their desk. Children know that they then have to count to 100 by ones, think about what they were doing wrong, and then get back to work. If I have to speak to them again during the day, they go to the time-out chair where I have a 3-minute egg timer. They have to sit for that length of time. They understand that this is a severe warning. The third time I have to talk with them I put their name on the board with a check and call their parent. This corrects the behavior most of the time.

I am able to enforce these rules most of the time without getting upset. I make sure the children know I expect them to behave better. One parent commented to me that her daughter liked my room because I was "fair and treated everyone alike."

TWO SPECIALTY SYSTEMS

Specialty System #1: Behavior Modification

Teacher: Constance Bauer

I had been teaching for 5 or 6 years before I ever understood what behavior modification was all about and what it could do for teachers. I had controlled my second graders through the usual stern-voiced admonitions, and had tried to motivate them by telling them how much fun we were going to have in school that day. Neither approach ever went over quite well enough to suit me.

Then, our school had an inservice training session on behavior modification and its uses in the classroom. Because our principal expected us to, I half-heartedly began to try out some of the approaches in my classroom—such things as finding a student who was behaving correctly and praising that behavior rather than scolding those who were misbehaving, and setting up a "bookworm" chart so that students who did their work could add another segment to their worm.

My students responded so well to those first efforts that I decided to see what more I could accomplish with positive reinforcement. I set up individual progress charts for my students so they could keep track of their improvement in reading, math, and spelling. I made little stuffed rabbits that could sit on desks where there were "good workers." I made note forms that I sent home each day with "good helper" students, so their parents could be proud of them.

Before long I found that I was controlling and motivating the class with these devices and everything was going much more smoothly and positively than ever before. I am told that it is easier to use such programs at the primary grade level than with older students. I don't know if that's so, but in any case behavior modification has made a believer out of me.

Specialty System #2: Token Economy

Teachers: Mike Straus and Roy Allen (team teachers)

For the first few years we taught, we used authority as our way of keeping discipline. We are large and can talk mean and order students to behave. But that was wearing us out and making the kids afraid of us. Nobody was enjoying school very much.

Then one year we decided to try a behavior control system based on fake money. We called our currency "Strallens" (our names combined), and we printed up several hundred bills of different denominations. A couple of years ago a student's mother took photographs of us and made up a batch of Strallens with our pictures on them.

Anyway, we decided to pay our students Strallens when they worked quietly, did their homework, finished work on time, did extra work, participated well in class, and so on. We also decided we would fine them when they didn't do their work or misbehaved or talked back. We have heard that in behavior modification you give rewards for good behavior, but don't do anything when the kids act bad. That's not real life, so far as we are concerned. In society when you break the law you get fined, and that was how we wanted it in our classroom.

We usually walk around the classroom with Strallens in our hand or pocket. We give them out personally. When students misbehave, like talking when they're not supposed to, we say, "Jack, that's a ten Strallen fine." Jack knows he has to go put 10 of his Strallens in the fine box.

As students accumulate Strallens, they can use them to buy special things we provide. Every couple of weeks, for example, we rent a video movie that the kids want to see. We charge admission. Those who don't have enough Strallens can't watch the movie. We have popcorn sometimes and field trips to interesting places and white elephant sales. Students can spend Strallens for those things, too.

After a while some of the students don't care to spend their Strallens—they want to see how many they can get. Some amass several hundred. We set up bank accounts, too, that earn interest, to teach students about interest, writing checks, and balancing check books.

Our system has worked for us. We almost never have to scold a student. They accept the rewards and fines as reasonable and everyone stays in a pretty good mood most of the time.

The Strallen system doesn't work for every student. We tell students at the beginning that they don't have to participate in it if they don't want to. They can have the usual praise if they behave and the usual scoldings and staying-in if they don't. An occasional student takes that option. Once in a while a student on the Strallen system misbehaves so much they go hopelessly in the hole. We take them off the system and use conventional controls with them.

All in all, we like our system. It is effective, easy to operate, and the kids react to it positively. It has made our teaching easier and more enjoyable.

CHAPTER 13

Classroom Scenarios
for Analysis and Practice

This chapter contains descriptions of ten classrooms with misbehaviors teachers are likely to encounter, presented for analysis and hypothetical correction. They also provide situations against which to test your own personal system of discipline once you have composed it.

Each classroom scenario consists of two parts: a general description of the class and then a recounting of typical occurrences. As you read the scenarios, ask yourself the following: (1) What is the problem behavior, if any, and why is it a problem? (2) What seems to be causing the problem? (3) What should the teacher do to stop the misbehavior(s)? (4) What can the teacher do to give positive redirection to the misbehavior(s)? (5) What tactics should be included in the correction so as to maintain student self-concept and good personal relations?

SCENARIO 1: FIFTH GRADE

The Class

Mrs. Miller's fifth grade enrolls students from a small, stable community. Since transiency rate is low, many of her students have been together since first grade, and during those years have developed certain patterns of interacting and playing of roles.

Unfortunately, many of those behaviors interfere with teaching and learning. During the first week of school Mrs. Miller noticed that four or five students enjoyed making smart-aleck remarks about most things she wanted them to do. When such remarks were made, the other students laughed and sometimes joined in.

Even when Mrs. Miller attempted to hold class discussions about serious issues, many of the students would make light of the problems and refuse to enter genuinely into a search for solutions. Instead of obtaining the productive discussion she hoped for, Mrs. Miller would find the class degenerating into flippancy and horseplay.

A Typical Occurrence

Mrs. Miller has begun a history lesson that contains a reference to Julius Caesar. She asks if anyone has ever heard of Julius Caesar. Ben shouts out, "Yeah, they named a salad after him!"

The class laughs and calls out encouraging remarks such as, "Good one, Ben!" Mrs. Miller tells Ben she does not appreciate such contributions. She waits for some semblance of order, then says, "Let us go on."

"Lettuce, continue!" cries Jeremy from the back of the room.

The class falls into a chaos of laughter and talk.

After waiting a while, Mrs. Miller slams a book down on the desk and yells for quiet. "Any more such comments and you will go straight to the office!" she asserts.

For the remainder of the lesson, no more students call out remarks, but most continue to smirk and whisper comments about Caesar salad. A great deal of giggling goes on. Mrs. Miller tries to ignore the display of disrespect, but because of the disruptions is not able to complete the lesson on time or get the results she hoped for.

SCENARIO 2: HIGH SCHOOL BIOLOGY

The Class

Mr. Platt teaches advanced placement classes in biology to students from middle- to upper-income families. Most of the students have already made plans for going to college. When the students enter the classroom, they know they are to go to their assigned seats and write out answers to the "questions of the day" that Mr. Platt has written on the board. After that, Mr. Platt lectures on text material that he assigned students to read before coming to class. During the lecture, he calls randomly on students to answer questions and requires that they support their answers with reference to the assigned reading. Following the lecture, students engage in lab activity for the remainder of the period.

A Typical Occurrence

Mr. Platt has begun his lecture on the process of photosynthesis. He asks Arlene what the word *photosynthesis* means. She pushes her long hair aside and replies, "I don't get it." This is a comment Mr. Platt hears frequently from Arlene.

"What is it you don't understand?"

"None of it."

Mr. Platt snaps, "Be more specific! I've only asked for the definition!"

Arlene is not intimidated. "I mean, I don't get any of it. I don't understand why plants are green. Why aren't they blue or some other color? Why don't they grow on Mercury? The book says plants make food. How? Do they make Twinkies? That's ridiculous. I don't understand the point of photosynthesis."

Mr. Platt stares at Arlene for a while, and she back at him. He asks, "Are you finished?"

Arlene shrugs. "I guess so." She hears some of the boys whistle under their breath; she enjoys their obvious admiration.

Mr. Platt says to her, "Arlene, I hope some day you will understand that this is not a place for you to show off."

"I hope so, too," Arlene says. "I know I should be more serious." She stares out the window.

For the remainder of the lecture, delivered in an icy tone of voice, Mr. Platt calls only on students he knows will give correct answers.

Lecture completed, Mr. Platt begins to give instructions for lab activity. He notices that Nick is turning the valve of the gas jet on and off. He says to Nick, "Mr. Turner, would you please repeat the rule about the use of lab equipment?" Nick drops his head and mumbles something about waiting for directions. Arlene says calmly, "Knock it off, Nick. This is serious business." She smiles at Mr. Platt.

Mr. Platt stares at the class for a moment, then completes his directions and tells them to begin. He walks around the room, monitoring their work. He stands behind lab partners Sherry and Dawn, who are having a difficult time. He does not offer them help, believing that advanced placement students should be able to work things out for themselves. But as they blunder through the activity, he shakes his head in disbelief, leaving the strong impression that he hopes the two girls will drop the class.

SCENARIO 3: MIDDLE SCHOOL LIBRARY

Setting and Students

Mrs. Daniels is a media specialist in charge of the middle school library. She sees her job as serving as resource person to students who are seeking information and is always eager to give help to those who request it. The students in her school are characterized as lower middle class. About half are white, the remainder African-American, Latino, and Southeast Asian. Each period of the day differs as to the number and type of students who come under Mrs. Daniels' direction. Usually, small groups have been sent there to do cooperative research. Always some unexpected students appear, excused from physical education for medical reasons but hating to be sent to the library, or else bearing special passes from their teachers for a variety of purposes.

Typical Occurrences

Mrs. Daniels has succeeded in getting students settled and working when Tara appears at her side, needing a book to read as make-up work for missing class. Mrs. Daniels asks Tara what kinds of books interest her. Tara sullenly shrugs her shoulders. Mrs.

Daniels takes her to a shelf of newly-published books. "I read this one last night," she says. "I think you might like it. It's a good story, and fast reading."

Tara only glances at it. "That looks stupid," she says. "Don't you have any good books?" She glances down the shelf. "These are all stupid!"

Another student, James, is tugging at Mrs. Daniels' elbow, with a note from his history teacher wanting the source of a particular quotation. Mrs. Daniels asks Tara to look at the books for a moment while she takes James to her reference books.

As Mrs. Daniels passes a table of students supposedly doing research, she notices that the group is watching Walter and Tim have a friendly pencil fight, hitting pencils together until one of them breaks. She admonishes Walter, who appears to be the more willing participant. Walter answers hotly, "Tim started it! It wasn't me!"

"Well," Mrs. Daniels replies, "if you can't behave yourself, just go back to your class." The other students laugh at Walter who feels he has been treated unjustly. He sits down and pouts.

Meanwhile, Tara has gone to the large globe and is twirling it. Mrs. Daniels starts to speak to her, but realizes that James is still waiting at her shoulder with the request for his teacher.

Somehow, before the period ends, Tara leaves with a book she doesn't want and James takes a citation back to his teacher. The research groups have been too noisy. Mrs. Daniels knows they have done little work and wonders if she should speak to their teacher about the students' manners and courtesy.

After the period finally ends, Mrs. Daniels notices that profane remarks have been written on the table where Walter was sitting.

SCENARIO 4: SECOND GRADE CLASS

The Class

Mrs. Desmond teaches second-graders in a highly-transient neighborhood. She receives an average of one new student each week, and those students typically remain in her class for fairly short lengths of time before moving elsewhere. Most are from single-parent, dysfunctional homes, and their poor behavior, including aggression, boisterousness, and crying, seems to reflect many emotional problems.

Typical Occurrences

The morning bell rings, and students who have been lined up outside by an aide enter the classroom noisily. Mrs. Desmond is speaking with a parent who is complaining that her son is being picked on by others in the class. When finally able to give attention to the class, Mrs. Desmond sees that Ricky and Raymond have crawled underneath the reading table, while a group of excited children is clustered around Shawon who has brought his new hamster to share with the class. Two girls are pulling at Mrs. Desmond's sleeves, trying to give her a note and lunch money. Mrs. Desmond has to shout above the din before she can finally get everyone seated. Several minutes have passed since the bell rang.

Mrs. Desmond, having lost much of her composure, finally gets the reading groups started when she suddenly realizes that the assembly scheduled for that morning has slipped her mind. She suddenly stands up from her reading group and exclaims, "We have an assembly this morning! Put down your books and get lined up quickly! We are almost late!"

Thirty-one students make a burst for the door, pushing and arguing. Rachael, a big strong girl, shoves Amy and shouts, "Hey, get out of the way, stupid!" Amy, meek and retiring, begins to cry. Mrs. Desmond tries to comfort Amy while Rachael pushes her way into the front of the line.

During the assembly, Ricky and Raymond sit together. They have brought some baseball cards and are entertaining the students seated around them. When the first part of the assembly performance is over, they boo loudly and laugh instead of applauding. Under the school principal's disapproving eye, Mrs. Desmond separates Ricky and Raymond, but for the rest of the performance they make silly faces and gestures to each other, causing other students to laugh.

Upon returning to the classroom, Mrs. Desmond, certain that the principal will speak to her about her class's behavior, tries to talk with them about the impropriety of their actions. She attempts to elicit positive comments about the assembly, but several students say it was dumb and boring.

The discussion has made little progress before time for recess. Mrs. Desmond sighs and directs the students to line up and orders them sternly to use their best manners. As they wait at the door, Rachael is once again shoving her way into the head of the line.

SCENARIO 5: HIGH SCHOOL SPECIAL EDUCATION

The Class

Mrs. Reed teaches special education English to high school students, all of whom have a history of poor academic performance, though some seem to her to have at least average intelligence. Some of the students have been diagnosed as learning disabled. For others, no specific learning difficulties have been identified. Several live in foster homes. About one-third are Latinos, bused from a distant neighborhood. Some of the students are known to be affiliated with gangs.

Typical Occurrences

The students enter the classroom lethargically, find their seats, and as directed, most of them begin copying an assignment from the board. Something is going on between Lisa and Jill, who shoot hateful glances at each other. Neither begins work.

When the students are settled, Mrs. Reed reviews the previous day's lesson and then begins instruction on how to write a business letter. She asks the class to turn to an example in their textbooks. Five of the fourteen students do not have their books with them, though this is a requirement that is repeated almost daily. Students without books are penalized points that detract from their course grade.

Mrs. Reed sees that Lisa has her book and asks her to open it to the correct page. Lisa shakes her head and puts her head down on the desk. Mrs. Reed gives her the option of time out. Lisa leaves the room and sits by herself at a table in the corner.

Mrs. Reed goes on with the lesson. She asks the students to work in pairs to write a letter canceling a magazine subscription and requesting a refund. She lets them pick their own partners, but finds after a while that several students have formed no partnerships.

Lisa's absence leaves an odd number of students. Jill asks if she can work by herself. Mrs. Reed grants her request, but Jill spends most of her time glancing back at Lisa.

Two other girls, Marcia and Connie, have taken out mirrors and are applying make-up instead of working on their assignment. Mrs. Reed informs them that she intends to call on them first to share their letter with the class.

After the allotted work time, Mrs. Reed asks for volunteers to read their letters. With prodding, a pair of boys is first to share. Mrs. Reed then calls on Marcia and Connie. They complain that they didn't understand how to do the assignment. Mrs. Reed tells them they must complete the letter for homework. They agree, but Mrs. Reed knows they will not comply and expects them to be absent the next day.

Other students read their letters. Some are good; others contain many mistakes. The students do not seem to differentiate between the correct and incorrect. Mrs. Reed tries to point out strengths and weaknesses in the work, but the class applauds and makes smart-aleck remarks impartially.

At the end of the period, Mrs. Reed asks that the letters be turned in, intending that the students refine their work the next day. She finds that two papers are missing and that Juan and Marco have written on theirs numerous A+ symbols and gang-related graffiti.

SCENARIO 6: CONTINUATION HIGH SCHOOL PHOTOGRAPHY LAB

The Class

Mr. Carnett teaches photography lab, an elective class, in a continuation high school, attended by students who have been unsuccessful for behavioral reasons in regular high school settings. Many of the students want to attend this particular school, as it is located in what they consider their "turf." Some of the students are chemically-dependent and/or come from dysfunctional homes. The photography lab class enrolls eighteen students and all are on individual study contracts.

Typical Occurrences

As students begin work, Mr. Carnett busies himself with a number of different tasks—setting out needed materials, giving advice on procedures, handing out quizzes for students who have completed contracts, examining photographs, and so forth. He sees Tony sitting and staring into space. He asks Tony if he needs help. Tony shrugs. Mr. Carnett asks if Tony has brought his materials to work on. Tony shakes his head. Mr. Carnett tells Tony he can start on a new part of his contract. Tony doesn't answer. Mr. Carnett asks what's the matter. When Tony doesn't respond, Mike mutters, "He's blasted out of his head, man."

At that moment, Mr. Carnett hears heated words coming from the darkroom. He enters and finds two students squaring off, trying to stare each other down. He asks what the problem is but gets no reply. He tells the boys to leave the darkroom and go back to their seats. They ignore him. As tension grows, another student intervenes and says, "Come on, we can settle it later. Be cool." Mr. Carnett calls the office and informs the counselor of the incident. The boys involved hear him do so and gaze at him insolently.

The class settles back to work, and for the remainder of the period Mr. Carnett circulates among them, providing assistance, stifling horseplay, urging that they move ahead in their contracts, and reminding everyone that they only have a limited amount of time in which to get their work done.

From time to time he glances at Tony, who does no work during the period. He asks Tony if something is bothering him. Tony shakes his head. Mr. Carnett asks Tony if he wants to transfer out of the class, since it is elective. Tony says, "No, man, I like it here." "That's fine," Mr. Carnett says. "But this is not dream time. You do your work, or else we will find you another class. You understand?"

"Sure, man. I understand."

Mr. Carnett turns away, but from the corner of his eye is sure that he sees Tony's middle finger aimed in his direction.

SCENARIO 7: SHELTERED ENGLISH KINDERGARTEN

The Class

Mrs. Bates teaches a sheltered English kindergarten class comprised of thirty students, only seven of whom speak English at home. The ethnic/racial make-up of the class is a mixture of Vietnamese, Laotian, Chinese, Samoan, Iranian, Latino, Filipino, African-American, and Caucasian. The emphasis of the class is rapid English language development. For the most part, the students work in small groups, each of which is directed by a teacher, aide, or parent volunteer. The groups rotate every half-hour so as to have a variety of experiences.

A Typical Morning

Shortly before school begins, a new Asian girl, Mei, is brought into the class. She speaks very little English and is crying. She tries to run out of the classroom but is stopped by the aide. When Mrs. Bates rings her bell, the students know they are to sit on the rug, but those already at the play area do not want to do so. Mrs. Bates calls them three or four times, but finally has to get up and bring two of them personally to the rug.

As the opening activities proceed, Mrs. Bates repeatedly asks students to sit up (they have begun rolling around on the floor). Kinney is pestering the girl seated next to him. Twice, Mrs. Bates asks him to stop. Finally, she sends him to sit in a chair outside the group. He has to sit there until the opening activities are finished, then rejoins his group for the first rotation at the art table.

As soon as the groups get under way, Mrs. Bates hears a ruckus at the art table, which is under the guidance of Mrs. Garcia, a parent volunteer. She sees that Kinney has scooped up finger paint and is making motions as if to paint one of the girls, who runs away from him. Mrs. Garcia tells him to put the paint down. Kinney, who speaks English, replies, "Shut up, you big fat rat's ass!"

Mrs. Bates leaves her group and goes to Kinney. She tells him, "You need time out in Mrs. Sayres' room (a first-grade next door to Mrs. Bates's kindergarten). Kinney, his hand covered with blue paint, drops to the floor and refuses to move. He calls Mrs. Bates foul names. Mrs. Bates leaves him there, goes to the phone, and calls the office for assistance. Kinney gets up, wipes his hand first on a desk and then on himself, and runs out the door. He stops beside the entrance to Mrs. Sayres' room, and when Mrs. Bates follows he goes inside and sits at a designated table without further resistance.

Mrs. Bates returns to her group, comprised mostly of Asian students. They sit quietly and attentively, but do not speak. Mrs. Bates is using a "Big Book" on an easel, trying to get the students to repeat the words she says, but with little success.

When it is time for the next rotation, Mrs. Bates goes quickly to Mrs. Sayres' room and brings Kinney back to the class. He rejoins his group. As Mrs. Bates begins work with her new group, she sees Ryan and Duy at the measuring table pouring bird seed on each other's heads.

Meanwhile, the new girl, Mei, continues sobbing audibly.

SCENARIO 8: JUNIOR HIGH WORLD HISTORY

The Class

Mr. Jaramillo's third-period world history class is attended by students whose achievement levels are average to below average. He paces his work slowly and keeps it simple. For the most part he enjoys the class, finding the students interesting and energetic.

Mr. Jaramillo's lessons follow a consistent pattern. For the first part of the period, students take turns reading aloud from the textbook. Mr. Jaramillo selects the student readers at random, from cards with students' names on them. If a student who is called on has lost the place in the textbook, or is unable to answer a question about material read by the previous reader, he or she loses a point, which affects the final grade.

For the second part of the period, the class is divided into work groups. Each group selects a portion from text reading and uses the information it contains as the basis for making something creative, such as group posters, to be shared at the end of the class if time allows.

Typical Occurrences

During oral reading, Mr. Jaramillo calls on Hillary to read. Although she has been following along, she shakes her head. This has happened several times before. Mr. Jaramillo, not wanting to hurt Hillary's feelings, simply says, "That costs you a point, Hillary," and he calls on someone else.

Unfortunately, Hillary's reluctance carries over into group work as well, in which she refuses to participate. The other students ignore her and complete the work without her involvement. Occasionally, Clarisse refuses to involve herself in group work, as well. When Mr. Jaramillo speaks to her about it, she replies, "You don't make Hillary do it." Mr. Jaramillo answers, "Look, we are talking about you, not about Hillary." However, he lets the matter lie there and says no more if Clarisse doesn't participate.

On this particular day, Deonne has come into the classroom looking very angry. He slams his pack down on his desk and sits without opening his textbook for reading. Although Mr. Jaramillo picks Deonne's card from the deck, he recognizes Deonne's mood and decides not to call on him.

Will is in an opposite mood. Throughout the oral reading portion of the class, he continually giggles at every mispronounced word and at every reply students give to Mr. Jaramillo's questions. Will sits in the front row and turns around to laugh, seeing if he can get anyone else to laugh with him. Although most students either ignore him or give him disgusted looks, he keeps laughing. Mr. Jaramillo finally asks him what is so funny. Will replies, "Nothing," and looks back at the class and laughs.

At the end of the period, there is time for sharing three posters. Will makes comments and giggles about each of them. Clarisse, who has not participated, says, "Will, how about shutting up!!"

As the students leave the room, Mr. Jaramillo takes Deonne aside. "What's the matter with you, Deonne?" he asks. "Nothing," Deonne replies with clenched jaw as he strides past Mr. Jaramillo.

SCENARIO 9: HIGH SCHOOL AMERICAN LITERATURE

The Class

Mr. Wong teaches an eleventh grade one-semester course in American literature. The course is required for graduation. Among Mr. Wong's thirty-three students are eight seniors who failed the course previously and are retaking it. The students at Mr. Wong's school are from middle-class affluent families, and many of them are highly motivated academically. At the same time, there is also a significant number who have little interest in school aside from the opportunity to be with their friends.

Mr. Wong's teaching routine proceeds as follows: First, he begins the period with a three-question quiz over assigned reading. The quiz items focus on facts such as names, places, and description of plot. Second, when the quiz papers are collected, Mr. Wong conducts a question and discussion session about the assigned reading. He calls on individual students, many of whom answer, "I don't know." Third, Mr. Wong has the class begin reading a new chapter in the work under study. They take turns reading orally until the end of the period. The remainder of the assignment not read orally is to be completed as homework.

A Typical Occurrence

The students enter Mr. Wong's classroom lethargically and begin taking the quiz from questions written on the board. Mr. Wong notices that many of the answers are obvious guesses. He notices Brian in particular, who has already failed the class and must pass it now in order to graduate. Mr. Wong says, "Didn't any of you read your assignment?"

When oral reading begins, Mr. Wong notices that Brian does not have his copy of *Huckleberry Finn*, the work being studied. This is nothing new. Mr. Wong lends Brian a copy. Brian follows along in the reading for a while, then begins doodling on a sheet of paper. Mr. Wong calls on Brian to read. Brian cannot find the place.

Mr. Wong says, "Brian, this is simply unacceptable. You have failed the class once; fail it again now and you know you don't graduate."

Brian does not look up but says, "Want to make a bet on that?"

'What?"

"I guarantee you I'll graduate."

"Not without summer school, you won't!"

"That's okay by me. That will be better. This class is too boring, and the assignments are too long. I've got other things to do besides read this stupid story. Who cares about this anyway? Why can't we read something that has to do with real life?"

Mr. Wong, offended, replies, "You couldn't be more wrong! Other students enjoy this work, and it is one of the greatest books in American literature! There is nothing wrong with the book! What's wrong, Brian, is your attitude!"

Brian's eyes are hot, but he says nothing further. His book remains closed. Mr. Wong struggles through the final ten minutes of class. Brian is first out of the room when the bell rings.

SCENARIO 10: SIXTH GRADE, STUDENT TEACHER

The Class

Denise Thorpe is a student teacher in an inner-city magnet school that emphasizes academics. Half of her students are African-American, and the other half, of various ethnic groups, have been bused in to take advantage of the instructional program and rich resources. All students in the class are academically talented and none has what would be called a bad attitude toward school.

Mrs. Warde, the regular teacher of the class, does not seem to rely on any particular scheme of management or discipline, at least none obvious to Denise. Mrs. Warde simply tells the students what to do and they comply.

For the first few lessons Denise teaches, Mrs. Warde remains in the room, acting the role of aide for Denise. The students work well as always, and Denise feels happy and successful.

When Mrs. Warde Left the Room

Mrs. Warde told Denise that she would leave the room during the math lesson so that Denise could begin getting the feel of directing the class on her own. Mrs. Warde warned Denise that the class might test her with a bit of naughtiness, though nothing serious was likely to occur. Just be in charge, Mrs. Warde counseled.

The math lesson began well, without incident. The lesson had to do with beginning algebra concepts, which Denise approached through a discovery mode. She told the class, "I want you to work independently on this. Think your way through the following equations and decide if they are true for all numbers:"

$$a + 0 = a$$
$$a + b = b + a$$
$$a(b + c) = ab + c$$
$$a + 1 - 1$$
$$a - 0 = a$$

The students began work, but within two minutes hands were shooting up. Denise went to help Alicia, who was stuck on the third equation. "What's the matter?" Denise whispered.

"I don't understand what this means."

"It was like what I showed you on the board. The same."

"Those were numbers. I don't understand these letters."

"They are the same as the numbers. They take the place of the numbers. I showed you how they were interchangeable, remember? Go ahead, let me see. Tell me what you are doing, step by step."

Denise did not realize it, but she spent almost five minutes with Alicia. Meanwhile, a few of the students had finished and were waiting, but most were holding tired arms limply in the air. Denise rushed to the next student and repeated her questioning tutorial.

Meanwhile, Matt and Alonzo had dropped their hands and were looking at each other's papers. They began to talk, then laugh. Others followed, and soon all work had stopped and the classroom had become quite noisy.

Denise repeatedly said, "Shhh, shhh!" but with little effect. At last she went to the front of the room, demanded attention, and told the class how disappointed she was in their rude behavior.

Index